AMBUSH VALLEY

Books by Eric Hammel

CHOSIN: Heroic Ordeal of the Korean War

THE ROOT: The Marines in Beirut, August, 1982

GUADALCANAL: Starvation Island
GUADALCANAL: The Carrier Battles
GUADALCANAL: Decision at Sea

KHE SANH: Siege in the Clouds, An Oral History

AMBUSH VALLEY

**I Corps, Vietnam, 1967 — the Story of a
Marine Infantry Battalion's Battle for Survival**

ERIC HAMMEL

★

PRESIDIO

For the Marines and Corpsmen
of the 3rd Battalion, 26th Marines,
Class of September 1967,
for Those Who Helped Them,
and, Especially,
for the Fallen.

Copyright © 1990 by Eric Hammel

Published by Presidio Press
31 Pamaron Way, Novato CA 94949

Distributed in Great Britain by
Greenhill Books
Park House, 1 Russell Gardens
London NW11 9NN

959.7
H21a

Library of Congress Cataloging-in-Publication Data

Hammel, Eric M.
   Ambush Valley: I Corps, Vietnam 1967: the story of a Marine infantry battalion's battle for survival / Eric Hammel.
     p. cm.
   Includes bibliographical references.
   ISBN 0-89141-365-0
   1. Vietnamese Conflict, 1961–1975—Regimental histories—United States. 2. United States. Marine Corps. Marines, 26th. Battalion, 3rd.—History. 3. Vietnamese Conflict, 1961–1975—Campaigns—Vietnam—Con Thiên Mountain Region. 4. Vietnamese Conflict, 1961–1975—Personal narratives, American. 5. Con Thi`ên Mountain Region (Vietnam)—History. I. Title.
DS558.4.H36   1990   90-30090
959.704'342—dc20   CIP

Printed in the United States of America

Contents

Guide to Terms & Abbreviations

A-4	Douglas Skyhawk jet attack bomber
AC-47	Douglas Skytrain propeller-driven gunship
AK-47	Soviet-pattern 7.62mm assault rifle
ALO	air liaison officer
amtrac	amphibian tractor (LVT)
AO	aerial observer
AP	Associated Press
arclight	B-52 high-altitude bombing program
Arty	artillery
ARVN	Army of the Republic of Vietnam
B-40	Soviet-pattern rocket-propelled grenade (RPG-2)
B-52	Boeing Stratofortress jet heavy bomber
Bird Dog	light observation airplane
CBS	Columbia Broadcasting System
CH-53	Sikorsky Sea Stallion heavy cargo helicopter
Chicom	Chinese Communist (NVA hand grenade)
Chopper	helicopter
CO	commanding officer
Comm	Communications
CP	command post
CWO	chief warrant officer
Delta-Med	Delta Company, 3rd Medical Battalion, aid station
DMZ	Demilitarized Zone
Doc	Navy medical corpsman
E-tool	light entrenching tool
Exec	executive officer
F-4	McDonnell Phantom jet fighter–bomber
FAC	forward air controller
fast mover	any jet aircraft
fixed wing	any aircraft not a helicopter
FO	artillery forward observer

G-2	intelligence officer (division or above)
Grunt	infantryman
Gunner	any Marine warrant officer
Gunny	gunnery sergeant
H-34	Sikorsky Sea Horse medium cargo helicopter
HE	high explosive
Helo	helicopter
H&I	Harassment-and-Interdiction (fire)
HM3	hospital corpsman 3rd class
HN	hospitalman
hooch	living quarters
hook	radio or radio handset
H&S	Headquarters-and-Service
Huey	Bell UH-1E light attack/transport helicopter
I Corps	I Corps Military Region
Illume	Illumination
Intell	Intelligence
KIA	Killed in Action
Klick	Kilometer
LAAW	U.S. M-72 light antitank assault weapon
LVT	landing vehicle, tracked (amtrac)
LZ	Landing Zone
M-14	U.S. 7.62mm rifle
M-16	U.S. 5.56mm rifle
M-48	U.S. medium tank
M-60	U.S. 7.62mm medium machine gun
M-79	U.S. 40mm grenade launcher
MAF	Marine Amphibious Force
medevac	medical evacuation
MIA	Missing in Action
MSR	Main Supply Route
Nape	napalm
NCO	noncommissioned officer

NROTC	Naval Reserve Officers Training Corps
NVA	North Vietnamese Army
Ontos	U.S. tracked 106mm recoilless rifle carrier
Opcon	operational control
PAVN	People's Army of Vietnam (NVA)
Pfc	private first class
Phantom	McDonnell F-4 jet fighter–bomber
PRC-25	U.S. infantry radio
Puff	Douglas AC-47 propeller-driven gunship (a.k.a. Puff the Magic Dragon and Spooky)
R&R	Rest and Rehabilitation (i.e., leave)
Recon	reconnaissance
RF-4	McDonnell Phantom reconnaissance jet
Rough Rider	convoy security escort
RPG	Soviet-pattern 40mm rocket-propelled grenade
S-1	personnel officer
S-2	intelligence officer
S-3	operations officer
S-4	logistics officer
Six	company commander (as in "India-Six")
Skipper	Captain or company commander
SKS	Soviet-pattern 7.62mm bolt-action carbine
snake	250-pound bomb
SOP	Standard Operating Procedure
tac	Tactical
TACP	Tactical Air Control Party
UH-1E	Bell Huey light attack/transport helicopter
UPI	United Press International
USMC	United States Marine Corps
VC	Viet Cong
VMO	Marine Observation Squadron
V Ring	center of a target; bull's eye
WIA	Wounded in Action
Willy-Pete(r)	WP (white phosphorous, or waterproof)

Prologue

In the late summer of 1967, the war in northern I Corps—South Vietnam's northernmost military region, bordering on North Vietnam—did not seem to be going badly for the American forces there. It did not seem to be going well, either. It did not seem to be going anywhere.

Manned by United States Marines and several Army of the Republic of Vietnam (ARVN) bastions, the northernmost tier of South Vietnam was among the hottest showplaces in Vietnam. The Marines deployed two full divisions and a reinforced regiment from another division in I Corps. They had long since been drawn into an attritional type of hit-and-run warfare with a growing number of North Vietnamese Army (NVA) units. The NVA were living full-time in the steep-sided brush-and tree-choked ravines that broke up the gently rolling fields that typified the lowland coastal plains along the Demilitarized Zone (DMZ), the nominal boundary separating the two Vietnams.

Over July and August, battles in northern I Corps centered on the Marine combat base on a hill called Con Thien. In that time, the NVA slowly gained fire superiority and, indeed, initiative over the two U.S. Marine regiments operating just south of the DMZ.

Con Thien. The news was abuzz with stories of the Marine stand at Con Thien. Television news footage focused on hard-bitten Marines telling TV reporters and, through them, the American public that Con Thien would not fall. Their words said, in effect, ''Let them come get us.'' But the NVA never quite obliged. Instead, they sent their artillery shells and rockets from the safe haven just across the narrow DMZ. And when the Marines inside the Con Thien Combat Base ventured out—when the timing was just right—elements of the NVA combat division *living* in the triple-canopied ravines south of the DMZ attacked them.

On July 2, 1967, at the start of Operation Buffalo, the Marine battalion in Con Thien left the combat base and was quickly attacked by all or part of an NVA regiment. However, three other Marine battalions waiting in the wings counterattacked the NVA force and, in bloody fighting that lasted until July 14, claimed to have killed 1,290 enemy soldiers against losses of 159 Marines killed and 345 wounded.

The war in northern I Corps ebbed and flowed around Con Thien. Both sides paid dearly for their mutual stubbornness. Each side grimly held the other hostage in a battle of attrition that could go either way— or nowhere at all. Both sides won a few, and both sides lost a few. Mostly, the two sides stayed about even but fought on like a pair of matched pit bulls—bleeding and dying for not much gain or obvious reason.

Throughout the early phases of Operation Kingfisher, which the Marines initiated on July 28, the NVA attacked road-bound convoys and were attacked in turn by nearby Marine infantry units. The Marines claimed more kills than they sustained, but real, dead NVA were always hard to find.

*

Another item that filled the newspapers and airwaves during the summer of 1967 was something the Department of Defense dubbed The Barrier but which everyone else called the McNamara Wall or McNamara Line, after its chief architect, Secretary of Defense Robert McNamara. The McNamara Wall was pure panacea, a brilliant ongoing show that reaped immense short-term political gains without actually achieving its least sanguine military goal.

Basically, the McNamara Wall was an American high-tech response to the NVA's low-tech effort to infiltrate men and supplies directly across the DMZ. The American effort entailed clearing a narrow strip of ground along about 20 kilometers of the DMZ, seeding the area with electronic detection equipment, and building several strong combat bases and artillery fire bases to interdict the illicit flow from the north.

High-tech—a term of the late '60s. During the '60s, a retired Air Force general named Curtis LeMay called for the United States Air Force to "bomb North Vietnam back into the Stone Age." Some Americans liked the line, but few realized that North Vietnam was only a few levels up from the Stone Age and that it could—and did—weather the fall. The United States, on the other hand, was an eon removed from the Stone Age, particularly in its thinking. Its leaders could never understand how Stone Age men (as it were) thought or how long they could hang in there by their fingertips, elbows, and teeth. High-tech. The Americans lived by it and the North Vietnamese and Viet Cong lived without it—in all but one important aspect.

The North Vietnamese Army fielded superb artillerists. Its Russian and Chinese benefactors provided the NVA with superb doctrine and training and, more important, with some of the best artillery field pieces in the world. Most deadly among those was the 130mm field gun. Mortally accurate and possessed of a range superior to virtually every land-based weapon in the U.S. inventory, the 130mm guns set in battery sites north of the DMZ simply dominated the battlefield or, as the Americans called it, the area of operations. Indeed, the domination of the area of operations, which included "rear" bases, by NVA artillery and frighteningly dense 140mm rocket coverage was the factor that shaped the war of attrition along the DMZ. Americans began thinking of the depth of the battlefield in terms of what they called the 130mm artillery fan. That is, if the 130mm guns set in north of the DMZ could reach a place, that place was on the battlefield. For practical purposes, everything within 20 kilometers south of the DMZ could be hit with accuracy by 130mm guns set in north of the DMZ. In addition, the NVA artillery and rocket positions were untouchable except by artillery counterbattery fire and aerial interdiction. For the most part, the governments of the United States and the Republic of Vietnam honored the DMZ as a valid international boundary; they sent no ground troops across. At least, they sent no large units across in flashy operations.

*

Incorporated into the battlefield defined by the 130mm artillery fan was National Route 9, the two-lane east-west all-weather road that knitted together a network of Marine base camps and artillery positions stretching from the coastal lowlands to the highlands around Khe Sanh. Nearly three regiments of Marine infantry and their vast supports lived in proximity to Highway 9. Dong Ha, at the junction of Highway 9 and South Vietnam's premier north-south highway, National Route 1, was the home of the forward headquarters of the 3rd Marine Division and the full-time headquarters of at least one Marine regiment. It was the main supply base in the area, and the largest artillery base. The 3rd Marine Division maintained a forward field hospital—hardly more than a triage center—underground at Dong Ha. Until they were quite literally blown off the runway by NVA artillery and rockets in the middle of 1967, Marine helicopters were permanently based at Dong Ha.

There was a small Marine position at the abandoned town of Cam Lo, which was on Highway 9 almost due south of Con Thien. There wasn't much around Cam Lo beyond a supply point and an unimposing artillery fire base called C-2 (Charlie-2), a few hundred meters to the north of the town.

Cam Lo was the southwest corner of an area the Marines had dubbed Leatherneck Square. The other corner points were Dong Ha, to the southeast; Con Thien, to the northwest; and Gio Linh, to the northeast. Gio Linh was a shabby fire base manned by the South Vietnamese. Leatherneck Square was really a rhomboid because Gio Linh was farther north than Con Thien.

It is easy to understand why Gio Linh was selected as the site for a combat base. The hill overlooks the so-called Peace Bridge, which carries Highway 1 across the Ben Hai River, the official frontier between the two Vietnams. At the Peace Bridge, each Vietnam maintained a showy little border post reminiscent of posts maintained by the munchkin states of Europe in the nineteenth century. Highway 1 had the potential of serving as an adequate invasion route should the NVA ever get around to launching an armored or mechanized assault against the South. (It did, in 1972 and 1975.)

Dong Ha made sense as a base because it was at the junction of Highways 1 and 9. Basing large units at Cam Lo did not make much sense because of its proximity to Dong Ha—they were about 15 kilometers apart—but there was an important bridge across the nearby Cam Lo River and it had to be guarded. Still, if there had been no Con Thien there would have been a smaller presence at Cam Lo.

Why *was* there a base and a major commitment at Con Thien? Because the 160-meter-high hill at Con Thien overlooked Dong Ha. If the NVA had had artillery forward observers on the hill, they would have been able to hit Dong Ha with an accuracy more telling than that with which they were already pasting the place. Con Thien became an issue because Dong Ha was an issue. Except for denying the hill to the North Vietnamese, there wasn't much reason to defend Con Thien.

Did the NVA gunners really need a forward observer team on the Con Thien hill? The question is moot. They did fine without the vantage point. Was there a larger purpose for their actions?

*

The commander of the NVA was the vaunted Senior General Vo Nguyen Giap. Giap was an innovator, a man given to planning so far ahead that it often took years before all the pieces fell into place. During the Indochina War, Giap had learned what it took to defeat a western force. With only a ragtag irregular army, he had brought down the French colonial empire in the Far East. After the French defeat in 1954, Giap oversaw the slow buildup of Viet Cong forces in South Vietnam. He also set about revamping the irregular army with which he had defeated the French. He modernized it, without abandoning the guerrilla elements that had proved so useful. Giap's new army, the People's Army of Vietnam (PAVN), was an elegant hybrid of modern army and guerrilla force. It was resource-poor but manpower-rich. In the summer of 1966, Giap deemed his army ready to begin "conventional" operations south of the DMZ. When used by Giap, however, the term *conventional* was, well, *un*conventional.

The NVA was composed largely of divisions, the divisions were composed of regiments, the regiments were composed of battalions, and the battalions were composed of companies. At almost all levels, including infantry supporting arms such as mortars and machine guns, an NVA division was structured much like a U.S. Marine division. Though lacking many of the service and support units that the Marines deployed, the NVA deployed many rocket units, which the Americans almost never used. The NVA had few tanks and almost never took trucks or other rolling stock into a battle area. An NVA division and its components were built to live and fight in the bush—something large American units never quite achieved.

NVA battle doctrines were based on an ironclad command structure: Everything started from the top and worked down in a well-defined order. The NVA often employed brilliantly conceived battle plans, but the plans often fell victim to reality when things started happening. Independent thought and action was frowned upon in the NVA, so North Vietnamese field-unit commanders were often at a loss when quick thinking was demanded. Selecting, training, and promoting flexible thinkers was something the NVA eschewed, and that was its greatest failing.

General Giap had a devious plan that centered on Con Thien, but first something must be said about what he did *not* have in mind.

In the Indochina War, Giap's greatest victory had been at Dien Bien Phu, a stunning defeat for France that ended the war by popular acclaim. It has been speculated that, in 1967, Giap sought to emulate Dien Bien Phu along the DMZ, within his vaunted artillery fan. (Artillery had played a major role in his strategic and political victory at Dien Bien Phu.) It has been said that the siege at Khe Sanh, which took place in early 1968, was the Vietnam War's conceptual analog to Dien Bien Phu, but that probably was not the case. It is also arguable that the confrontation centered on Con Thien was an analog to Dien Bien Phu, but that is also doubtful. The conditions were different.

The Americans possessed overwhelming aerial assets; the French had had almost none. Dien Bien Phu was isolated. Its garrison was cut off from outside assistance, particularly resupply. Con Thien was less than 10 kilometers north of Highway 9, in a relatively flat and largely accessible area. Although under constant artillery threat, the Main Supply Route (MSR) from Highway 9 at Cam Lo through Fire Base C-2 was almost never cut. At Dien Bien Phu, Giap had conducted a siege in the classic sense, with army facing army. At Con Thien, the NVA spent most of its time under cover. Portions of one infantry division, the 324B Division, waited for choice game to step into the open. Except for frequent, vicious artillery bombardments, Con Thien cannot be described as being under siege. It was under pressure—as were all American and ARVN bases within the 130mm artillery fan—but it was not under siege. Indeed, throughout the summer of 1967, Con Thien was never attacked *except* by indirect-fire weapons: artillery, mortars, and rockets.

Was Giap simply intent upon drawing blood? Certainly, the bombardment of Con Thien and the bases supporting it—chiefly Dong Ha and C-2—was ongoing, as were bombardments of traffic on Highway 9 and the Con Thien–Cam Lo MSR. And the regiments of the 324B Division certainly tried to bleed Marine and ARVN units that could be caught in the open. But was that all? Was drawing American blood a sufficient reason for sacrificing so much North Vietnamese blood? There is no evidence to suggest that Giap wanted the hill badly enough to attack it. So, what was the focus on Con Thien all about?

Giap wanted to *test* the Americans—their will, their ability to respond, their methods of response. He had to find a sore spot at which they were bound to respond with vigor. As anyone reading an American newspaper in mid 1967 could divine, Con Thien was the place the Americans seemed most determined to defend. But why run a test?

The North Vietnamese had a pet plan they called the General Offensive–General Uprising. In the West today, we know its execution phase as the Tet Offensive of 1968. Before launching it, Giap needed to know the probable reactions of his adversaries. The Con Thien confrontations in the summer of 1967 were one part of the discovery phase. Into early autumn Giap launched similar probing operations against American and ARVN forces elsewhere in South Vietnam. Since one major portion of the General Offensive–General Uprising called for the outright annexation of South Vietnam's two northernmost provinces, Quang Tri and Thua Thien, it made a great deal of sense to test the major battle force in those provinces, the United States Marines.

*

For the Americans, Con Thien certainly represented a major investment in the McNamara Wall, but not much else. It was merely a high place in a relatively flat region, and Americans had come to believe that he who held the high ground controlled everything within his view. Within the constraints of American war-fighting doctrine, Con Thien was a good position to hold.

In addition, Con Thien became a media symbol or, as Americans started calling such things around that time, a "media event." In a war whose political phase at home was just about all media event, media attention often led tactical planning. It is safe to assume that at least part of the Con Thien "game plan"—another expression of the time— was shaped by media attention.

Whatever the reasons for putting Marines in that exposed position, they were there and they were bleeding and drawing blood. No one was winning and no one was losing. The battle would not end until much larger events emerged—until the bloodbath known as the Tet Offensive changed the complexion of the war.

*

The Con Thien Combat Base was large enough to billet only a single Marine battalion and a single Marine artillery battery at a time. Most of the American troops and guns that took part in the ongoing Con Thien event were based outside the combat base, at a network of camps and fire bases close to Con Thien. In addition to Dong Ha, Cam Lo, and C-2, Marine infantry and artillery (including U.S. Army long-range 175mm self-propelled guns) were based to the west, along Highway 9, at Camp Carroll and The Rockpile. From a few companies at C-2 to the battalion at Con Thien to several battalions at Dong Ha, many U.S. Marine units were tied down defending or patrolling around the permanent bases.

At almost all times, Marine infantry battalions operated in the field on both sides of the Con Thien–Cam Lo MSR. All the battalions of the 3rd Marine Division were at one time or another liable for operations—"sweeps"—along and on either side of the MSR and for garrisoning Con Thien. The infantry battalion and artillery battery based inside the Con Thien Combat Base usually stayed for about a month before being rotated. The units garrisoning the other bases came and went more frequently as they rotated in and out of the field.

The sweeps in the field were central to the U.S. plan. It was the job of the U.S. Marine "maneuver" battalions to prevent the 324B NVA Division from blocking the Con Thien–Cam Lo MSR or concentrating for a direct assault. However, there was a rub. The need to secure Dong Ha, C-2, Camp Carroll, and The Rockpile kept enormous resources tied to fixed locations. The need to garrison and guard those bases turned the Marines' maneuver doctrine on its ear and gave rise to the concept that later came to be called the set-piece strategy.

*

The objective of the American "search-and-destroy" doctrine was to locate an elusive enemy, pin him, and destroy him. To do the job in I Corps, the Marine Corps had deployed by mid 1967 a force amounting to 21 infantry maneuver battalions supported by 9 artillery battalions and a wide variety of support and service units.

For practical purposes, the 3rd Marine Division operated in Quang Tri and Thua Thien provinces, South Vietnam's two northernmost states. The 3rd Marine Division consisted of three infantry regiments of nine infantry battalions and an artillery regiment of four battalions, plus supports. The 3rd Marine Division oversaw the 26th Marine Regiment (26th Marines) and a battalion of artillery from the 5th Marine Division, which was still forming in the United States. The 1st Marine Division operated in three neighboring provinces to the south of the 1st Marine Division. The III Marine Amphibious Force (III MAF), a corps headquarters based at Danang, oversaw all Marine units in Vietnam.

The 21 Marine infantry battalions in I Corps should have had an easy time controlling the countryside. There were more Marine battalions than there were NVA battalions, and each NVA battalion was only about one-third the size of a Marine battalion. But, though the Marines called their infantry battalions "maneuver" battalions, the bulk of the Marine infantry in northern I Corps was actually tied down defending fixed bases, which were occupied by the service and support units. Most companies of most Marine maneuver battalions spent most of their time in or near the bases. Through 1966 and the first half of 1967, the Marines tied down maneuver battalions to defend the bases required to keep maneuver battalions maneuverable. The Marines had paralyzed themselves. They were the frozen game pieces of the set-piece strategy.

At the time, the Marines saw their weakness as a virtue. The *stated* policy was to draw the NVA battalions and regiments into battles in which they could be pinned by artillery and air attacks and then attacked by Marine infantry sallying from the fixed bases. The enemy was expected to act in a certain way, and Marines were to respond in a certain way; the enemy was expected to throw himself on the wire around a massively defended position, and the Marines were to wipe him out. This was the American view of the set-piece strategy.

The NVA were not stupid. The Marine bases were self-defending and mutually supporting by virtue of their massive artillery firepower—not to mention fixed-wing combat air support. Therefore, the NVA never launched a direct assault on a Marine base through the summer of 1967. However, though the bases were heavily defended, there were never enough Marine maneuver battalions in the field along the DMZ to locate or destroy the growing number of NVA regiments and independent battalions in the area. Therefore, the NVA were largely free to attack the convoys linking the fixed bases. Amply supplied from the north by circuitous means and accustomed to living underground in deep canopied ravines, the NVA were rarely bothered by Marine sweeps and probes. They attacked when they wanted to attack—when a convoy or a Marine unit in the field was particularly vulnerable or, rarely, when some important issue needed resolution.

The 324B NVA Division suffered extremely high losses whenever it attacked American convoys or roving Marine infantry units, yet it persisted in doing so through the summer. (Most of the losses the NVA suffered were inflicted by the air and artillery units that routinely supported Marine infantry in the field.) Though the price in lives was high, the losses bought something that General Giap needed badly: battlefield information. To get it, he was willing to sacrifice thousands of his best-trained soldiers in what otherwise would have been futile attacks.

*

By the end of August 1967, Marine intelligence analysts were coming to believe—correctly—that the 324B NVA Division was getting ready to cut the Con Thien–Cam Lo MSR in preparation for a major direct assault on Con Thien. To prevent or deflect such a move, the commanding general of the 3rd Marine Division decided to call in extra units to relieve the infantry battalion inside Con Thien. In addition, the extra units were to act as spoiling forces along the MSR.

One of the fresh battalions drawn into the fray was the 3rd Battalion, 26th Marines (3/26), which had been operating out of the Khe Sanh Combat Base since early June. Two of 3/26's four infantry companies and its advance battalion command post had been operating east of the Con Thien–Cam Lo MSR for several weeks as part of an ad hoc 9th Marines task force charged with routinely sweeping that area.

The alert call for 3/26 to move to a position west of and about midway along the Con Thien–Cam Lo MSR came on September 4, 1967. One company was detached for convoy–guard duty. The two companies from Khe Sanh were to meet the battalion command group and the other company at the abandoned village of Nha Tho An Hoa, a spot known as The Churchyard. The Churchyard had been manned for two unexciting and uneventful weeks by about half of the 1st Battalion, 9th Marines (1/9).

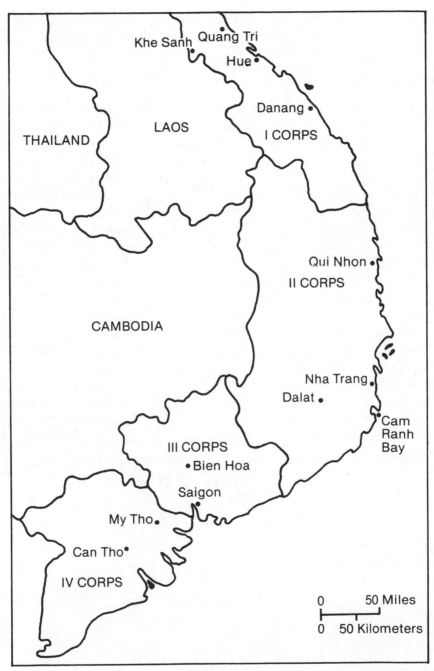

KHE SANH

DONG HA

QUANG TRI

QUANG TRI

SOUTH

CHINA

SEA

THUA THIEN

HUE

PHU BAI

DANANG

QUANG NAM

HOI AN

TAM KY

QUANG TIN

CHU LAI

QUANG NGAI

QUANG NGAI

K.W.White

I CORPS TACTICAL ZONE

NORTHERN QUANG TRI PROVINCE

E.L. WILSON

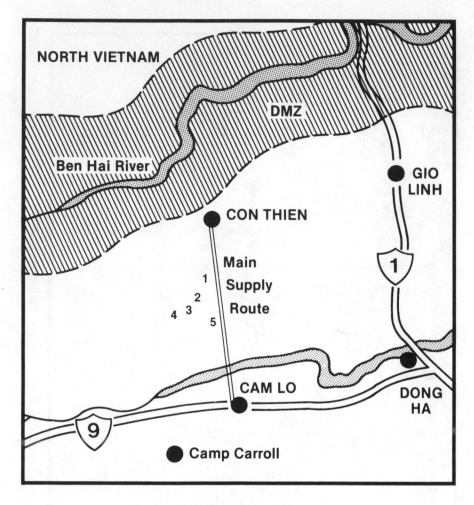

3rd Battalion, 26th Marines
September 6-11, 1967

Key:

1. The Churchyard
2. Bivouac, night of September 8-9
3. Hill 48
4. Hill 88 (NVA regimental command post)
5. Artillery Fire Base C-2

3rd Battalion, 26th Marines
September 7, 1967

Key:

CP	— 3/26 Command Post
81	— 3/26 81mm mortars
⊗	— India Company contact
◍	— India Company perimeter
⊥□	— Church
▦	— Rice paddy area
⤵	— Mike-2 move

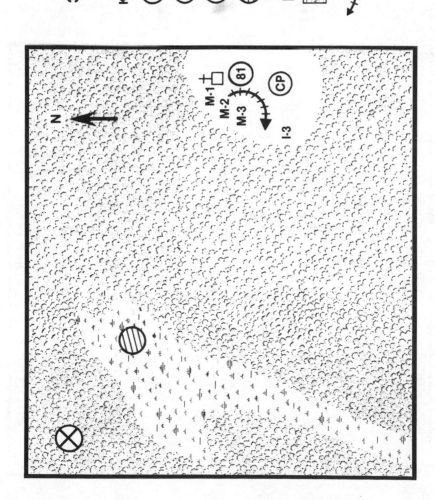

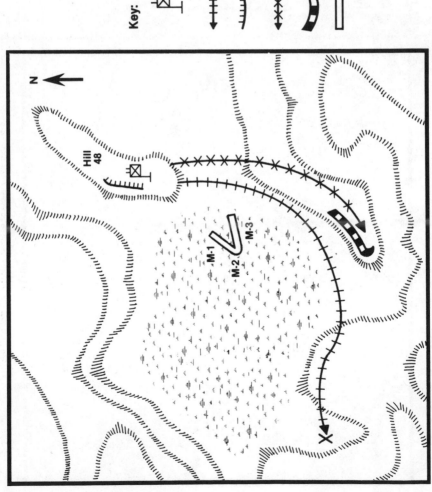

3rd Battalion, 26th Marines
September 10, 1967
0730-1430

Key:

⊠ — 3/26 Command Post

— India Company advance to contact

— Kilo Company position

— Lima Company advance

— Lima Company position

— Mike Company position
(with platoons as indicated)

N

Hill 48

⊠

M-1
M-2
M-3

3rd Battalion, 26th Marines
September 10, 1967
1500-2030

Key:

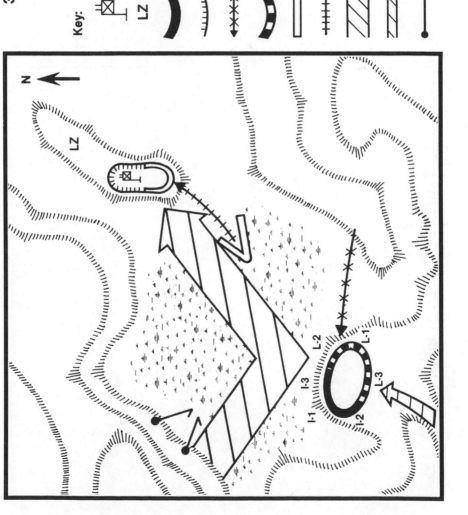

⊠	— 3/26 Command Post
LZ	— Landing Zone
	— India Company position (with platoons as indicated)
	— Kilo Company position
	— Lima Company advance
	— Lima Company position (with platoons as indicated)
	— Mike Company positions
	— Mike Company withdrawal
	— NVA primary attack
	— NVA secondary attack
	— NVA .51-caliber machine guns

PART I

The Churchyard

Chapter 1

The 26th Marine Regiment was first commissioned near the end of World War II and, as part of the 5th Marine Division, fought at Iwo Jima. Immediately after the war, the 5th Marine Division and all its regiments were decommissioned. Rather than call up the Marine Corps Reserve division, the 4th, for the Vietnam War, Congress authorized the recommissioning of the 5th Marine Division, the start of a tedious buildup. The first of the new division's regiments to be recommissioned was the 26th Marines. As its three battalions were formed at Camp Pendleton, California, each was sent to Vietnam and attached administratively to the 3rd Marine Division.

After serving from early October as III MAF's shipborne Special Landing Force, 3/26 arrived in Vietnam on December 11, 1966. Thus, the first members of the battalion eligible to be sent home following standard 13-month tours—those who lasted that long—would leave Vietnam in late September 1967.

The battalion's first operation in Vietnam comprised a number of sweeps in Thua Thien Province, in the Co Bi-Thanh Tan area, on Highway 1 about 13 kilometers northwest of Hue. The U.S. battalion skirmished with a Viet Cong (VC) main force battalion and then was attacked by the Viet Cong unit two days before Christmas 1966. The green Marine battalion stood its ground. The officers and men turned in a creditable performance and learned the ropes.

Following many small clashes in the Co Bi-Thanh Tan and other coastal areas, 3/26 was dispatched to the western highlands of Quang Tri Province on June 13, 1967. The move was made to bolster the permanent garrison at Khe Sanh—mainly 1/26—in the weeks following a major NVA move to capture the high hills that dominated the base.

*

On June 27, 1967, India Company, 3/26, was searching for NVA mortar positions on Hill 689, west of the combat base. Two NVA infantry companies attacked. Lima Company landed from helicopters to cut off the enemy force. The two Marine companies accounted for 35 known enemy dead, but they suffered in kind. Several Marine officers, including the Lima Company commander, were among those killed.

Heavy patrolling and several sharp skirmishes ensued during the remainder of the summer, but the immediate threat to Khe Sanh receded. Many in the battalion felt that 3/26 was merely marking time.

*

1st Lieutenant BOB STIMSON
India Company, 3/26—Executive Officer

3/26 spent the entire summer at Khe Sanh. As the months progressed, and certainly during August, it became clear to me that contacts with the enemy were getting larger and progressively closer to the Khe Sanh perimeter. Anyone who was paying attention could see that they were building up. They were building up everywhere—all around us and on out to the east, toward Con Thien and Gio Linh. The battalions that were down in the lowlands along the DMZ were experiencing the same thing—more frequent engagements with larger NVA units. There was a sense on my part that we would be seeing a big action sooner or later.

2nd Lieutenant CHAN CRANGLE
Mike Company, 3/26—1st Platoon Commander

During the first part of September 1967, 3/26 was split between Khe Sanh and the Cam Lo–Con Thien areas. Mike Company (affectionately known as "Medevac Mike"), H&S Company, and India Company were at Khe Sanh. The remaining companies, Lima and Kilo, and a battalion forward CP were operating in the Cam Lo–Con Thien area.

At the beginning of September, Mike Company spent a lot of time and effort trying to quietly insert into the hills southeast of the Khe Sanh Combat Base, south of Highway 9. The NVA had nailed several recon teams attempting to insert into the area.

Captain ANDY DeBONA
Mike Company, 3/26—Commanding Officer

On September 2, Mike Company went out to an area east of Khe Sanh in which recon teams were constantly getting hit. We decided to pull a fake helicopter insertion—an artillery prep of the area, the fake insertion, and an ambush.

2nd Lieutenant CHAN CRANGLE
Mike Company, 3/26—1st Platoon Commander

Andy DeBona's scheme was to have the helos make several touch-and-go landings, the recon insert profile. But a company, not a four- to six-man recon team, would be waiting for the bad guys.

Captain ANDY DeBONA
Mike Company, 3/26—Commanding Officer

The fake insertion was set for the morning of September 3. Meantime, Mike Company left Khe Sanh the night of September 2 and humped about 13 klicks to set an ambush for any NVA who tried to attack the fake insertion.

2nd Lieutenant CHAN CRANGLE
Mike Company, 3/26—1st Platoon Commander

This was no minor effort, especially since we were far from water. They had to make some helo drops to resupply us, but with only marginal success.

Captain ANDY DeBONA
Mike Company, 3/26—Commanding Officer

After we marched all night through treacherous terrain and got set in, the arty prep began at 1000 and the birds arrived at about 1030. A half hour later, we got the word that we had to be out on the road—Highway 9. That made me a little unhappy after all the effort we'd put in getting there.

2nd Lieutenant CHAN CRANGLE
Mike Company, 3/26—1st Platoon Commander

Andy didn't take too kindly to throwing away a lot of time and effort spent on this project.

The orders were to get our fannies to the highway as fast as possible, straight through some mean countryside—jungles and hills. We had no contacts, but we did have more than a few heat casualties on that forced march.

Captain ANDY DeBONA
Mike Company, 3/26—Commanding Officer

We humped down to the road at about 1400, just in time to catch a ride with Lima Company as it made the final leg of a Rough Rider run from Dong Ha into Khe Sanh.

We sat around in Khe Sanh all day on September 4.

*

Major CARL MUNDY
3/26—Executive Officer

3/26 had been split for about a month. As the executive officer, I was with two companies up at the Khe Sanh Combat Base, with the 26th Marine Regiment CP and the 1st Battalion, 26th Marines. The decision had been made in August to pull the Alpha Command Group—the battalion commander and the principal staff officers—and two of the companies down to operate under the operational control of the 9th Marines at Dong Ha. They had been down there operating for several weeks. As the 3/26 executive officer, I was left up at Khe Sanh.

We received an operations order, a frag order, on about September 1 to prepare to move down for a link-up with the remainder of 3/26. The move was to commence on September 5.

The move out of Khe Sanh was very welcome because we were very isolated up there. Our only connection with the rest of the world was an occasional trip over to the Lang Vei Special Forces Camp, which we had the mission of reinforcing. I was the task force commander for that reinforcement plan, so I used to get out there to Lang Vei a couple times a week. Other than that, there wasn't a great deal around Khe Sanh except the daily patrols that we ran. Life was kind of dry. We had had some limited contact, but not a lot.

When the alert came to move out for an operation southwest of Con Thien, we were very excited.

2nd Lieutenant JOHN PRINCE
Lima Company, 3/26—2nd Platoon Commander

3/26 was sort of the bastard outfit over there. We had the 1st Marine Division and the 3rd Marine Division in Vietnam, but we were part of the 5th Marine Division, so we were *always* opcon—under operational control—to somebody else. It wasn't uncommon to be administratively controlled by one or another of the regiments of the 3rd Marine Division, the 3rd, 4th, or 9th Marine regiments.

Captain ANDY DeBONA
Mike Company, 3/26—Commanding Officer

On the morning of September 5, we got the word we were going to reinforce Con Thien. I was told we were going in south of Con Thien and, possibly, we were going to take over the position inside Con Thien.

1st Lieutenant BOB STIMSON
India Company, 3/26—Executive Officer

We got the word we were moving east, down off the plateau to the lowlands. I was not a member of the battalion staff, so I was never given the full details, just that the operational needs in that sector were greater than they were around Khe Sanh. About all I knew was that it wasn't a routine rotation, that we were going there because of increased enemy activity.

Lance Corporal CHUCK BENNETT
India Company, 3/26, 1st Platoon

On September 5, we all of a sudden got orders for a big move: "Get your gear, we're going." I don't think anyone knew what it was all about. They moved us to the airfield and a huge helicopter—a CH-53—that could hold 50 to 60 troops came to pick us up. It was the only time I ever flew on a CH-53. We were packed in like sardines, in full gear.

1st Lieutenant BOB STIMSON
India Company, 3/26—Executive Officer

September 5 was just at the beginning of the rainy season. Someone had reported there was one or more bridges out along Highway 9 on the way down from Khe Sanh, so we flew with some of our vehicles from Khe Sanh to Camp Carroll in CH-53 choppers.

Major CARL MUNDY
3/26—Executive Officer

Clouds began to come in, which usually would knock off flight operations out of Khe Sanh. I went out on about the next-to-last lift. We were flying out on a CH-53 aircraft, which in peacetime carried 30 to 35 troops. That's what there were seats for. In those days in Vietnam we didn't use the seats. When we rode in a helicopter, we usually got in and plopped down on the deck. On that particular day, we were trying to get the last of the elements down to Camp Carroll before the weather closed us down. From time to time, weather would settle in Khe Sanh for several days at a time. The clouds were ominous as they came in from the sea, and I was advised that air operations out of Khe Sanh were due to be shut down shortly.

We stacked ourselves in the CH-53s like cordwood. The helicopter I went out on had 65 to 70 troops aboard. We had to lean up against each other—stand up and lean against the man behind you and the next man would come in and lean against you.

*

Lance Corporal CHUCK BENNETT
India Company, 3/26, 1st Platoon

We knew something big was coming up, but no one knew what it was. We'd heard there was a lot of stuff going on up at Con Thien, but we didn't know if we were going there. We were wondering, but we didn't know.

At Camp Carroll, I went through the chow line and found a guy serving food who I'd grown up with in Dayton, Ohio. After I ate, he took me outside and showed me around. Camp Carroll was up on a big hill. It had a lot of elevation.

My friend and I were standing around talking and he pointed out to the distance and asked me, "See that dark spot out there?" I could see a big spot where they'd dropped bombs and napalm. It was all burned up. "That's Con Thien. You don't want to go there."

1st Lieutenant BOB STIMSON
India Company, 3/26—Executive Officer

The artillery base at Camp Carroll was on a prominent rise overlooking quite a large area. After we ate, another officer and I walked out to the corner of the camp to see what we could see. I could see all the way to the South China Sea, across the entire lowland plain of northern I Corps and the DMZ. I could easily see Quang Tri City, Dong Ha, and

Cam Lo. I could also see plainly all the fighting out there. I could see tracers and explosions from artillery and mortar fire. And I could hear the rumbling of it. It was the one and only time I ever saw a war from such a vantage point. It was a crystal-clear day in the lowlands. I looked up and even saw a B-52 dropping his bombs. I had been around Arclights a lot, but I had never seen anything like I saw that afternoon—the airplane flying and the bombs coming down. It was like watching a war on the stage. What a show! It occurred to me, "This is where we're going *tomorrow*." I wasn't afraid, but I had an uneasy feeling. I could see that it was going to be a pretty rough proposition.

Lance Corporal CHUCK BENNETT
India Company, 3/26, 1st Platoon

Later on that night, they got us together in a big tent and told us we were going to Con Thien. They said there was a big suspected movement of an NVA regiment around there and that we were going out there with the whole battalion. Someone said it was going to be the first time we'd have the whole battalion operating together.

Staff Sergeant DAVE NUGENT
3/26, 81mm Mortar Platoon

The only thing I knew was that we were going down to relieve 1/9 and set up by a church. No one told us anything else.

Staff Sergeant RUSS ARMSTRONG
India Company, 3/26—1st Platoon Commander

We got the troops dispersed and looked after, and then the officers and staff NCOs gathered in a cluster of hard-backed hooches for the evening. We all spent the evening smoking Philly cheroots and sipping beer from cans someone got for us. It was a very pleasant way to spend the evening, one of the best.

Chapter 2

2nd Lieutenant CHAN CRANGLE
Mike Company, 3/26—1st Platoon Commander

I'm not sure what the purpose was of our frantic race to Camp Carroll. I gathered that the intell folks had decided that the NVA was up to something serious—attacking Con Thien, or perhaps Cam Lo. I knew only that our mission was to move into 1/9's position south of Con Thien, stay out of trouble for a few days, and then move into Con Thien as the palace guard. There were no briefings highlighting specific enemy buildup or recent unusual activity. I knew that Con Thien was a dangerous place under any circumstances, but I didn't hear anything specific at the time.

Captain TOM EARLY
3/26—Communications Officer

We were originally supposed to replace the battalion that was physically inside of Con Thien, but it was decided someone else would do that. I wasn't aware of all the high-level reasons for the changes, but we were sent in to replace the battalion that was in a place called The Churchyard.

2nd Lieutenant PAUL DRNEC
Bravo Company, 3rd Tank Battalion—2nd Platoon Commander

Two companies of 1/9, with my platoon attached, were working out of The Churchyard for a few days or a week going into September. The NVA in that area were under their own artillery umbrella. They could

20

use some pretty bold tactics because they were being supported right out of North Vietnam. They had a lot of flexibility. The 1/9 people were very experienced in that area; they knew it like the back of their hands. They knew how to work the area, but they didn't have one contact the whole time we were around The Churchyard. We swept up and down, but found nothing. Nothing happened.

*

Major CARL MUNDY
3/26—Executive Officer

Nothing unusual happened at Camp Carroll. On the morning of September 6, we got up and found that it was raining. We had escaped the rain at Khe Sanh when we moved down to Camp Carroll, but it rained on us there the next morning as we boarded our organic vehicles and the motor transport that was provided.

In heavy rain, we drove down to Cam Lo, which was the turnoff point for the road that led up to Con Thien and the artillery fire base at C-2. We drove straight up the road. At that time, it seemed a little exciting to me.

2nd Lieutenant CHAN CRANGLE
Mike Company, 3/26—1st Platoon Commander

On the way, north of C-2, we saw an LVT off the edge of the east side of the road. It was thoroughly shot to hell. What was so remarkable was the number of RPG hits. It was a thoroughly blasted and burned hulk. To an infantryman, tanks and LVTs look almost invulnerable. I was aware that the NVA could kill tanks, but I had not seen the results before. Both the fact of the destroyed vehicle and the ferocity of the kill brought home the fact that Con Thien was going to be a far different war than we had previously experienced. I told my platoon sergeant that we were about to get into a very different war from the farmer-and-pitchfork stuff down south!

Captain ANDY DeBONA
Mike Company, 3/26—Commanding Officer

As we drove up the MSR from the Cam Lo bridge, I saw Major Jim Woodring stopped beside the road in a jeep. Jim was then the CO of 3/9, but he was the former S-3 and exec of 3/26. I was very happy to see him, so I pulled my jeep out of the column to say hello. Jim said that he had heard that 3/26 was moving in. He had driven over to tell us that we were moving into a "bad-guy area" and that we should not go out unless we had to, and if we had to, we should go out only as a battalion and with a lot of supporting arms planned.

Lance Corporal CHUCK BENNETT
India Company, 3/26, 1st Platoon

The trucks dropped us on the road. We had to hurry because it was getting dark. We knew there was movement out there, a big NVA force. We wanted to get under cover as quick as we could, before it got dark.

2nd Lieutenant CHAN CRANGLE
Mike Company, 3/26—1st Platoon Commander

By the time we reached the dismount point 2 to 3 miles north of C-2, the weather had closed in. Heavy overcast, drizzling rain, fog, ground visibility down to less than 100 yards.

The guides from 1/9 were wearing ponchos, and as they moved out ahead of us, it seemed surreal, with these green ghosts walking toward the treelines. Noiseless. No chatter. No clatter of equipment. The silence was striking.

I was somewhat of a nut on maps. I had taped the map sections of the Cam Lo–Con Thien area together, and during the ride to Cam Lo, I was doing some intense map reading. Andy DeBona spotted the maps, thanked me for doing such a good job for the company commander, and promptly appropriated them for himself.

With no landmarks to guide on, all I could do was follow the guides in. Part of my unease was not knowing where I was, being mapless for the moment, not having a good handle on the NVA situation. The hair wasn't crawling on my neck, but I didn't feel comfortable.

Staff Sergeant RUSS ARMSTRONG
India Company, 3/26—1st Platoon Commander

As near as I could tell, we stopped in the middle of nowhere, next to a leveled village, Nha Tho An Hoa, and started trading places with a unit of the 9th Marines. The other unit had its leaders, down to the squad level, out on the road to meet their counterparts. The other unit's people took us out to their positions and showed us where to set in. As far as I could see, the emplacement of their positions made no particular sense, so there was no particular merit to all the trouble everyone went to to effect the relief on line. Even worse, we had more people than they did, so the perimeter with which we were left was too restricted.

Captain TOM EARLY
3/26—Communications Officer

On the morning of September 6, I was at Dong Ha with the battalion forward command group and Kilo Company. It was SOP [standard operating procedure] for me to double as the H&S commandant in the field. Since we left much of H&S Company in the rear, the H&S Company commander remained as the officer in command of the rear CP. Hence, all the detachments—flamethrowers, 106mm recoilless rifles, 81mm mortars, and the headquarters section itself—needed someone in charge of them while they were in the field in a mobile situation. So, with the real headquarters commandant remaining in the rear, the acting headquarters commandant in the field usually was me. In this particular situation, I was also serving as the battalion S-4. I had the logistics chief along with me, but I wore the hat when it came to answering questions when an officer thought he had to stick his nose into the resupply situation.

I was not worried as we moved out of Dong Ha in a northerly direction toward the Con Thien area. We were in very good shape. I felt very comfortable with the people and I felt comfortable with the safety of our equipment.

We mounted out from Dong Ha and traveled 3 to 4 miles, until we got to The Churchyard area. It struck me that we didn't see any people. In the whole area, once we cleared Dong Ha, we saw a few people up toward Cam Lo, but north of that was just a wasteland. The only people up there were us little green people. There were absolutely no locals whatsoever.

Going by us after we left C-2 was part of 1/9, which had occupied the position we were going to move into. As we drove up the road from C-2, our former battalion exec, Major Jim Woodring (who now had 3/9, which was up in that area), met us with his sergeant major. Major Woodring took the battalion commander, Lieutenant Colonel Harry Alderman, and a few other folks aside and explained the local situation to them. I think he told them not to go over a certain rise because when anyone did, the 152mm guns across the DMZ would start pounding away.

After meeting with Major Woodring along the road, we continued in truck convoy up to a point southeast of The Churchyard, which was 3½ klicks south of Con Thien.

The area we were in was absolutely new to each and every one of us. Other than a map reconnaissance, none of us had been over this terrain or had patrolled or even seen it in a helicopter or reconned it in any way. It was absolutely new ground.

When we arrived at the dismount point, we immediately began moving out to the left of the road, toward The Churchyard. The only one who had voiced any "be carefuls" was Major Woodring, but I wasn't privy to exactly what he had said.

Major CARL MUNDY
3/26—Executive Officer

I met Lieutenant Colonel Alderman beside the road. We stood in the rain and exchanged greetings, and I turned his other two companies over to him. About the only guidance he gave me was "Go back to the rear. Go back to Dong Ha and set us up a good battalion rear."

I left feeling a little bit like a dog with its tail between its legs as the combat elements of the battalion moved into position and I went to Dong Ha to set up the battalion rear base.

*

Staff Sergeant RUSS ARMSTRONG
India Company, 3/26—1st Platoon Commander

The troops from the 9th Marines we had relieved had had no contact during their stay in the destroyed village. The unofficial word, grunt to grunt during the relief, was that there was nothing around there—no VC, no NVA, no action.

Captain TOM EARLY
3/26—Communications Officer

It concerned me that we immediately began to move into the exact positions that the 1/9 Marines had occupied. At this time, it was late in the afternoon. I think our people were doing it because they were tired and it looked defensible. It was a lot easier to get into somebody else's foxhole than dig your own.

We went to relieve a unit and we found a prepared area with holes dug. Unfortunately, it's sometimes easy to take the lazy way out and put yourself into prepared positions, put yourself into a hole that's already been dug, and just try and change things around a little bit so that maybe you won't take fire from the enemy.

1st Lieutenant RON ZAPPARDINO
3/26—Forward Air Controller

The perimeter we occupied on September 6 was tiny. We were up on a little mound—a slight grade, real small—but it was the highest ground around there. On the outskirts of the little perimeter were some bushes— some low scrub—and lots of trees. It was nicely landscaped, with rice paddies on the other side of the trees. It was really very pretty. I guess the last guys who were there cleared the mound when they dug in.

The church was right off a movie set. One side was blown up, the steeple was sticking up over everything, there was no wall on the other side. It was right out of a John Wayne movie. I remembered it from my early days in Vietnam, when I was flying a Huey gunship with VMO-2.

1st Lieutenant BOB STIMSON
India Company, 3/26—Executive Officer

The position was too small for us because it had been occupied by a smaller unit. The first thing we did was get security out while the rest of us were positioning ourselves. Some positions we took over were deemed satisfactory, but others were not. The perimeter had to be expanded a bit.

Captain ANDY DeBONA
Mike Company, 3/26—Commanding Officer

I didn't like the position Mike Company occupied. It was too damn loose. I was spread out over hell's half-acre and back. By the time we got in there, it was almost dark. By the time we got 1/9's fields of fire, I realized we weren't going to move that night. I didn't like it, but the 1/9 company commander I talked to said they hadn't had any action, that they'd seen about two bad guys in the last three days. The position Mike was in was so big that my CP was about 100 meters behind my center platoon's line.

We were tied in with Kilo Company on my right and India Company on my left, and they were tied in together on the south side of the perimeter. If India and Kilo complained that their positions were tight, then what I think happened was that Mike took over the entire position of the 1/9 company we relieved. India and Kilo wound up squeezing in together in the position of the other 1/9 company. They were too tight and we were too loose.

1st Lieutenant BOB STIMSON
India Company, 3/26—Executive Officer

We were an experienced company. The troops knew what they had to do. The officers and NCOs checked, of course, but the machine-gun teams and 60mm mortarmen knew where to set in their weapons and how to do it without having to be told. Some of the men, and certainly most of the troop leaders, had been doing it for nearly a year. The company commander might have told the mortars which way to lay in, but he and I left it to the gunners to get the job done. We had faith in them. I was the only officer remaining in India Company from when we shipped over; I knew the men better than the others, so I walked the line during the set-in and spoke with them.

2nd Lieutenant BILL COWAN
India Company, 3/26—3rd Platoon Commander

There was a lot of moving and shuffling as the perimeter got expanded so there would be room for our three companies. It was a mess. We walked all the way across the perimeter and then someone told us to go back, that we had to set in on the other side. There were a lot of real thick hedgerows and brush, which slowed us down and added to the confusion. My platoon—and all of India Company—finally set up on the west or northwest side of the perimeter. Mike Company was on our right flank and Kilo Company was on our left.

Staff Sergeant RUSS ARMSTRONG
India Company, 3/26—1st Platoon Commander

There was nothing left of the village, but there were flowers growing. I had the feeling that, by Vietnamese standards, it was a wealthy village. It was different than most of the standing villages in the immediate area, where attention to survival in that economy left no time for aesthetic touches. But this place had sidewalks and the remnants of flower gardens and grassy lawns. There were birds living there. Seeing the flowers and hearing the birds got me thinking about why a place like that could have been touched by war, much less destroyed by it.

As soon as we got there, everyone went to work expanding the cramped battalion perimeter, building positions for our mortars and machine guns, and cutting fields of fire. I have no idea why that spot was picked for a battalion position. There was no vista, no high ground to defend. It was bordered on two or three sides by dense growth we did not control and in which I was afraid enemy soldiers could conceal themselves.

Comfort was paramount to most of us, particularly the old-timers. Many of us were due to rotate home in about three weeks, and we sensed that this was going to be our last trip to the field. No one had given us a clue as to the importance of Con Thien, the nature of our mission, or the potential risks we faced. Cutting fields of fire and setting in our supporting arms was done as a matter of course, of ingrained habit. Expanding the perimeter was done as a matter of comfort.

The position I selected for myself was in the foundation of what had been a small building. What remained was only about 18 inches high, but my position was enclosed on all four sides except for where the door had been. The little foundation allowed me to use heat tabs to cook some coffee that night without the fire being observed.

2nd Lieutenant CHAN CRANGLE
Mike Company, 3/26—1st Platoon Commander

We spent the remainder of the day with patrols out and improving the company positions.

Our arty FO, Lieutenant Crenshaw, who Andy DeBona called Baby Huey, was shooting white phosphorus to mark planned concentrations north of my platoon. Either he was off or the guns were. The first round impacted close enough to get everyone in their holes. Unfazed, Baby Huey called a second shot on the same coordinates—with the same or closer results! By that point, I convinced our cannon cocker that something wasn't right and he should add a few meters to his plot.

*

Staff Sergeant DAVE NUGENT
3/26, 81mm Mortar Platoon

Chief Warrant Officer Dick Holycross was executive officer of the 81mm mortar platoon, but he was in command of the forward section when we left Khe Sanh; the CO, the platoon sergeant, and two gun sections were on an emergency mission somewhere else. We went out with only four of our eight guns—one two-gun section for India and one two-gun section for Mike. We had about 15 people in each section and forward-observer teams out with the companies—no more than 35 mortar people total.

No one led us into the mortar position. Gunner Holycross came back from a battalion officers' meeting and said, "We gotta set up by the church." We didn't like the mortar positions. The church was still there. Anyone looking at a map was going to know we were digging in by the church. It was like a giant aiming stake. Anyone could bring in artillery on us with no problem at all. Also, there were big old trees there that masked our guns in one direction. If anything came from that direction, we wouldn't be able to get the guns on them. I complained to Gunner Holycross and he agreed, so he went up to the battalion CP to complain. Then he came back and said they wanted us where we were, so we began setting up.

Captain TOM EARLY
3/26—Communications Officer

The 81mm mortars were beginning to set up in the exact position that the other battalion's 81mm mortars had been in. This concerned me because I was sure that the position was targeted by the NVA. At my urging and that of Captain Bill Wildprett, the battalion S-3, the battalion commander moved them from the prepared positions to other positions.

Captain ANDY DeBONA
Mike Company, 3/26—Commanding Officer

Gunner Holycross moved his people into a treeline about 30 meters off to the left flank of my company CP position. I didn't know anything about the 81s' move until I looked over and saw them digging their new positions.

*

Lance Corporal CHUCK BENNETT
India Company, 3/26, 1st Platoon

We heard some movement during the night, but not much. They were testing us, I think. They were out there, in front of our perimeter. I could hear movement, but I didn't see anything.

Captain ANDY DeBONA
Mike Company, 3/26—Commanding Officer

The night of September 6 was uneventful.

1st Lieutenant BOB STIMSON
India Company, 3/26—Executive Officer

There was stuff going on away from our position that night. I was not conscious of any specific action in the neighborhood, but C-2 was firing a lot of artillery. There was a lot of noise, but nothing happened right around us. There was nothing significant or out of the ordinary that night.

As far as I was concerned, we were just there. No one communicated to me what our mission was. The captains and above might have known, but I don't think any of the lieutenants or platoon sergeants knew if we were there for a specific reason.

Chapter 3

Staff Sergeant RUSS ARMSTRONG
India Company, 3/26—1st Platoon Commander

September 7 was the anniversary of my leaving the States for Vietnam.

India Company was ordered to run a patrol out in a northwesterly direction. Lieutenant Bill Cowan's 3rd Platoon was left behind to man the company position, but the rest of the company went out, including the skipper, Captain Wayne Coulter, and the exec, Lieutenant Bob Stimson.

Lance Corporal CHUCK BENNETT
India Company, 3/26, 1st Platoon

On the morning of September 7, Staff Sergeant Armstrong went up to a meeting at the company CP. When he came back, he said we were going out on patrol. He was a real gung-ho Marine and liked to volunteer us for stuff. He said we'd be leading the patrol out. It was all "Hurry up! Get moving!"

1st Lieutenant BOB STIMSON
India Company, 3/26—Executive Officer

The company was good at running itself, so my job as executive officer was more tactical—an assistant company commander—than it was administrative. I went out with the patrol on September 7 because I usually went out when all or most of the company was on patrol.

A standard infantry company at the time was 210 officers and men.

Going into The Churchyard, we couldn't have been more than 165. We were way down. With Lieutenant Bill Cowan's 3rd Platoon staying back to man the entire company sector, we would be going out short of officers. The 1st and 2nd Platoons were both commanded by NCOs. Captain Coulter, the artillery FO, and I were the only officers on the patrol. We went out about 80-strong.

*

Staff Sergeant RUSS ARMSTRONG
India Company, 3/26—1st Platoon Commander

It was a very nice day. There was still a lot of dew on the grass and the rolling terrain looked peaceful, tranquil. The birds were singing, the sky was clear, the flowers were waving in a little breeze. It reminded me of home, of eastern Nebraska. It was so pleasant it kind of scared me. The tranquillity of what I was seeing and the chaos of the war I was in didn't fit together.

As far as we were concerned, our job was to take a morning walk in the sun, see what we could see, and return to the battalion perimeter.

1st Lieutenant BOB STIMSON
India Company, 3/26—Executive Officer

The last civilians had been forcibly evacuated from the DMZ area about a year earlier. I had flown over the area once in a helicopter just when we arrived in-country. There were then some people living in the area, but not many, because there was already saturation bombing going on. Consequently, because there was no one living there except Marines and NVA, the cultivated areas were dormant and badly overgrown.

Several times on the patrol, squads moved out to check areas we were not able to see from the main body. Many such detachments were for purposes of security—for example, before the main body could cross a clearing or a trail. These were routine occurrences and saved us time, though the overall pace was very slow. We'd have had to go slow even if there were no danger of enemy troops being around. It took us three to four hours to go only 1,000 to 1,200 meters, though we certainly didn't cut through in a straight line. The ground was very uneven, and the hedgerows blocked us everywhere. That terrain was as tough to move in as any I had ever experienced. It was very confining, very scary. I had a very bad feeling about being in such dense growth.

Staff Sergeant RUSS ARMSTRONG
India Company, 3/26—1st Platoon Commander

We marched out about a klick and the two platoons split. I was supposed to reconnoiter in one direction and the 2nd Platoon was supposed to reconnoiter in the other. We worked our way through fields and battered little villages. We had a general direction in which to head and a general area to reconnoiter, but there were lots of obstructions—buildings, woods, and heavy brush—so we got pretty fragmented.

My method was to send two or three Marines ahead of the main body at a faster pace while the rest of us scattered out to the sides. Everyone was very relaxed. Often as not, as we worked through a tiny built-up area, I joined a fire team and worked with them as they checked through abandoned houses and sheds, seeing what we could see, looking for signs of occupation or military activity.

The terrain was not especially rough. The ground meandered around into little rises here and there. Everything that was low had been rice paddies and everything from the edge of the paddies to the top of each knoll was covered with foliage. I couldn't tell if the growth was natural or if it had been planted by the Vietnamese. It was a combination of trees and bushes such that we couldn't see into it without *going* into it. It was fairly difficult to navigate in, because we couldn't see far enough to locate landmarks on our maps or shoot a resection on to pinpoint our position. Also, our map sheets converged in this area, so it was doubly difficult to be sure a feature on the map was the feature we could see. It was not difficult to walk, but navigating was difficult and tedious.

Another factor that slowed us down was that this was our very first trip out into this new area. We had had a very short turnover with 1/9 the previous afternoon, not enough time to get any details from them about local topography or places to be wary of. It was a rule to move through a new area with trepidation, so it took longer to move across relatively short distances because we tended to be more careful. Also, I was not sure what our purpose in being there was. I did not know what I was supposed to be looking for or doing.

After a while, we came to a grassy area and found four very distinct beaten-down trails in the grass where a military unit had marched through four abreast. I knew we were somewhere near the area of responsibility of a unit of the 4th Marines, but I didn't know quite where their area began. As soon as I recognized the trails in the grass for what they were—signs of a large passing military unit—I thought, "My God, I had no idea the 4th Marines are this close to us!" I filed that away and kept the platoon moving.

Lance Corporal CHUCK BENNETT
India Company, 3/26, 1st Platoon

After we'd been out for a long time, we saw some smoke. It was over by a rice paddy, in some high grass. We came across a big black kettle. There were no VC or NVA or anyone around, but there was rice cooking in the kettle.

Staff Sergeant RUSS ARMSTRONG
India Company, 3/26—1st Platoon Commander

A little later, we came out of some undergrowth within sight of two blown-out churches, about 75 meters apart. Portions of both steeples were still standing. I located two destroyed churches on my map, but visibility was so lousy that I couldn't figure out if these were the same churches. I led the platoon over to the nearest church and climbed up into one of the dilapidated lath-construction steeples to try to find a land feature I could zero-in on so I could determine our position on my map.

I climbed as high as I could to get a look over the treetops. My years as a mortarman had ingrained in me the habit of knowing my position precisely so I could call in fire if I had to. And I wanted to see if I could find the 2nd Platoon. We were in radio contact but had not seen it since splitting up with it. The vista, which was both gorgeous and tranquil, allowed me to pinpoint our position, but I was unable to see the 2nd Platoon.

Shortly after I climbed down from the steeple and we started moving again, Captain Coulter's radioman called and ordered us to rejoin the command group and the 2nd Platoon. I set a direct vector, and we headed out at a good pace along a little trail. The link-up was accomplished without incident, and the company headed northwest.

Eventually, we cleared a treeline and started crossing a large, open rice-paddy area. The open area was open out to only about 250 meters in front of us, to a wooded area to the west, but we could see forever to the left and right—north and south.

The paddy area was dry; it probably hadn't been cultivated in years. We crossed with the 2nd Platoon in the lead and entered the wooded area. It was getting on toward midday and I began expecting to hear the CO order us to break for chow, but he apparently wasn't ready.

As we entered the woods we found a large, dry watercourse or drainage ditch, probably 8 feet deep and about 10 feet across. It did not look man-made. It had a rounded bottom and the sides were semi-sloping. It would take some effort to climb up and out of it. The bottom was dry. There were trees growing up to the edges.

Lance Corporal CHUCK BENNETT
India Company, 3/26, 1st Platoon

We checked the ditch out because it would have been a good spot for an ambush.

Staff Sergeant RUSS ARMSTRONG
India Company, 3/26—1st Platoon Commander

After putting out flankers to walk along the top of the ditch and more flankers partway up the side to keep visual contact with the outer flankers, the bulk of the patrol walked right into the ditch and proceeded along it. It was easier to move in there than in the broken terrain on either side.

1st Lieutenant BOB STIMSON
India Company, 3/26—Executive Officer

Even though part of the company was able to use the drainage ditch, progress remained slow because fire teams and squads had to advance through the brush on either side to provide security for the rest of us. The going for them was every bit as tough as it had been getting out to the ditch.

Lance Corporal CHUCK BENNETT
India Company, 3/26, 1st Platoon

I was a flanker. It was very confined up above the ditch, so most of the time I was up on the rim of the ditch, inside.

Staff Sergeant RUSS ARMSTRONG
India Company, 3/26—1st Platoon Commander

All of a sudden, at 1150, our flankers on the left began taking some sporadic fire—burst, burst, burst, then nothing.

Lance Corporal CHUCK BENNETT
India Company, 3/26, 1st Platoon

There was shooting. It was a bunch of shots—several automatic weapons. I hit the deck and started returning the fire.

Lance Corporal Gary Lindsay was the next guy to my left, about 20 feet away. I saw him go down. I knew he was hit, but I didn't know how bad. I was trying to get fire out to where they were shooting at us from. They were dug in. They were only 75 to 80 feet from me. As soon as I could, I hollered at Lindsay, but the guy never responded. I crawled over there, firing a few bursts as I went. Lindsay was hit in the head. He was already dead. He never knew what hit him.

The NVA kept firing at us and I kept firing at them, but I felt I had to get Lindsay into the ditch. I couldn't leave him out there.

*

Staff Sergeant RUSS ARMSTRONG
India Company, 3/26—1st Platoon Commander

We had no way of telling how many NVA were out there—one lone sniper, a fire team, or whatever. In the direction from which the fire was coming, to our left and left front, was a flat meadow, and behind that, 75 to 100 meters out, was another thick treeline through which I could see no daylight. The fire seemed to be coming from that treeline, but the vegetation was so thick I could not see muzzle flashes.

1st Lieutenant BOB STIMSON
India Company, 3/26—Executive Officer

The company command group was in the middle of the column in the ditch. As soon as the flankers got hit, Captain Coulter started reacting, but the troops reacted on their own, too.

Staff Sergeant RUSS ARMSTRONG
India Company, 3/26—1st Platoon Commander

We instantly set up a hasty defense. More or less instinctively, the unit leaders pushed troops out of the ditch to form a perimeter 20 to 30 meters in circumference in the direction of our march. If forward was twelve o'clock, the perimeter was from nine o'clock to three o'clock by way of twelve o'clock. The 2nd Platoon was on the right, from twelve o'clock to three o'clock and my 1st Platoon was on the left, from nine o'clock to twelve o'clock. The company command group, both platoon command groups, and some of the troops stayed in the middle of the perimeter, down in the ditch.

I passed orders for everyone to stay in place and not to try to attack the enemy position. There were some low shrubs near the ditch, about waist high. The troops used them for cover.

My radioman told me that the word on the company net was that the 2nd Platoon had had three of its flankers wounded in the initial flurry of fire. No one said so, but I assumed that Captain Coulter was calling in a medevac on the battalion net and that we would wait until the WIAs had been flown out.

There was some shooting going on and some explosions—RPGs or grenades—but I don't think anyone in the ditch could see the enemy. I couldn't.

*

Captain TOM EARLY
3/26—Communications Officer

When India Company made contact at 1150, the first news we had at the battalion CP was the noise of the small arms on the battalion tactical radio net. Then we received verbal reports that they were in contact. We found out where they were and that they were pinned down.

1st Lieutenant BOB STIMSON
India Company, 3/26—Executive Officer

The official radio complement at the time provided radios only to the platoon level. We did not rate squad radios. By the book, the exec of an infantry company didn't rate a radio. Based on our experiences, though, we had acquired more than we rated.

Captain TOM EARLY
3/26—Communications Officer

The radio we used as a mainstay was the Marine PRC-25. To anybody who had been around longer than a year or two—through the transition from the PRC-8, -9, and -10—suddenly even a communications guy looked good because of his radios. The PRC-25's main advantage was that when you turned it on, it worked. That kept everybody not only happy but shocked, because that was not the case with the previous radios.

The PRC-25 was a VHF frequency-modulated radio, and we depended on it. It was used not only in the battalion communications net, which connected the battalion commander with all his company commanders, but also by each company's tactical net. I would give each company the number of PRC-25s they needed; I had extras that I could dole out, so anybody who presented a good reason got a few. In many cases, the company tactical net would not only include the company commander and platoon commanders, but as far as those extra radios would go. It would encompass the squad leaders and platoon sergeants also.

1st Lieutenant BOB STIMSON
India Company, 3/26—Executive Officer

I had my own radioman and we had radio communication down more or less throughout the squad level, though I doubt every squad had one. The result was that the demand on everyone to report was great. People just got their butts chewed if they didn't immediately get on the radio and tell the next level up what was going on. Everybody in the chain of command was wary of this—I know I was—so the natural inclination was to immediately get on the horn and report to the next guy up the chain of command because, if you didn't, you knew there was going to be a voice coming over the channel asking why you hadn't reported.

Militarily, the adherence to reporting procedures resulted in a lot of missed opportunities to exploit situations. The North Vietnamese weren't constrained by similar requirements, so they could keep moving. It was the hallmark of the NVA to engage us, for instance, on one side and within a minute or two you had to be prepared to have them coming at you from the rear. They were experts at this. So, while the Marines were screwing around with this onerous reporting of situation, casualties, number and type of rounds expended—all the stuff that was kept in the statistical morass that *was* the Vietnam War—the NVA infantry was firing and maneuvering at us. They were figuring out how to beat us while we were encumbered with all the statistical stuff the Marine Corps and the Department of Defense needed so they could figure out whether we were winning the war and by how much. It was lunacy!

Captain TOM EARLY
3/26—Communications Officer

The word was passed from India Company to our battalion CP group over the battalion tactical net. In Vietnam, very few of our nets had security devices on them. So, when anything was reported over an unsecured net, the enemy, who had captured many PRC-25s, was assumed to be dialed in on that frequency. We assumed the NVA was monitoring everything that was being said and that they knew exactly what we were doing. This gave the NVA a tremendous advantage since they knew exactly how India Company was pinned down, where they were pinned down, what they were calling for fire support, and what help they needed. The NVA knew all the essential elements of information, probably as quickly as the battalion CP group.

*

1st Lieutenant BOB STIMSON
India Company, 3/26—Executive Officer

As soon as the shooting started, some of the more adventurous squad leaders fired and maneuvered and did the things crack infantrymen are supposed to do. But others and their seniors—the platoon commanders, Captain Coulter, and me—had to report the situation up the chain before we could do anything about the battle. Once we got that done, it was too late to exploit whatever it was we were involved with. Meanwhile, I'm sure *all* the NVA were either firing or maneuvering or trying to size up what they had come up against.

The NVA nearest to my position were very close, certainly no farther than 25 yards. There were little open areas out there, but mostly it was high brush, high grass, and trees. If they had been any distance away, they never would have seen us. Their vision was as encumbered by the thick vegetation as ours was. I'm sure the guys who first ran into us hadn't seen us until they were right on top of us. I'm sure they didn't know if we were a platoon, a company, or a battalion. While they were trying to find out what we were, most of our leadership was *not* doing the same. We were all trying to report.

I made sure that information from the platoons and squads got to Captain Coulter, and up to Battalion. Only when we completed the initial rush of reporting did we start trying to push squads and fire teams out in an organized, centrally controlled manner to see what we were up against. We were doing what they were doing, but later.

*

Staff Sergeant RUSS ARMSTRONG
India Company, 3/26—1st Platoon Commander

Shortly after we set out our hasty defense perimeter, I asked my squad leaders to report. Two of them responded instantly, but the last one, Sergeant Alexander Chisholm, of my 2nd Squad, did not respond.

Scotty Chisholm was an interesting fellow. He was 28 years old and a native of Scotland. He had served for five or six years in the British Army, in a Highland unit, and was a college graduate. I believe he might have been an officer. He was not a U.S. citizen, but he had a green card and was thus prime for the draft. He was an exceptional land navigator; I depended on him a lot. I don't think there was anywhere in Vietnam he couldn't navigate us to. Because of him, the 1st Platoon was almost always the company's point element when we were on a move.

Scotty didn't respond when I asked the squad leaders to report, so I had to ask him again to report. He finally came to me and said, "I think Lindsay may have been hurt." That was Lance Corporal Gary Lindsay, the 2nd Squad's 2nd Fire Team leader. Chisholm and Lindsay were boot-camp buddies, very tight.

I asked, "Do you know for sure?"

"No, I'm not sure," he replied.

I yelled over across the field on the left side of the ditch, toward where we thought Lindsay was. At about the nine-thirty position, I could see someone's shoulder and boots. They were about 15 meters out. There was no response, so I climbed up on the bank of the ditch and put on a burst of speed. I hit the ground, rolled, got up, and ran again. I did that a few times until I got to within a few feet of Lindsay, then I yelled, "Lindsay, goddammit!" There was still no answer, so I crawled up beside him, reached over, and grabbed onto him. He was limp. I rolled him over and saw that his head had a big gaping hole in it. He was dead, but I yelled for a corpsman and added that I wanted some men to help pull him in. One of the docs responded, and he and two or three Marines did what I had done, ran and rolled until they reached us.

Lance Corporal CHUCK BENNETT
India Company, 3/26, 1st Platoon

Gary Lindsay was one of the finest guys I met in Vietnam. He was there when I got there, and he took me under his wing. He taught me the ropes. He was a good talker and a really strong man, a bodybuilder. He was always laughing. Lindsay was a damn good Marine and a good friend. He'd taught me not to make friends over there, but he was my friend.

1st Lieutenant BOB STIMSON
India Company, 3/26—Executive Officer

Lance Corporal Lindsay had been one of the all-stars in the Hill 689 battle at the end of June. He had really come into his own there, had showed a lot of fortitude that afternoon.

Lance Corporal CHUCK BENNETT
India Company, 3/26, 1st Platoon

Lindsay had a powerful build and big bones; he was muscular and heavy. And he had all his gear on. It was hard to move him.

Staff Sergeant RUSS ARMSTRONG
India Company, 3/26—1st Platoon Commander

The troops took off their belts and looped them under Lindsay's arms. When they were ready to move him, I led the way back, crawling toward the ditch.

Most of the men were manning a perimeter. Only the company command element and a squad or two were still in the ditch. So was Scotty Chisholm. As the troops who were dragging Lindsay in pulled him down the bank of the ditch, I looked right at Scotty, who was sitting erect on the bank. He had piercing blue eyes, but now they seemed to be staring 5,000 meters into the distance. Inside his head, I was sure, he wasn't anywhere near Vietnam. Scotty had been the most effective squad leader I had. He was due to rotate with me and most of the rest of the "old" battalion. I decided then and there that, as soon as we got back to the battalion perimeter that evening, I was going to find him a job in the rear. He was used up; he'd had enough.

*

1st Lieutenant BOB STIMSON
India Company, 3/26—Executive Officer

They kept probing us with fire. This was to get a response from our M-60s and mortars, to see how large a unit we were. I'm sure—I *know*—they were moving around us and maneuvering progressively closer and closer to learn what we were.

I was busy. I also was very wary and frightened. However, I think the professional skills we had developed worked for us. Though we were late getting started because of the reporting, we knew what had to be done, and we did it. Everyone knew and everyone did it. Captain Coulter and I never worked in the same place, so I'm not sure what he was doing besides answering questions from Battalion. While the captain continued to speak with Battalion, I started moving around, helping the platoons and squads tactically. The company command group stayed in the ditch, but I moved everywhere outside the ditch.

I believe we were probed initially by several very small NVA units—fire teams. I was never sure because my view was restricted by the undergrowth. But what I heard—flurries of small-arms fire at intervals from different places—led me to that conclusion. They seemed to move around a lot, so I had no idea how many fire teams there were. The whole NVA force might have been only a squad or two altogether, but they kept us very busy and confused by firing from a lot of different places all around our position.

Staff Sergeant RUSS ARMSTRONG
India Company, 3/26—1st Platoon Commander

I was very concerned. I had no idea what lay in store for us, no idea what was out there. I knew that most of my men had only two or three weeks left. One of my short-timers was dead, and another seemed to have lost his effectiveness.

Whatever enemy were out there, we were holding them with fire from our weapons. They were close, but too far away to reach us or be reached by us with hand grenades. Our fire was reactionary; whenever they fired out from the woods, we fired back. We didn't know what we were shooting at; we couldn't see anyone. All we did was fire at the source of their fire, at muzzle flashes when we could see them. When their fire stopped, ours stopped. We didn't fire again until they started firing again.

In time, the 2nd Platoon's three wounded flankers and Lindsay were brought into the ditch, but another Marine, who did not respond to calls, could not be recovered from a bomb crater into which he had fallen. The enemy fire was so intense that no one could get to him.

I heard that the skipper had called for a medevac chopper, but there was quite a bit of delay.

Captain TOM EARLY
3/26—Communications Officer

It took a long time to get the helicopters from Phu Bai or wherever they came from. Our request had to go up through the helicopter request net, had to be confirmed, and then they had to send the helicopters.

Staff Sergeant RUSS ARMSTRONG
India Company, 3/26—1st Platoon Commander

I also heard that the skipper had put in a request for fixed-wing air support, but, like the medevac, it got delayed.

Captain TOM EARLY
3/26—Communications Officer

There was an AO [aerial observer] up. The AOs were always on the same frequencies. We knew what those frequencies were; we all had them in our little notebooks. Any CP could come up and talk with him, ask him any questions they wanted. The AO was an artillery officer who could either help our FOs on the ground or call artillery fire himself. He could also call naval gunfire if there was a ship on station, or he could run fixed wing if there were fixed-wing aircraft in the area, or he could assist the arty FO on the ground in spotting exactly where the rounds should go into the enemy positions. So, we were in a position to control air either from the ground position with the FAC or from the air with the AO. It certainly was simpler for the AO because he was up there and could observe more from that little bird dog airplane.

*

The AO was aboard a single-engine light "Bird Dog" observation plane. He had arrived over the India Company position within about 30 minutes of the initial exchange of gunfire. Circling over a wide area, he located an NVA bunker and six NVA soldiers in fighting holes. He also reported that one of the NVA soldiers had an automatic weapon. The AO requested immediate air support. Typically, Marine jet fighter–bombers based at Danang, on the coast, needed at least 30 minutes to take off and get on station along the DMZ. They were thus due to arrive at about 1300, about 70 minutes after the first shots were fired.

Lance Corporal CHUCK BENNETT
India Company, 3/26, 1st Platoon

The NVA kept firing at us. They'd fire and then they'd move and fire again. It was sporadic fire. They were probing, trying to find out what we had.

There were fast movers coming in, dropping bombs near us. They had to give us cover so we could move out of there. They were dropping right on top of us, close in. They were shaking the ground real bad.

Staff Sergeant RUSS ARMSTRONG
India Company, 3/26—1st Platoon Commander

The 2nd Platoon managed to recover the Marine from the bomb crater. When they got to him, he was dead.

1st Lieutenant BOB STIMSON
India Company, 3/26—Executive Officer

It suddenly quieted down. I think they left because they found out what they wanted to find out.

We had to move the wounded to an LZ [landing zone] about 100 meters from where we had been engaged. They were all serious enough to have to be carried. An H-34 came in and picked them all up, but they didn't take the two dead Marines.

The medevac took place at 1320, 90 minutes after the first shots were fired and at least an hour after medevacs were requested. At 1325, the AO directed an additional fixed-wing strike. The pilots claimed four confirmed NVA deaths. At 1400, as India Company was moving back toward the battalion main body, the AO sighted a squad of NVA about 400 meters northwest of the original point of contact. He called for an artillery fire mission. The guns were fired, but the AO was unable to determine the result. At about the same time and several hundred meters to the southwest of the original point of contact, the AO located a new foot trail and, nearby, "many new bunkers."

*

Though 1/9 had reported that there had been no contacts around The Churchyard, it was well known that many NVA were living in the area. India Company's contact and the AO's sightings were not deemed significant. It was inevitable, given the number of NVA in the area, that Marines would run into them from time to time.

Chapter 4

Captain ANDY DeBONA
Mike Company, 3/26—Commanding Officer

Mike Company's patrol on the morning of September 7 was directed generally south, a little to the east of the battalion perimeter—about 4 klicks altogether, out and back, roughly parallel to the MSR between C-2 and Con Thien. Being out in that open, rolling terrain was a tad bit eerie. I had had that talk with Major Jim Woodring, the former 3/26 exec, the previous afternoon, and he had told me specifically to stay put in our positions unless the entire battalion moved. I wanted to get out and back into the battalion perimeter as quick as I could. While I was out, I wanted all the fire-support protection I could get.

The only signs of people we found were old NVA fighting pits. They were easy to tell from Marine fighting holes because they were symmetrically so much better. The terrain was a series of rice paddies cut up by treelines, something like squares. We tried to cover two or three treelines at a time with our flankers all the way out. The flankers were on the inboard side of the treeline as we moved.

On the way out, we reconned by fire. We put our artillery on the high ground and had 60mm mortars pop off quite a few rounds. We went out about 2 klicks and turned around. On the way back in, it was completely quiet. We did not recon by fire on the way back in.

Mike returned to the battalion CP location and occupied our old positions late in the morning, about 1100. As soon as we got back in, I sent out a water run. A few Marines from each of the platoons and some of the attachments got together with a security squad and went down to a stream near the position. We also had a redistribution of ammunition.

Before the water was passed out, India Company reported on the battalion tactical net that they were in contact. There were no details. All they said was that they were in contact. Approximately 20 minutes later, when our water detail came back in and everybody got their water, India Company was still in contact. I monitored the battalion tac net and alerted my platoons to get ready to go to the aid of India Company. Then I gave a call to Battalion, saying that we were ready to go out to aid or support India if they needed us. The S-3, Captain Bill Wildprett, told me to wait. I didn't hear anything, so I called in again. Wildprett told me that Kilo Company was going to go. I continued to monitor the net.

*

2nd Lieutenant PAUL DRNEC
Bravo Company, 3rd Tank Battalion—2nd Platoon Commander

I arrived in Vietnam in July 1967 and was assigned directly to Bravo Company, 3rd Tank Battalion, which operated out of Camp Carroll and spent most of its time working with the 9th Marines. During my first five to six weeks in-country, my platoon constantly worked south of Con Thien, mostly with the 9th Marines.

A normal tank platoon was composed of five M-48 gun tanks equipped with 90mm main guns. Because of breakdowns and other damage, my platoon went into September with only three gun tanks. We also had a flame tank attached. It was a battalion asset, one of two that were normally based with Bravo Company out of Camp Carroll. Also under my nominal control were two Ontos, which belonged to the 3rd Antitank Battalion. They were placed under my control because they were *tracked* fighting vehicles, but they had to be specially supported and supplied because they were completely incompatible with tanks. They used gasoline instead of diesel, and they each had six 106mm recoilless rifles while we used 90mm ammo.

On the afternoon of September 7, I heard that one of the 3/26 patrols had made contact west of The Churchyard and that there were casualties. The entire tank platoon—all three gun tanks and the one flame tank— was assigned the mission of linking up with India Company. Kilo Company, reinforced by all the tanks, left the battalion perimeter heading in a westerly direction.

*

Staff Sergeant RUSS ARMSTRONG
India Company, 3/26—1st Platoon Commander

At about 1330, after the medevac birds lifted out the three 2nd Platoon WIAs (they had to leave the two dead Marines), Captain Coulter told us that Battalion was sending Kilo Company and a few tanks to link up with us.

Kilo and the tanks originally were supposed to come all the way out to where we were. But after a long wait they told Captain Coulter that the tanks couldn't get across a paddy area, that we would have to move back to where they had had to stop. Captain Coulter ordered us to withdraw and link up with Kilo Company.

With my platoon in the lead and me only three places behind the point, we went back down the drainage ditch to about where we had entered it on the way out.

1st Lieutenant BOB STIMSON
India Company, 3/26—Executive Officer

The India Company column was going slow because a lot of things were limiting us: We had to carry the two KIAs, everyone was dog tired, the terrain was bad.

We retraced our route over the same ground we had gone in on. Most important, we had been in contact and *knew* there were NVA out there who knew what we were and where we were; we had to be super cautious. I felt as I had never felt before. I kept thinking, "Man, they are *here.*" That feeling came, not only because of the small engagements we had just had, but because I had been sensing "something" in the air the whole time we had been out on patrol. From the start, I could just *sense* that we were in the wrong place to be with such a small unit.

I was toward the rear of the column and Captain Coulter was toward the front. I knew we were coming up on the big paddyfield and would have to cross in the open. The "big" paddyfield was really quite small as paddyfields went—only about 100 meters wide—but it was all open ground. At the time, it *seemed* huge. There was no way around it. By then, we realized our situation was critical. The shortest and quickest way back was the way we had come—across the open ground.

Staff Sergeant RUSS ARMSTRONG
India Company, 3/26—1st Platoon Commander

When my platoon had the point, it was my policy to travel right behind our point so I could see what was going on and be there to make decisions instantly if we walked into anything. I had Kilo Company's call sign and radio frequency, so I decided to switch frequencies so I could call ahead and find out if they could see anything. There was a Guamanian staff sergeant in Kilo, and he had a very pronounced accent. I asked for him just to be sure I was talking to the right people—our side.

As it turned out, Kilo Company and the tanks were not very far away. As we reached the break in the woods and saw the big, wide-open paddyfield, I could hear the tank engines. I don't know why, but I was hesitant to just leave the ditch and start moving across the big open area.

The paddyfield was about 150 meters across to Kilo Company's position, east of us, but it was much wider to my right and left, from approximately north to south. It was a very long, relatively narrow open area, somewhat rolling, divided up into small paddies by dikes and berms the Vietnamese used to control irrigation. Like everything else in the area, the paddies had been abandoned long before.

I looked down into the open area to my right. About 400 meters out I saw a man in a Marine helmet and flak jacket motioning for me to come to him. Something didn't seem right. The man was to my right front, but the tank engine noises sounded like they were coming from straight ahead. I could also see uniformed men straight ahead, but not as clearly as I could see the man to my right front. I could not see the tanks at all, presumably because they happened to be behind or below some of the intervening rolling terrain, or they might have been inside the trees on the far side of the paddyfield.

I said to the Guamanian staff sergeant, "Hey, we're standing on the edge here. Can you see my pointman?"

He told me to wait a minute, and when he came back, he said, "Yes, I can see him."

"Okay. If we keep coming straight from here, are we going to link up with you?"

"Yes. Come right across that berm and we'll be together."

"Okay, then, I'm checking out of your frequency." I immediately forgot about the guy who had been motioning at me from the right and headed straight out. I thought back to the beaten-down trails in the grass we had located during the early part of the patrol and came to the conclusion that the man in the flak jacket was from the unit in the adjacent sector, a battalion of the 4th Marines.

We had put the dead into body bags. It was taking six people to carry each of the bags. As we started across the paddy area, the men tried to stay on the paths on top of the paddy dikes, but the paths were extremely narrow and, invariably, the men on one side of the body bag or the other had to step down onto the sloping side of the dike. It had been a long day, everyone was tired, and the bodies were very heavy, very hard to hold even at knee level. The heads of the dead men, which were lolling around even lower, kept getting caught in the mud. It was terrible. Everyone felt terrible. I kept thinking how chickenshit it was for not sending medevac helos to lift out our dead.

1st Lieutenant BOB STIMSON
India Company, 3/26—Executive Officer

While the forward elements of the company moved across the paddyfield, I stayed back with the rearguard and set them in to cover the rest of the company. We were very anxious to get moving, to complete the crossing. I was sure there were NVA breathing down our necks. Soon, Captain Coulter contacted me to say that he was in sight of the tanks that had come out with Kilo Company.

When the lead elements established a base of fire on the other side to cover us, the rearguard finally got the word to cross. Also, the tanks came out partway into the paddyfield to cover us across the open ground.

2nd Lieutenant PAUL DRNEC
Bravo Company, 3rd Tank Battalion—2nd Platoon Commander

The surface of the paddies looked dry, but there was a lot of water underneath the surface crust, so the paddies could not support the weight of the tanks. The tanks skirted the paddies by heading in a northerly direction until we made contact with India Company close to the northern treeline, about two-thirds of the way across.

1st Lieutenant BOB STIMSON
India Company, 3/26—Executive Officer

I was of the opinion that tanks were more of a hindrance in Vietnam than they were a help. The terrain, the hedgerows, the vegetation, the inability of tanks to go across certain areas such as rice paddies had the effect of channelizing the infantry's moves. They were noisy and they attracted artillery, mortars, and rockets. I always felt I didn't need them when I was out on a patrol. They were fine as a defensive weapon, but I wasn't crazy about having them out on patrols.

Staff Sergeant RUSS ARMSTRONG
India Company, 3/26—1st Platoon Commander

As we approached the middle of the paddyfield, the tanks came out to meet us. When we reached them, they were sitting behind a natural berm at the edge of the open area, one behind the other, with their main guns pointing over our heads, back toward the way we had come.

Lance Corporal CHUCK BENNETT
India Company, 3/26, 1st Platoon

My fire team was carrying Gary Lindsay's body. He was heavy and it was very slow going. We had a hard time moving with him because the ground was soft. His head, which was hanging down, kept getting stuck. We finally put Lindsay's body down where we were told—beside one of the tanks—and kept on going.

2nd Lieutenant PAUL DRNEC
Bravo Company, 3rd Tank Battalion—2nd Platoon Commander

As the grunts hiked past us, I saw that they were placing two dead bodies on one of the other tanks.

1st Lieutenant BOB STIMSON
India Company, 3/26—Executive Officer

We were all very concerned that we were going to be attacked from the rear.

Staff Sergeant CHARLES OWENS
Kilo Company, 3/26—Company Gunny

We set up a base of fire in the treeline along the eastern edge of the paddyfield. Our captain told the India Company captain to go ahead and we would follow in trace, but their captain told us to go ahead and they would follow in trace of us, so we went in.

1st Lieutenant BOB STIMSON
India Company, 3/26—Executive Officer

My rearguard element was successful in getting across the paddyfield without any problems, and we joined up with the rest of the India Company patrol. I did not see anyone from Kilo Company then, but I knew we were in touch with them.

As I moved across the paddyfield, I passed the tanks, on which our dead had been placed. Captain Coulter told me to change positions with him in the company column: "You go forward," he said, "and keep our forward elements in contact with Kilo. I'm going to be firing the 90mm guns on these tanks back across the paddy." I thought the captain's idea was okay; it would give us additional protection and time to get through the thick vegetation between our position and the battalion main body. He was heading back toward the tanks, and I kept right on going to assume control of the front of our column.

The India patrol had turned itself inside out. The 1st Platoon had been on the point during the retrograde across the paddyfield, but it had provided my rearguard with cover as we crossed. When the column started back to the battalion perimeter, the 1st Platoon stayed in position to provide rearguard cover and the 2nd Platoon passed through it and went to the head of the column to link up with the rear elements of Kilo Company.

2nd Lieutenant PAUL DRNEC
Bravo Company, 3rd Tank Battalion—2nd Platoon Commander

Kilo Company and the lead elements of India Company had moved into the eastern treeline and started back to the battalion perimeter on a due easterly heading. As far as I was concerned, the tanks were now under the operational control of India Company.

Staff Sergeant RUSS ARMSTRONG
India Company, 3/26—1st Platoon Commander

It took about 20 minutes to complete the link-up, load the dead, and get Kilo Company started back toward the battalion perimeter. While that was going on, I sent Corporal Heyward O'Neal's 1st Squad ahead to take up a covering position at the point of a woodsy finger protruding into the paddyfield north of the tanks. The 2nd Platoon extended itself east to maintain contact with Kilo Company, and part of my 1st Platoon started extending itself behind the 2nd Platoon to maintain contact with it. I ran my platoon from a little diked paddy about 50 meters from the tanks. I stayed there because the tanks did not move and because Captain Coulter, who was over by the tanks, did not tell me to follow the 2nd Platoon back toward the battalion perimeter.

*

1st Lieutenant BOB STIMSON
India Company, 3/26—Executive Officer

Captain Coulter was a great big, massive guy, a former Midwest football player. He was very much a soft-spoken gentleman. He joined the battalion just about the time we got to Khe Sanh in June 1967, just in time for our big battle on Hill 689. He proved himself a good leader then.

Staff Sergeant RUSS ARMSTRONG
India Company, 3/26—1st Platoon Commander

Captain Coulter still looked every bit a member of the defensive team. He was relatively tall, about 6 feet, and very stocky and chunky. He ate as though he was still a football player. He wasn't overweight, but he was certainly a big man. He kept a very close crew cut, and I always noticed that he didn't have a neck. His head and his shoulders were right together. He had a broad back and kind of cauliflower ears.

I watched him as he climbed up onto the lead tank and thought he still looked fit enough to play football. When he was on the turret, he stood straight up and sort of straddled the 90mm gun tube.

2nd Lieutenant PAUL DRNEC
Bravo Company, 3rd Tank Battalion—2nd Platoon Commander

The India Company commander told me that he wanted me to fire rounds out toward the area in which the company had made contact earlier. I told him that I'd prefer having all his people out of the open paddyfields and back in the treeline before I started shooting, but he said, "No, let's start shooting now."

The commander of my tank was Sergeant Vining, who served as the loader when I was aboard. Sergeant Vining was very experienced. In fact, he was on an extended tour and had worked the same area for a long time. He came up with some pretty good dos and don'ts. As soon as the company commander said, "Let's start shooting now," Sergeant Vining said, "Oh, for Christ's sake, whatever you do, get the troops the hell out of the open!"

Vining was the expert; he knew what was going to happen next. At that, I told the captain, "Hey look, sir, let's get the hell outta here and *then* we can start playing games." But he said, "No." Vining kept talking: "Don't play around in the open. Let's get the hell outta here." We went a few more rounds, until I realized that the quickest way out of there was doing what the captain wanted me to do. "Okay, sir," I finally agreed, "We'll do your shooting." The captain pointed back to where he wanted the fire.

*

1st Lieutenant BOB STIMSON
India Company, 3/26—Executive Officer

I was extremely concerned that we stay in touch with Kilo. It was late in the afternoon—it was getting dusk—and I knew that our speed was going to be very slow over the last 400 to 500 meters to the battalion perimeter.

Staff Sergeant RUSS ARMSTRONG
India Company, 3/26—1st Platoon Commander

With the skipper pointing the way, the tank traversed its turret a little bit and fired a round. Then Coulter adjusted, and the tank fired again.

1st Lieutenant BOB STIMSON
India Company, 3/26—Executive Officer

As I moved toward the front of the column, I heard the sound of a 90mm tank round being fired. Captain Coulter called me on the radio and told me he was going to stop and fire. I assumed he was moving to the eastern edge of the paddyfield when he called. I replied that Kilo was moving farther and farther away from us, but he said, "That's all right. We're going to keep firing." I had no way of communicating with Kilo because my radioman was not tied into the battalion net; all I could talk to were other radios in India Company.

In hindsight, I suppose I could have switched frequencies and come up on the battalion net, but that was something we *never* did; only the company commander did that. It wasn't something I thought of, or would have thought of. It would have been very unusual. Net discipline was always very difficult to maintain, so lower echelons were discouraged from breaking into the battalion net. It all had to be done through channels. Besides, I had to assume that the captain knew what he was doing, that he was in control of the situation, notwithstanding my report that I was concerned.

I was concerned that if Coulter stopped, I would have to stop, and that we then would lose contact with Kilo. I thought to myself, "Oh, Christ, we have to stop. We're part of India Company; we can't go with Kilo." I knew that we were making a mistake, but I had to stop. I had to. It was our unit that was out there. We couldn't split up. We were already only two platoons and in a very precarious situation. I was extremely concerned that Kilo was still moving away from us, like a train going down the tracks. I could see them—the tail end of Kilo—disappearing.

I disagreed with what Captain Coulter was doing. That was not the time or place to stop. I didn't believe Captain Coulter intended to take much longer, though; I think he just wanted to do a little more firing. I didn't know if he saw something over there, or what.

2nd Lieutenant PAUL DRNEC
Bravo Company, 3rd Tank Battalion—2nd Platoon Commander

We had cranked off three or four rounds when, *KaBOOM,* mortars started falling in around us.

Staff Sergeant RUSS ARMSTRONG
India Company, 3/26—1st Platoon Commander

As soon as the third round was fired, all hell broke loose. A volley of 140mm rockets just came raining out of the sky on us. Captain Coulter, who was more exposed than anyone else, was one of the first casualties.

1st Lieutenant BOB STIMSON
India Company, 3/26—Executive Officer

I was 15 to 20 meters into the brush, east of the eastern edge of the paddyfield, when we lost contact with Kilo. It was then that the NVA

82mm mortar rounds started to come in on the rear of the company: Captain Coulter, the tanks, and Russ Armstrong's 1st Platoon.

Lance Corporal CHUCK BENNETT
India Company, 3/26, 1st Platoon

I was in the open, past the tanks, when we started getting everything— mortars, RPGs, artillery, rockets, small arms. It was all going toward the tanks. Around the tanks was no place to be, so I moved out as fast as I could. There was no cover in the open. I was still running when the tanks moved on through us, toward the eastern treeline.

Chapter 5

2nd Lieutenant PAUL DRNEC
Bravo Company, 3rd Tank Battalion—2nd Platoon Commander

As soon as the incoming started, I ducked into the turret and pulled the hatch down over me—an automatic reaction. The last I saw of the India Company captain, I assumed he was about to dive under the tank.

We were safe for the moment. It was only mortar fire.

Staff Sergeant RUSS ARMSTRONG
India Company, 3/26—1st Platoon Commander

Except for low paddy dikes and the natural berm where the tanks were, there was no place to take cover from the mortar rounds, so we just spread out and, in the confusion, managed to set up some type of a perimeter. I don't know what we would have done without the berm and dikes.

1st Lieutenant BOB STIMSON
India Company, 3/26—Executive Officer

Very quickly, as soon as the mortar rounds started landing around the tanks, I distinctly heard NVA rocket batteries firing from the north, and then their 140mm rockets also started falling in around the tanks and the rear element of the company.

Rockets are ordinarily considered area weapons of only marginal accuracy. The fire that was falling in on us was so accurate that I believe it was registered. We were in a place that any astute commander could see he could inflict a hell of a lot of damage on any enemy force that passed there. I believe the enemy commander had it registered as a contingency and that we obliged him by stopping there as long as we did.

Someone on the company net told me that the Six—Captain Coulter—was down. Whoever contacted me said that the captain was hit in the head and that I better get back there to take charge. Though nothing had fallen in on us, the Marines all around me were taking cover. I started to move back along the column with my radioman.

One of the first Marines I ran into in the open was Sergeant Larry Flora, who had been with me since the battalion was formed. He was nicknamed Mad Dog, and he was just that—absolutely fearless, and a first-rate leader. He was then a squad leader in the 2nd Platoon, newly promoted to sergeant. I thought he was with his squad, and I yelled at him to try to draw him in with me. Flora was half on his knees and half standing, yelling things about what was going on, but it was obvious he was not responding to me. I had thought he recognized me, but I finally realized that he was out of it and alone—out of contact with his squad. He was not wounded as far as I could see, but he was badly shocked. I think a mortar round or rocket must have near-missed him. I should have grabbed him and dragged him along, but my mind was on getting up to Captain Coulter and I didn't think of taking Flora with me. The next day, we found his body. I'm sure he was killed out there, all alone. Larry Flora had been in my platoon from the beginning and had always come through for me. It is my greatest regret that I didn't take him with me.

Staff Sergeant RUSS ARMSTRONG
India Company, 3/26—1st Platoon Commander

A second 140mm volley followed the first. By then, I was leaning up against the high natural berm, which was to my left, and my radioman, Lance Corporal Thomas Moore, was facing me. I had the handset, and I was trying to talk to someone. An explosion went off just to my right rear and shrapnel penetrated underneath my right arm and struck me in the right side of my face. Another piece went all the way through my left leg, which started jumping around all by itself. The hole in my leg was huge. I dropped the radio handset and grabbed hold of the leg to try to control it.

I knew that Moore was hurt. He had defied my standing order to keep his flak jacket closed at all times, and he had taken a spray of shrapnel from his crotch to the lip of his helmet. The force of the blast had thrown him over onto his back, so he was resting on top of the radio.

There I was, trying to control my runaway leg, trying to retrieve the handset I had dropped so I could talk to my squads, and Moore was on top of the radio, worthless because he hadn't kept his damn flak jacket closed. I wasn't in any pain, but I was experiencing a lot of apprehension. As I watched, Moore settled a little and started blowing bloody bubbles out of his nose and mouth. He was unconscious. I was so mad at him I almost started cursing out loud.

2nd Lieutenant PAUL DRNEC
Bravo Company, 3rd Tank Battalion—2nd Platoon Commander

As soon as I was sure all the friendlies were to our rear, I turned the tanks around and started moving them back toward the eastern treeline. We fired a few rounds into the treeline to make sure we kept down any RPG teams if any were out there. That's what we feared the most— their RPG teams. They were our worst enemy.

I kept my eye on things through the vision blocks. I saw no enemy soldiers, but I could see our grunts moving across the paddies.

Lance Corporal CHUCK BENNETT
India Company, 3/26, 1st Platoon

The NVA were putting everything they had on the tanks, and the tanks were maneuvering to evade the fire. One of them almost ran right over me. I had to roll out of its way. I think I saw one or two Marines who did get run over by the tanks. Everything was hitting around the tanks, and the tanks were buttoned up—running every which way to get out of the open.

1st Lieutenant BOB STIMSON
India Company, 3/26—Executive Officer

My radioman and I were a third or halfway back to Captain Coulter's last known position when the second 140mm rocket salvo fell in on the company. As it came in, I dived to my left, under the rear of a tank that was facing south, down the long axis of the paddyfield. At the same moment, the tank started to turn back toward the treeline I had just left. I was always pretty optimistic. I was never one to think I wouldn't make it home. But I have to admit that, as that tank started turning, I thought I had had it, that I was either going to get killed by rocket shrapnel the size of dinner plates or be run over by the tank.

I wasn't hit by shrapnel and the tank didn't run me over. My radioman and I took off again, moving in a series of up-down moves to try to evade the incoming. We were alone, running from one little pocket of Marines to another. I could see that the unit was badly fragmented and that there were casualties.

The company was in as vulnerable a position as anyone could have feared—strung out, burdened with casualties, in incredibly bad terrain, part in the open, and with no one in charge of everyone in the company. The mortar and rocket fire was inflicting a lot of damage on us, disrupting everything. All we needed was an NVA infantry push through the rocket and mortar volleys. They could have run right over us.

Staff Sergeant RUSS ARMSTRONG
India Company, 3/26—1st Platoon Commander

As I was trying to gain control of myself, my wounded leg, my radio, and the situation—as the rockets and mortars were still coming in—the NVA launched their ground assault.

Lance Corporal CHUCK BENNETT
India Company, 3/26, 1st Platoon

A guy in the turret of one of the tanks was firing his .50-caliber heavy machine gun at some NVA who had just started getting out in the open, coming across the paddyfield. I could hear bullets ricocheting off the tank.

Staff Sergeant RUSS ARMSTRONG
India Company, 3/26—1st Platoon Commander

I managed to climb up to the top of the berm and look across the paddyfields. I saw a dozen to about 20 people in green uniforms *trotting*—double-timing—across the paddies, from back the way we had come. I distinctly thought, "Jesus Christ, this is the end of the line."

The Marine Corps attack philosophy was that you bombarded your target, softened it, moved up to your final protective line, shifted fire, and assaulted your objective. The NVA assaulted *through* their own supporting arms.

I could see those guys coming across, through their own fire. That, to me, was incredible. I thought, "This is crazy; you don't do it that way." I knew I sure wouldn't have been able to get *my* platoon to do it.

I really thought that it was end of the line. A whole raft of complex thoughts and issues ran through my mind in the very brief moment I stayed up to stare at all those NVA. I have never been religious, but I distinctly thought that I needed to say a prayer. Then I thought, quite clearly, "You've never asked for help before; it's not the best time to do it now." I felt like a hypocrite. Then I began thinking about my son, who was just starting kindergarten that week in San Diego. I kept thinking, "You're not going to make it." Then I *accepted* that I wasn't going to make it. I was struck very hard by remorse, by guilt. I wasn't going to be there for my son; I wasn't going to be around to get him going in the right direction at that important juncture in his life. I was only a few weeks away from getting home. I had seen so much death, had weathered so much grief, had come so close—and now I was going to die violently at the end of a day that had started out in beautiful sunlight, with the sound of birds singing and the vision of flowers growing.

At that point I began fading, going in and out, getting a little shocky from trauma and blood loss. I still didn't feel any pain, but I was definitely failing.

I don't know what happened to all those NVA. I vaguely sensed that some of them overran us and kept on going, but I thought that many were stopped before they got to the berm. I'm not sure.

Lance Corporal CHUCK BENNETT
India Company, 3/26, 1st Platoon

I got separated from my squad along with the other two guys in my fire team, Lance Corporal Joseph Juaire and Lance Corporal Robert Pugh. They had helped me carry Gary Lindsay's body in. The NVA were coming at us. Some Marines were pinned down out in the paddyfield. But Juaire, Pugh, and I got to flat ground on the edge of the paddyfield. There were some guys from another squad of our platoon already in the treeline. There were about a dozen of us altogether. We wound up in some thin trees off to the side of the paddyfield.

There were human waves of NVA coming at us from back the way we'd come across the paddyfield. It sounded like they had us completely surrounded. White phosphorous rounds hit near us. They burned and blinded two Marines. We wrapped bandages around their eyes and burns, but there wasn't much we could do for them. They were in a lot of pain.

*

Captain ANDY DeBONA
Mike Company, 3/26—Commanding Officer

India-Six [Captain Coulter] was reported hit. Over the radio I heard a lot of *cracks,* which signified to me from my experience that there were people shooting outgoing at that time. I could not actually hear the firefight.

I offered to fire my 60mm mortars in support of India Company, but they were beyond range. It seemed strange to me at the time that I didn't hear any of the battalion 81mm mortars shooting, nor did I hear artillery being called in support of India.

*

1st Lieutenant BOB STIMSON
India Company, 3/26—Executive Officer

I wasn't sure where Captain Coulter was. There were no real guideposts, because the unit was so fragmented. No group I passed was larger than a fire team, and a lot were individuals alone. At that point, in addition to the incoming, we were being engaged by NVA infantry. They were in and behind their own mortar and rocket fire, moving on us.

My radioman and I were the only Marines moving around in the open. We could have run into some NVA! They were all around us. I was conscious that there were NVA soldiers to the north, in the treeline, and around to the east of us, in that treeline. I couldn't see them, but I knew they were in there as well as moving on us in the open.

I finally found Captain Coulter, way out in the paddyfield, in one little paddy section surrounded by low dikes. The captain was prone in the middle of the paddy, obviously badly injured. He had a wound in the back of his head; I could see a pressure bandage beneath the edge of his helmet, which was tipped to the side. He was laying there, in obvious pain. To his credit, he was still trying to command his unit. He was lucid; he recognized me.

I immediately got down on my stomach, facing him, with a map between us. He said, "I'm not feeling very well; I want to tell you some things." His speech was slurred and I could see that he was in very bad shape. He didn't come out and say so, but I was sure he was going to turn the company over to me. I think he thought he was going to die, but he was trying to hang in to tell me what he thought I needed to know.

I needed to know a lot. I didn't know where half the unit was. In fact, I didn't know where three-quarters of the unit was. All I had seen in the run I had made were fragments and individuals and a lot of casualties, mostly from the 2nd Platoon. I had no idea where elements of Armstrong's 1st Platoon were. About all I knew for sure was that our unit integrity was pretty bad. I was hopeful that Captain Coulter could at least tell me where the main elements of the company were. He was pointing to the map and out to the edge of the paddy we were in, trying to tell me what he knew about who was where.

The captain and I had been talking for less than a minute when a mortar round landed right beside the two of us. We were face-to-face, shouting over the din of the battle. A piece of shrapnel hit him on the forehead, right under the front lip of his helmet. It was like a razor blade cut him across the forehead. I was looking right at him and saw it—a gash appeared across his forehead. He kind of moaned and toppled over. I didn't know if he was dead or not. Then I could hear him breathing. A corpsman was nearby, and he started to attend to the captain.

At that point, I certainly was in command of India Company. I had known the captain was leading up to turning it over to me, but he hadn't quite done that when the mortar round ended our discussion. He was out of it and I was in command.

My situation was that I didn't know where a large part of my unit was. We had virtually no tactical integrity. At some point, I was finally able to assess that we were separated into three principal groups, but I didn't even know if they were intact squads or just individuals who had come together somehow. It seemed to me that there was the group I was with and two other groups in other paddies. In addition, there were fire teams and individuals who were separate from these three groups. It was an exceedingly grim situation.

Captain Coulter at that point was lapsing in and out of consciousness. I asked the corpsman to move him to another part of the paddy, behind a berm, to keep him out of the direct fire. I also knew I had to move him because, in addition to the danger he was in, his presence in what passed for the CP would be disruptive to my efforts to get control of the company. There was the chance that people who needed to report to me would not know I was in charge.

We had a large but undetermined number of wounded and dead. I would have preferred getting them all in one place, under cover, but the situation was too chaotic then to make the effort. Foremost in my mind was arranging some tactical integrity. The NVA were pushing; we were being attacked pretty heavily by their infantry. The main infantry attacks were coming from the north, but, without question, there were NVA soldiers to our east, between us and the battalion position. I knew there was a hell of a lot of NVA infantry in that area; I could see them all over the place. We were also getting .51-caliber heavy machine-gun fire from the west and southwest, from the treeline back the way we had come. I'm not exactly sure where the machine guns were, but they were to our west. There definitely were two of them there, keeping us pinned down, preventing us from getting organized.

Anybody who would demean the professionalism and capabilities of the North Vietnamese Army doesn't know what he's talking about. I am sure the NVA attack was reactive to our being there, but its strength, the short notice on which it was launched, and the accuracy of the opening rocket attack suggest that they had planned to attack, trap, and annihilate any American unit that blundered into that particular spot. We were struck by a battalion, minimum. That kind of attack takes plenty of planning, plenty of thinking ahead.

*

2nd Lieutenant PAUL DRNEC
Bravo Company, 3rd Tank Battalion—2nd Platoon Commander

We pulled the tanks back about 100 meters, into the eastern treeline. All four tanks got back into the trees without incident. By then, the barrage had lifted.

I had a PRC-25 aboard my tank so I could communicate with the infantry. They were talking to us, but I never heard anything definite from anyone in authority. I knew they wanted to pack up and go back to the battalion perimeter, but that was about it. No one told me, but I knew we were going to be the rearguard. That was standard procedure.

Someone was talking to me on the PRC-25, but I didn't know who it was. I told him, "Okay, you guys go ahead and start working back to the battalion. We'll bring up the rear." I told him that I wanted him to provide us with an infantry screen to help keep NVA off the tanks as we moved through the thick underbrush, and I thought he agreed to that.

The tanks were just maneuvering into position to start the move. The idea was to put the flame tank in a position in which he could be protected by the gun tanks. That was standard procedure. I was going to lead, the flame tank was going to follow me, and the two other gun tanks were going to be the rear. I thought it was all set with the infantry— that they were going to mutually support us—but the flame tank commander, Corporal Guy Wolfberger, came up on the hook and said, "For Christ's sake, they're all around me!"

"What," I asked, "Who's around you?"

"NVA!"

"Are you sure they're not Marines?"

"No, sir, they're NVA."

"Look again." It seemed impossible that any NVA could be there.

"No, sir, they are definitely gooners. Can I zap them with the flame?"

Firing the flame was the last thing I wanted to do in that underbrush. I was sure there were NVA soldiers out there, but I was just as sure that there were Marines out there, too. I didn't know what the hell was going on, but a flame is very hard to control. "No, use your .50-cal if you're sure you're not firing on Marines. Spray them with .50-cal." I made it abundantly clear that I did not want the flame fired.

We had not completed our maneuver to get in line yet, so Wolfberger backed down the flame tank to pull in with the gun tanks. I still wanted to get in line. None of us knew what was going on. The only thing I was sure of was that there were NVA up by the flame tank. I just wanted to punch out of there and link back up with the battalion main body. However, I got a call on the PRC-25 from someone I believed to be an infantry officer. I suggested that we form up together and beeline back to the battalion position, but he told me that his unit had suffered many casualties and was unable to move or maneuver out of the exposed paddy area. I did not know where he or his men were— they sure weren't with the tanks—but I felt morally obliged to stay in the area so I could support them. I certainly had to give up thinking about punching through the woods to rejoin the battalion main body. I asked my expert, Sergeant Vining, what he thought we should do. He said what he had been saying right along: "We better get the hell outta this brush. We're sitting ducks."

Vining was right. Since we couldn't move deeper into the trees for fear of running into more concealed NVA, our only choice was to pull back out into the open so we could see any RPG teams they might be trying to maneuver in on us. That was the threat—the RPG teams. If we could see them, we might defeat them. If not, they would definitely get us.

I sent the flame tank out first because it was the most vulnerable. Then I sent the other gun tanks out, and I brought up the rear. We had moved about 25 yards into the open when my tank simply stopped. I called my driver on the intercom. "Let's get moving." Nothing. "For Christ's sake, don't stop. Get going!"

"I can't," he yelled back. "I can't get the damn thing moving. I got zero transmission pressure."

I couldn't figure out why.

As I quickly sifted through possibilities, I kept looking around through the vision blocks in the commander's cupola. The gun tube was trained forward and—as always in that type of close-in, immediate-action situation—a canister round was in the breech. The danger was in the treeline, to the rear, so I was getting ready to bring the tube around 180 degrees when I happened to glance out the back. I spotted an RPG team just as it stood up in full view, right at the edge of the treeline—less than 25 yards behind my tank. Without giving it any thought, I grabbed the tank commander's override and swung the gun around. As it got there, I pulled the trigger and blew those NVA away with the canister. When the smoke cleared, there was no one there.

We got that team, but by then other RPG teams had hit us. As I found out much later, their first shot had gone through the ass end of the engine compartment, on the left side, and had taken out our transmission, dumping out 25 gallons of hydraulic fluid. Another shot had hit right on the weight-bearing knuckle hinge of the immensely heavy access panel doors. It had sheared the hinge right off. If that RPG hadn't hit that knuckle, it would have come straight through the rear of the turret, straight into my back.

When Corporal Wolfberger, in the flame tank, saw that we had been disabled, he swung back around and asked if he could spray flame into the treeline. Meanwhile, the other gun tanks also turned to face the treeline. They pulled up alongside my tank and engaged the enemy in the treeline with their machine guns and, I believe, several canister rounds. I knew that there were plenty of NVA in those trees, but I still didn't know what the hell had happened to the Marine grunts. I couldn't let Wolfberger fire; I had to tell him there might be Marines pinned down in there. It was a very tough call.

*

Staff Sergeant RUSS ARMSTRONG
India Company, 3/26—1st Platoon Commander

It was mass confusion. We had been taken by surprise by the indirect-fire weapons. Many of our people were out in the open. They were in defilade positions to the NVA direct fire, but the mortars and rockets could and did get them in many cases. We were vulnerable. We were very vulnerable.

The 140mm rockets stopped coming in, but we were taking lots of .51-caliber machine-gun and 60mm and 82mm mortar fire. They might have been firing 120mm mortars at us, too.

I was thinking about how to control my platoon and trying to pull myself together when I saw this guy wearing a green uniform and a steel helmet stand up out of the grass only 30 feet away. When I noticed that he was pointing his rifle the wrong way, I tried to figure out which of my men he was, but I couldn't. That was because he was Asian. He stood up, fired a shot, and hunkered back down into the grass.

I knew that one of the tanks was somewhere behind me, knocked out by an RPG, but I didn't know then where the other tanks were. Marines were scattered all over the place around me, on my side of the berm clear back to the treeline to the west and up to the treeline to the immediate north.

For the longest time, I felt that I was on my own. My injuries were affecting me and I knew I wasn't as sharp as I needed to be. I was sure I had seen the company commander fall off the tank, but I had no idea what had become of him. I didn't know if he was running the company, or if Lieutenant Stimson was, or if they were both dead or incapacitated.

In times like these, I had learned, the people you least suspect rise to the occasion. One such was HM3 Albert Butsko, one of my two platoon corpsmen. He was a slightly effeminate character, the object of much speculation. When one of my corporals yelled over to me that Butsko was cowering next to the berm, not helping the wounded, I yelled, ''Butsko, you son of a bitch, get up and get with it.'' He did. He came over and pulled my wounded radioman, Lance Corporal Moore, off of the radio, freed the radio, treated Moore's wounds, and dragged Moore away from the berm to wherever they were collecting the casualties. After that, whenever I saw Butsko, he was moving around in the open like you wouldn't believe—dressing wounds, helping the injured—with complete disregard to his own safety.

My other platoon corpsman, HN Robert Davis, was injured early in the fight, but not so badly that he couldn't help the other wounded men. Davis had an interesting story. He was in the Navy assigned to the Marine Corps, and he had a brother who was in the Marine Corps assigned to sea duty with the Navy.

*

Lance Corporal CHUCK BENNETT
India Company, 3/26, 1st Platoon

I was in the treeline north of where the tanks got hit. We got hit by a small force of NVA. At about 1735, they fired their mortars at us, and while we had our heads down, they attacked through their own mortar fire so they could get in close to us while we were pinned down. It was something they always did. When they were getting in on top of us, they quit firing the mortars to keep from hitting their own guys. In fact, I think they did kill some of their own men with the mortars. We caught them on open ground and had a mad moment, squeezing off rounds at them. I could see their faces.

We repulsed the attack.

Staff Sergeant RUSS ARMSTRONG
India Company, 3/26—1st Platoon Commander

There were trees and brush about 100 meters behind me, and I saw Marines in there. I somehow knew that a squad from the 2nd Platoon that was supposed to be connected with Kilo Company was lost, that we had no contact with it at all. Then I learned that my platoon's 1st Squad, under Corporal Heyward O'Neal, was more or less lost, too. I had sent it into the woods about 50 meters north of our position to observe and provide cover from a little high area. I realized that the men I could see in the woods were probably O'Neal and his men. It eventually dawned on me that I had sent a radio with O'Neal, so I called him. He reported that his position had been attacked by about a platoon of NVA assaulting through their own mortar fire. The enemy had been repulsed, but the squad sustained several casualties, including two Marines who had been blinded, probably by a mortar blast.

The next thing I knew, it was getting dark. I was speaking with Corporal O'Neal on the radio, trying to guide him back out of the woods to rejoin the main body of the platoon. They were having lots of trouble because it was getting dark, because they had to help the blind Marines, and because no one knew exactly where anyone else was.

Lance Corporal CHUCK BENNETT
India Company, 3/26, 1st Platoon

My group of about a dozen 1st Platoon Marines moved out of the treeline to rejoin the main body of the company. We passed a few dead Marines on the way, but there was no time to pick them up. We were rushing to get out of the open.

Staff Sergeant RUSS ARMSTRONG
India Company, 3/26—1st Platoon Commander

One of the blind Marines turned out to be a draftee who had been caught up in the Black Power movement. He had exhibited extreme hostility toward whites the whole time I had been with the platoon. He had an Ace bandage wrapped around his head and he was completely dependent on men he could not see and who, in large part, he had spent most of his tour in Vietnam offending and even threatening. He seemed so pathetic that I briefly relinquished all other thoughts to say to myself, "You poor pathetic bastard, I wish you could see who's saving your life."

*

1st Lieutenant BOB STIMSON
India Company, 3/26—Executive Officer

My first thought on assuming command was that I needed to find Russ Armstrong. Until he had come to India Company as a platoon commander in March or April, Russ had been the chief of the 81mm mortar section that was usually attached out to India Company. I had had a great deal of contact with him then, when I commanded India Company's 2nd Platoon. We were in a lot of little actions together. In fact, I always requested Russ when I had the opportunity. We were about the same age and both had Midwest backgrounds. I always liked him. We became good friends—as much as a staff sergeant and a lieutenant could be. He was extremely formal and was very conscious of the fact that he and I had an enlisted-officer relationship. He always addressed me in the third person: "Does the lieutenant want. . . ." He was very professional, very competent. His knowledge of what he was doing was impressive. When he came to India to command our 1st Platoon, I knew we had an exemplary performer. He was a 100 percent Marine—demanded a lot of the troops, was a stern disciplinarian, insisted on proper appearance and clean weapons all the time. He was right. He was very much the classic noncommissioned officer.

Knowing well and appreciating Russ's capabilities with indirect fire and map work, I realized that I would get a lot farther a lot faster if I could get him to the CP to handle indirect fire support. I had not seen him, didn't know where he was, or that he was wounded. I didn't even know if he was still alive. But I knew if he was still functioning and if I could get him to the CP, then I could start moving around and put our unit back together. The fact that Russ was a platoon commander made no difference to me then; formal organization—platoons and squads—meant nothing at that moment. My only thought was to get our position consolidated, and I needed someone to handle fire-support coordination so I would be free to do that.

I put out the word and, somehow, Russ and I got together. It was obvious that the man was badly injured, but he could talk. I asked him if he could help and he said, "Yeah, I can." And he did.

While Russ tried to get 81mm mortar support from the battalion main body and air and artillery support from anywhere he could, I started moving around to see what we had to work with and to start pulling people in.

Staff Sergeant RUSS ARMSTRONG
India Company, 3/26—1st Platoon Commander

The NVA had us pinned with mortars, heavy machine guns, and small arms.

We needed artillery support, and it was available from Fire Base C-2. But our company's artillery FO, a newly arrived lieutenant, was dead, killed in a freak incident at the onset of the NVA rocket barrage. One of my platoon's machine gunners, Lance Corporal Wayne Gordon, was carrying a can of M-60 ammo. As always, every fifth round was a tracer. Shrapnel from an enemy mortar round or rocket penetrated the ammo can and blew it up. Gordon lost the fingers of the hand in which he was carrying the ammo can. The FO, who was next to Gordon, was killed.

Since I had had plenty of experience calling 81mm mortar fire, I was able to help Lieutenant Stimson by calling in some artillery fire. My radioman was down and out, but I still had his radio. The FO was a casualty and his radioman turned yellow; he was of no use.

It took some doing in the failing light, but I eventually got a few registration rounds on target. I was able to shoot an azimuth to the target and give a grid coordinate that approximated the enemy position based on my best estimate of my own position. When the first round hit, I was able to give adjustments based on range and deflection. When I had the target bracketed, I requested HE impact rounds and ordered the battery to fire for effect.

*

1st Lieutenant BOB STIMSON
India Company, 3/26—Executive Officer

It was very intense. I didn't give a moment's thought to reporting our situation to Battalion. I was afraid that if I took the time, we wouldn't have a situation.

I felt we were in pretty grim straits. I knew we were up against a large enemy unit with a lot of horsepower. I was very concerned that I still didn't know where everybody was. I wasn't really certain about the level of ammunition we had retained, and I knew we had taken and were still taking heavy casualties. I had to get it across to the remaining squad leaders and fire-team leaders that we needed to get the three main groups and an unknown number of splinter groups and individuals consolidated in and adjacent to the paddy in which I had established my CP.

Eventually, we got one perimeter—more or less—put together. The ground was like concrete; entrenching tools were useless. The only cover was the paddy dikes. We didn't even really form a perimeter per se. Our position had an amorphous shape. My main concern then was not the shape of the perimeter but its strength—just getting something fairly substantial put together before the NVA launched their next major ground attack. Or before the indirect fire took a much greater toll.

It took quite awhile to get everything pieced together, and there were still people who could not be accounted for. Individuals kept drifting in. There were so many gaps to be filled that I had to ask all the wounded men who could to take up firing positions. Men who were hit but could still fire—even if they couldn't move around—represented a large proportion of our manpower.

A corpsman who was only a few yards away from me was shot through the throat. He was the most undisciplined guy I had ever seen in my life. Very sloppy. He got shot right through the throat. He wrapped a pressure bandage around it and carried on. It was one of the most incredible things I have ever seen.

After a while, just around dusk, the NVA infantry pressure suddenly didn't seem to be as intense as it had been a few minutes earlier. But we were still feeling the pressure, still receiving heavy small-arms fire from the north and from the .51-caliber machine guns across the paddyfield to the west and southwest. We also continued to receive indirect fire, from mortars.

The big machine guns were taking the biggest toll. They were really raking our position, really playing havoc with us. We couldn't move. You got above the top of the paddy berm at your peril. They had me crawling on my belly as I moved around putting the unit together and trying to keep it together.

Lance Corporal CHUCK BENNETT
India Company, 3/26, 1st Platoon

I was on flat ground, in the open, firing at the treeline in front of us, the northern treeline. Lance Corporal Robert Pugh, from my fire team, was to my left 10 to 12 feet. He hollered, "Ben! Ben! I'm hit." It was hard to hear him, even though he wasn't far away, because of all the noise of the gunfire. I looked over and he yelled, "I'm hit! I'm hit bad, I think." I crawled over and saw he was hit in the back. There was a big hole in there, down low, near his spine. It had gone in underneath the edge of his flak jacket, but the flak jacket wouldn't have stopped it anyway. It looked like a .51-caliber round. There was a lot of blood. Pugh said his legs felt numb. I yelled back for a corpsman, and while I waited, I tried to stop the bleeding. So much was going on, I'm not even sure if a corpsman came out or if we pulled him back to a corpsman. The next thing I remember, I was at the aid station with Pugh and a corpsman was working on him. Pugh was still alive, but he was in bad shape. He kept asking, "Am I gonna be all right? Am I gonna make it?" I tried to comfort him. I kept telling him, "Yeah! You're gonna be okay. Just stay here and relax." There wasn't much else I could do. It looked bad. I didn't think he was going to make it.

*

1st Lieutenant BOB STIMSON
India Company, 3/26—Executive Officer

My concerns continued to be the tactical integrity of the entire unit, fire discipline, and our ammunition supply. For example, our 60mm mortars were out of ammunition, even though every rifleman had been carrying a couple rounds in addition to the mortar section's basic load. I was extremely concerned about ammunition. It wasn't quite dark yet, and I was sure that we were facing a long night of firing. I could not depend on being resupplied. I knew that something was going on to our east, around the battalion main body. That much was clear from my exchanges with Captain Bill Wildprett, the S-3.

Lance Corporal CHUCK BENNETT
India Company, 3/26, 1st Platoon

They had us outnumbered. They had everything we had except air support. We were running low on ammo. We usually carried 300 rounds for our M-16s, but going up there that morning, they told us to carry extra— 100 to 200 extra rounds. So, I was carrying maybe 500 rounds of ammo. It was heavy to carry, but it was worth having out there.

We were so shorthanded, we'd lost so many men, that we had wounded guys up on the line, manning positions.

Lieutenant Stimson kept moving around through us, seeing what was going on, talking to us. He kept asking how many bullets we had so he could even out the supplies. Some guys didn't have many and other guys had a lot. It seemed to be according to where you were, which side of the perimeter you were on and if that side was getting hit a lot.

1st Lieutenant BOB STIMSON
India Company, 3/26—Executive Officer

I was feeling desperate. I even ordered my Marines to fix bayonets. In

Vietnam in 1967, that was an order based on desperation. Then I worked to impose fire discipline. I passed the word for all M-16s to be put on semi-automatic and for squad and team leaders to check every man's weapon, to see that it was done and maintained. I emphasized to everyone down the chain that we had to make *every* shot count—to think sight picture and sight alignment, which is basic shooting technique.

There were NVA in the next rice paddy. I could see their faces. They were throwing hand grenades at us and we were throwing hand grenades at them. I was glad to see that my order regarding fire discipline was being observed; in my travels, I saw a number of NVA as close as 10 to 15 meters away get picked off by Marines firing the proverbial single, well-placed round.

Jammed weapons were a terrible problem. The M-16 was a problem weapon. Powder fouling the chamber allowed the round to be fired, but the bolt ejecting the spent cartridge tended to stop halfway out, ripping the rim of the cartridge, and then going all the way back. It was a classic pose: a rifleman sitting there working with a spent cartridge that was effectively welded in the chamber. The only way to clear a weapon in that situation was to assemble the cleaning rod and punch the cartridge out from through the barrel. It happened all the time. As in every other engagement I had ever been in, I gave my M-16 to a rifleman whose own M-16 was jammed. And all the M-16s we could recover from the nonambulatory wounded and dead were recycled.

*

1st Lieutenant BOB STIMSON
India Company, 3/26—Executive Officer

The NVA heavy machine guns to our west and southwest continued to play havoc with us. They were just devastating. They were antiaircraft weapons and they were *very* accurate. I raised the AO and he was telling me that he could see a company-size NVA unit to the north, in the treeline. I couldn't see them, but he could. He gave me a landmark and a distance. They were close enough that they could have been used to attack us at any moment. I told the AO about the .51-cals and asked if he could see them. He definitely was able to identify one of them. I asked for air to hit the NVA company to our north and the .51-cal he could see to our west.

Lance Corporal CHUCK BENNETT
India Company, 3/26, 1st Platoon

It was hell all over. We were getting rounds from every direction, but most of the heavy fire—most of the .51-cal fire—was coming from a clump of trees to the north of our position, from the direction I was facing. It seemed like there was a little hill up there. I guess they could see down on us. The jets were dropping all kinds of stuff on there and the .51-cals were firing on the jets. Those .51-cals were firing at anything big—the jets and the tanks. There were other .51-cals firing in behind us, from the other direction.

1st Lieutenant BOB STIMSON
India Company, 3/26—Executive Officer

The first F-4 made its run along an east-west axis—or west-east—and dropped all his HE on the NVA company on one run. It sounded like an atomic bomb. The earth shook. Then his wingman came in and worked on the .51-cal the AO had seen. He made several southwest-northeast passes until the AO said, "We got one of the guns." From that point on, I was conscious of a reduction in the .51-caliber fire, which finally ended altogether.

That was a big event, silencing those machine guns. We could move around better. We weren't going to gain fire superiority over so many NVA, but having the .51-cals out of the way certainly helped.

*

2nd Lieutenant PAUL DRNEC
Bravo Company, 3rd Tank Battalion—2nd Platoon Commander

It was getting dark. My tank was disabled. I didn't know where any of our infantry was and I didn't know what to do. I did know that the NVA had stopped bothering us, so we just sat there, ready to fire at the enemy if they showed themselves.

There was a lot of stuff going on. I talked with Battalion. I told them there were NVA out around us and asked them to send a relief out to link up with us and the India Company troops who were pinned down. They told me they couldn't because they were being attacked. Scratch that idea.

I had the two operable gun tanks guarding our flanks, so I felt pretty secure, and, if push came to shove, we always had the flame. But we couldn't stay in that exposed position forever. It was getting dark. I decided to bail out of my tank, B-21, and withdraw to the India Company position.

It was a 3rd Tank Battalion SOP that whenever you bailed out of a tank you were supposed to destroy the gun tube. That was ridiculous. Really, all we had to do was take the firing pins out of the machine guns and drop the main gun's breech. Hell, it would have taken the NVA three years to figure out how to put that damn thing back together again. I knew what a pain in the neck it was trying to get any type of major equipment replacement, so I decided, no, I was not going to comply with the battalion SOP. Disabling the weapons was enough. The breech was a vertical sliding breech. All I had to do was disengage it and drop it on the deck. It weighed a few hundred pounds, so I was sure no one was going to steal it or, more important, put it back. We grabbed the machine-gun firing pins and Sergeant Vining screwed up the electrical system to disable the radios. Vining took the .45-caliber grease gun and I took my maps, but I forgot to grab the bag of extra .45-caliber ammunition as we left the tank.

As we hit the ground, two of us ran to one gun tank and two of us ran to the other gun tank. Vining and I stuffed down into the turret of the gun tank we boarded. It was cozy. When my whole crew was safe, the two gun tanks and the flame tank drove farther out into the rice-paddy area to link up with India Company.

We couldn't see the infantry positions well enough in the failing light to complete the link-up, so we had to stop short. All the communications were jumbled, so on the PRC-25 we couldn't raise anyone in authority. There was no small-arms or other fire hitting us by then, so I turned the tank over to Sergeant Vining and got out to walk into the infantry position. I wanted to find someone in authority who could tell me what was going on and direct the tanks into the perimeter.

I did eventually find someone—I have no idea who he was—and he told me that the company had taken many casualties and was not yet fully consolidated under central authority in one perimeter. I got enough information to bring the tanks in safely, and I guided them in.

When we linked up, I threw the tank commander and loader out of the B-25 tank to make room for Sergeant Vining and me, and then set both gun tanks—B-25 and B-22—and the flame tank into the India Company perimeter. We couldn't cover everything, so we concentrated on the south and east, from which we could keep our eyes and our guns on B-21, which was about 100 meters away from the India Company position. It became fully dark shortly after we tucked in with India Company.

*

1st Lieutenant BOB STIMSON
India Company, 3/26—Executive Officer

By dusk, it felt as if our situation was improving slowly. I knew we were in better shape than we had been only a few minutes before dusk. I knew it wasn't good, but it was better. We had some tactical integrity, we had good communications, and the tanks were in with us and were providing moral as well as some real support. We had an AO and plenty of fixed-wing, and we were also getting artillery fire support, thanks almost entirely to Russ Armstrong.

I was aware that rounds were landing, but I wasn't even sure if all of them were ours or if some of them weren't misdirected rounds meant to support the battalion main body. Our battle was being fought in a very small area, in some cases within less than one incremental correction of an artillery tube. I do know that every friendly fire base in range was contributing to the effort.

At the last glimmer of sunlight that evening, we started getting illumination rounds, but it's hard to tell who benefited most from them, us or the NVA. After dark, I'd hear "Rounds on the way" from the artillery and then I'd hear explosions—mainly to our north, where we thought we knew there were NVA concentrations. But I can't say that we actually hit anything.

Russ Armstrong really performed for us. He took a lot of pressure off me, allowing me to do other things. He was a man I knew I could depend on, a solid known quantity who wasn't ever going to let us down. As badly hurt as he was, he helped me keep my spirits up. He was an inspiration. We owe him our lives.

I was automatic. I didn't doubt my abilities for a moment; I never gave the subject a moment's thought. I had been well trained and I had weathered nearly a year of combat. As much as anyone who has ever been in combat, I was ready to command that unit in that place at that time. That is not saying anything about me. The Marine Corps had molded me, my experience had molded me, the situation was molding me. If anything, I was better trained and better prepared than I thought myself to be. I just did things. I never gave it a second thought at the time. I do now, but I didn't then.

I was comforted by the fact that the tanks were there, occasionally firing and in a position to fire more if the NVA attacked again.

I had not been looking forward to sunset. I was never that crazy about fighting at night, but I realized that it could provide a major advantage in some situations. I was concerned because I wasn't sure where and how many NVA there were out there. The AO had told me about a company of them in the trees to our immediate north, and I wasn't sure the air strike had done enough damage to prevent or discourage them from launching a direct assault on us. I wasn't certain, either, if there were *other* NVA companies out there, ready to attack. I was quite worried about that.

We certainly were not a full-strength infantry company, nor even a full-strength company minus a platoon. We were the remnants of two platoons that had been understrength going into this battle. On the other hand, we were no longer vulnerable; we had good tactical integrity, we had the tanks, the air, and the indirect fire. And we had taken a heavy toll on the NVA. The time for them to turn it on full bore had been at the beginning, when we were strung out. That was when they could have gotten us, no question. They missed the opportunity.

Chapter 6

1st Lieutenant RON ZAPPARDINO
3/26—Forward Air Controller

On the morning of September 7, I went out with Mike Company. Whenever I could, I went out with Mike because the skipper, Captain Andy DeBona, was aggressive. I liked the way he operated. Not much happened on the patrol. We just went out hill hopping.

Late in the afternoon, I went out again, with Kilo Company. As we were coming back into the battalion perimeter, I was near the front of the company and could see the battalion CP—we couldn't have been more than 100 yards away—so, as far as I was concerned, the patrol was over. I told the company commander, "You don't need me anymore; I'm going in." I broke away from Kilo Company and started heading for the battalion CP, where my hole was located.

Staff Sergeant CHARLES OWENS
Kilo Company, 3/26—Company Gunny

There were hedgerows that slowed us down as we returned to the battalion perimeter from trying to bring in India Company. I was walking drag for the company. As I was following the company around a right turn, I saw this bush that didn't look right, so I fired a shotgun blast into it. I killed an NVA soldier in there. Just the one.

Staff Sergeant DAVE NUGENT
3/26, 81mm Mortar Platoon

I was the 81mm forward observer for Mike Company until I made staff

78

sergeant in April 1967. Then I moved over to become a section chief. I was in charge of two guns.

The 81 FO assigned to Kilo Company came over when Kilo got back and told me he had seen NVA on the way back in. He told me, "They wouldn't let me fire on them. They told me they wanted to sucker them in." He also said he heard an AO on his radio saying he saw 30 NVA coming our way. I told him, "We got no problem. We have Mike sitting right in front of us, and we have guns we can train right on them. We're all set."

2nd Lieutenant BILL COWAN
India Company, 3/26—3rd Platoon Commander

When the India Company patrol went out on the morning of September 7, my 3rd Platoon remained behind to cover the company position. I stretched my platoon out to cover the entire company line.

In the late afternoon, I heard some shooting off in the distance and my radioman called me: "Hey, Lieutenant, you oughta come over and listen to this for a minute." An AO was up on the net, talking about all these guys running along trenchlines—stuff like "I see 50 of 'em here and 20 to 30 of 'em there." It was all kind of surrealistic, that some guy could be up there seeing those people. It just doesn't make sense to a guy on the ground. I asked my radioman, "Where is that airplane?" He pointed up in the sky to the west and said, "Right there, that plane right up there." The bird dog was up at about a 45-degree angle, right up over our guys.

Staff Sergeant CHARLES OWENS
Kilo Company, 3/26—Company Gunny

Just about the time our company got back inside the battalion perimeter, the enemy hit India Company and split the force. I had shot an NVA in the bushes. I can't understand why, if they were in there, they didn't launch an attack on Kilo Company while we were in there with them. I guess they wanted to wipe out India Company, so they let us go by.

1st Lieutenant RON ZAPPARDINO
3/26—Forward Air Controller

The NVA must have been waiting in a hedgerow off to the left. They must have been waiting for Kilo Company to get close, but not quite in position. I was just moving through the front-line Marine fighting holes when the shit started.

*

Captain TOM EARLY
3/26—Communications Officer

When we set up at The Churchyard, the battalion CP was in the middle of the perimeter, with the church tower just off to our right. Also off to our right was Mike Company, set up in a wide perimeter in front of the church tower. Directly in front of the battalion CP was the India Company position. Kilo Company was to the left and behind us. We also had the H&S Company security detachment, which came from the 106mm Recoilless Rifle Platoon and the flamethrower section, neither of which had brought its weapons. We just brought the people with us as extra battalion CP security. Rather than having an inner ring of CP security, we lent these people to the infantry companies to make a 360-degree perimeter around the battalion CP as best we could.

The Churchyard was up on a ridge; we weren't on low ground. We had trees and paddies to our front—west—and we had paddies to our rear. We had come over ridges to get there, and as far as I saw, we were at an elevation—as much elevation as would be in that area. There were hedgerows in front of Mike Company's position. The area was kind of a green pastoral setting with trees all around. That made it fairly easy to defend.

*

2nd Lieutenant BILL COWAN
India Company, 3/26—3rd Platoon Commander

I was walking back toward the battalion CP, which was not too far from our lines, and I heard the *boom-boom-boom* sound of outgoing. I thought it was Con Thien firing at something. Then, all of a sudden, I heard *shwew*—the incoming sound—and a tremendous explosion behind me, about 50 meters.

I wasn't smart enough to get down. Though I had led or was on numerous patrols, I had never been in contact with—had never shot at—any enemy soldiers from the time I joined the battalion in June until we left Khe Sanh for Camp Carroll and the Con Thien area on September 5. This was the first time I'd ever been under fire.

I turned around and saw red from shrapnel and fire. My first thought was, "Goddammit, Con Thien's firing on us." Then I heard the company gunny yell, "Hey, Lieutenant, you better get down." Then four or five more rockets—big ones—came in and hit right along my perimeter. By then, all my people were down in their holes, waiting for what was going to happen. At that time, we'd had no activity on the ground, but we'd get a series of rockets now and again. We could hear the fighting that was going on to our front—the India Company patrol.

Captain ANDY DeBONA
Mike Company, 3/26—Commanding Officer

Beginning at about 1720, the battalion area started getting spasmodic heavy-caliber fire, which impacted in the vicinity of the positions that India had vacated, to the left of my Mike Company position. We also began getting light infantry probes and sporadic heavy fire across our company front.

2nd Lieutenant CHAN CRANGLE
Mike Company, 3/26—1st Platoon Commander

We could hear the India Company fight quite clearly, then I started to take incoming mortar, rocket, and small-arms fire. The tension went up a few notches.

When the shooting started, my 1st Platoon got a few 140mm rockets, which made a very loud blast, fire, and black smoke. I was sitting in the bottom of a foxhole, watching the incoming going off and thinking what the odds were of one of them coming into the hole with me.

Staff Sergeant CHARLES OWENS
Kilo Company, 3/26—Company Gunny

They hit us with rockets as we were getting back into the battalion perimeter. I had one arm in my flak jacket and I had my helmet in my left hand. I was diving into a hole headfirst when I saw the flash of a rocket as it went off. The last thought going through my mind was "Oh, no, not in the *stomach!*" I had always been afraid of a belly wound because they're horrible. When I woke up, my other arm was in the flak jacket and my helmet was on my head, buckled. I asked if anyone had helped me, but no one had even been close to me, no one had helped me. The Lord was taking care of me.

Captain TOM EARLY
3/26—Communications Officer

The 140mm rounds received at 1720 came from a good distance away, as far as I could figure, because of the range of that indiscriminate area weapon. We could, of course, hear the attack on India Company, but we were taking about 130 rounds of mixed 140mm rocket and 82mm mortar. An 82mm mortar is going to come in from much closer, so that had to be fired pretty much right in back of the attacking units. I'm not sure if the heavy rounds were all 140mm rockets or if there was 152mm artillery fire coming out of the DMZ.

Staff Sergeant DAVE NUGENT
3/26, 81mm Mortar Platoon

I heard explosions from up by the battalion CP. We never got hit at the 81s position, but they got hit up at the CP.

Between 1720 and 1749, the opening barrage—three volleys composed of an estimated sixty 140mm rockets and seventy 82mm mortar rounds— killed 2 and wounded 16 members of H&S Company, wounded 6 members of Mike Company, and killed 1 and wounded 3 members of Kilo Company. During the last mixed volley, NVA infantry already in position west of the perimeter attacked through their own supporting-arms fire.

Captain TOM EARLY
3/26—Communications Officer

The NVA infantry attack on the battalion perimeter was mainly against India-3 [India Company's 3rd Platoon] and Mike Company. I think everybody in the battalion CP just knew we were in some real heavy stuff, but India-3 was deployed to cover as much of the perimeter to our front—to the west—as it could. Everybody from H&S Company who was along for battalion security already was deployed on the front lines. Marines from the 106mm Platoon were sent out at about 1745 to help cover the India Company sector.

2nd Lieutenant BILL COWAN
India Company, 3/26—3rd Platoon Commander

The terrain in my sector was pretty flat, with minimal brush inside the perimeter. To our immediate front, the brush was thicker but the terrain was still generally flat. In essence, the enemy who approached my sector were coming to us concealed by brush, which allowed them to get within 10 yards in some areas. In front of one part of my line was a small depression between us and the brush.

As the only officer in India Company in the main battalion perimeter—in my first action—I was trying very, very hard to pay attention to everything that was going on with the whole battalion. Pretty soon, I heard from the troops on my line—the India line—that they were being probed a little. Our guys started doing some shooting, which I tried to get under control. My major concern was that I thought we had friendlies—the rest of India Company—somewhere out in front of us.

*

1st Lieutenant RON ZAPPARDINO
3/26—Forward Air Controller

It was mass confusion. Lots was going on, lots of people were moving around. My first reaction was to try to get some air immediately. I got right on the radio and started calling to see what was around. We were right in the middle of a big contact, so I thought it would be only a matter of getting in touch with someone and bringing them in.

The sky was overcast and it was starting to get dark. I jumped into my hole in the middle of the perimeter, but I jumped right out again and ran over to get orders from the S-3, Captain Bill Wildprett, who was fully running the show. I had to find out what was going on so I could figure out what to call the air in on.

We couldn't get air because of the weather. It remained overcast.

Captain TOM EARLY
3/26—Communications Officer

The artillery unit at Camp Carroll was 1/12, but the U.S. Army owned the 175s there. There were 105s at C-2, and 8-inch self-propelled guns at Dong Ha. We tried to get as much of that as we could, but there was a lot going on throughout the area that night. Con Thien and Gio Linh were being shelled.

These things didn't happen in isolation. The troops attacking us were not local VC who put down their water-buffalo plows and picked up their rifles. These people were coordinated and they knew what they were doing. They were not only coordinated within their battalions and regiment, they were coordinated within their division. They knew exactly how to do three or four things at once—and they could do them very effectively. So, the first guy to ask for the air cover and artillery got it while everyone else waited because there were multiple offensive areas.

1st Lieutenant RON ZAPPARDINO
3/26—Forward Air Controller

There was a big problem with controlling our artillery support. When I noticed how much trouble Bill Wildprett and the battalion arty FO were having getting the artillery coordinated—we had support from every gun at every fire base that could reach us—I said, "I'll take care of it," and started relaying firing information to the guns that were supporting us from Dong Ha.

*

Captain ANDY DeBONA
Mike Company, 3/26—Commanding Officer

By about 1800, the India patrol was still unable to disengage from its contact, so I called Battalion and suggested pulling one platoon of Mike Company over to cover India Company's spot in the perimeter in case they didn't get back in that evening. I was granted permission for this, and I pulled Lieutenant Bob Gall's 2nd Platoon out of the center of my company's defensive position. I gave it the mission of occupying India's positions, making contact with Kilo on their left and Mike-3 on their right. I told Gall to spread his people thin because he was occupying the position of a company with only his platoon. I did not realize at that time that India-3 had remained in the perimeter to cover the India Company sector.

Lance Corporal RON BURKE
Mike Company, 3/26, 2nd Platoon

My squad was a little ahead of the platoon, on a listening post. A machine-gun squad leader came running up and told our squad leader that Lieutenant Gall wanted us to move. When we got to the new position, we stayed low and stretched thin.

2nd Lieutenant CHAN CRANGLE
Mike Company, 3/26—1st Platoon Commander

When Andy shifted Gall's 2nd Platoon out of the Mike Company center to cover the gap between Mike and India-3, he also ordered Lieutenant John Manzi and me to spread our platoons toward Gall's former position, toward the center of the company position. Manzi had to spread Mike-3 to his right and I had to spread Mike-1 to my left. My platoon was spread thin to begin with. I rapidly ran out of Marines to put in holes. I got down to one man per hole, with me and my .45 holding one hole. A few holes were unoccupied.

Lance Corporal RON BURKE
Mike Company, 3/26, 2nd Platoon

The squad radioman was hit. He told me to give the radio and his maps to someone else who could attend to it, but I couldn't find that person. That left me with the responsibility.

I could see the enemy periodically, leapfrogging toward us. We kept getting rocketed and mortared. Somebody obviously had a bead on us, so we were all trying to get lower, digging in a little as well as we could without getting up. It was extremely hot and very difficult to dig, but we finally got our positions to where they were deep enough.

I was calling in artillery at someone's request, talking to somebody in an artillery battery. It seemed to me I was in touch with Dong Ha. I used the grid maps I'd picked up from the squad radioman when he was hit. This was the first time I had ever called an artillery fire mission. I could only hope I had it right. I was trying to call it in on the hedgerow where I last saw them and then advanced it up a little closer to us because I figured they'd moved up toward us. It worked. I thank God for his assistance. I didn't get everything I wanted, but we were grateful for anything we could get. They put it right where I wanted it. The grids were right on.

2nd Lieutenant CHAN CRANGLE
Mike Company, 3/26—1st Platoon Commander

We started taking small-arms fire from my front. I didn't see anybody shooting at us, but it was clear that we were taking direct fire, not just stray rounds. We were shooting at muzzle flashes to our front and ducking incoming. Some small-arms fire was impacting from our rear, making it a bit hazardous to keep our heads up to our front. I saw one of my squad leaders bracketed on both sides by stray small-arms rounds coming from the rear.

My platoon took a fair amount of incoming, but there was no direct assault as such, on my position.

Captain ANDY DeBONA
Mike Company, 3/26—Commanding Officer

No sooner had I passed the word for Mike-2 to move than the order was implemented. It took only 4 to 5 minutes. Almost immediately, Mike-3 reported it was in contact with an unknown-size enemy force. Apparently, what had happened was that, when Mike-2 pulled out, a platoon- or company-size force of NVA came right in behind it and got inside the battalion perimeter. They might have just accidentally fallen into the vacuum or they might have seen Mike-2 pull out. When Mike-3 started spreading out to fill Mike-2's sector, the right-hand squad of Mike-3 ran into the NVA almost in a heartbeat.

I started firing the 60mm mortars on the former Mike-2 sector.

There were a lot of bullets flying. It was a little bit disorganized.

2nd Lieutenant CHAN CRANGLE
Mike Company, 3/26—1st Platoon Commander

I suspect I was in a good position to make a counterattack on the assault on Manzi's [Mike-3's] flank, but everyone was too busy to think of it. Plus, I think the situation was thoroughly confused at that point, with India Company in heavy contact and Manzi's platoon and H&S Company in heavy contact. There was the distinct possibility that something was about to show up on my doorstep. The incoming mortar and rocket fire was pretty intense and pretty damn close. So long as you were in a foxhole, you were reasonably safe—except for concussions.

Staff Sergeant DAVE NUGENT
3/26, 81mm Mortar Platoon

Sergeant Bill Riggle, our FO with Mike Company, ran down to the mortar pits and told me they wanted all our rifles to help protect the battalion CP. I didn't know what he meant by that, but Gunner Holycross and I sent all the rifles we had except two, along with most of our ammo humpers. Except for the gunner, me, our guncrews, radiomen, and two ammo humpers, everyone left. We had only two rifles left— the gunner's and one ammo humper's. We sent all the others up to Battalion, which was on the other side of the church.

Captain TOM EARLY
3/26—Communications Officer

Everybody in the battalion CP who didn't have to have a handset in his hand and a radio stuck in his ear was given a weapon and put on the line around the CP area. Some of them just backed up Mike Company, where the hardest point of that contact was coming in, manning a second line of defense.

Once the enemy attacked and penetrated into the trees, especially in the night, we had a tremendous problem of identification and trying to get any type of clear field of fire.

I thought we were very directly threatened. I threw a couple Hail Marys and an act of contrition in as I watched this whole thing going on. I guess the only person who knows how directly threatened I was would be the laundry officer who had to take care of those things later.

Captain ANDY DEBONA
Mike Company, 3/26—Commanding Officer

We were not getting any 105mm illumination, so the 81s started firing illumination. They quickly expended their supply. Battalion had requested a flareship, but in the meantime I told them that I could fill in the illumination gap with my 60mm mortars. I had about 60 illume rounds with me at this time, which was my standard load. When all but about 10 rounds had been fired, I told Battalion that my illumination was expended and suggested to them that they have the other companies go ahead and start filling in the gap for me. However, that never came about. I don't know the reason for that.

*

Captain ANDY DeBONA
Mike Company, 3/26—Commanding Officer

As Mike-1 and Mike-3 and the 60s worked to seal the gap where Mike-2 had been, I glanced over at the 81s, which were within 30 meters of me, to the left rear of my CP. I noticed that the mortarmen were firing their small arms in the direction of Mike-3. I got pissed. I thought they were shooting at my guys, so I went running over there to tell them to cease fire.

Staff Sergeant DAVE NUGENT
3/26, 81mm Mortar Platoon

I never knew they'd pulled that platoon of Mike out.

The NVA started opening up on us and Gunner Holycross was yelling, "I think they're up in the trees!"

One of the mortar gunners, Sergeant Roy O'Neal, asked me if I wanted him to run the guns while I helped take care of the NVA. I told him I'd do both and that he should help the gunners defend the guns because we had no rifles. He went forward. I later learned that Sergeant O'Neal attacked the NVA with his .45 and the NVA killed him—shot him between the eyes.

One of the two ammo humpers who remained in the 81s perimeter, a big blond kid who still had his rifle, ran up to me and yelled, "I been shot in the leg!" I told him to get down in the hole so I could have a look. There was a big hole in his left thigh and it was just pumping blood out. An artery had been cut. I pulled off my belt and tightened it around the leg to stop some of the bleeding. Before I was done, I saw this Chicom grenade coming. It had to have come from the treeline. The ammo humper was blocking my right hand, so I reached around with my left to try to bat it away. I never caught it. It blew up just before I could get my hand on it.

The grenade destroyed my left hand and tore up the upper left side of my head. It tore up the skin on my temple. This is when I got scared. My big fear had always been losing my sight. There was skin and blood and powder in my eyes. I thought, "Oh shit! I can't see!" But, two seconds later, I rubbed my eyes and my vision cleared. I could see! I'd rubbed the loose skin and stuff out of my eyes.

The first thing I did was look at my hand. It was ruined. With my right hand, I pulled the big elastic band off my helmet—the band we used to hold our shit paper. I wrapped it around my left hand, to hold it together and stop some of the bleeding.

I'd always heard that the enemy always attacked after they threw grenades, so I took the wounded ammo humper's rifle. But they never came.

I turned around. Two radio operators were right behind me. They both said they couldn't see because of the grenade blast. I said, "Don't worry about it. Your sight'll come back to you. It's just the shock of the blast. Just hold still." I checked both of them out. One of the radio operators was Gunner Holycross's radioman. The radioman said he was blinded, but I couldn't find any other wounds. The other one, Lance Corporal Thomas Warren, had been wounded in the back. I told him, "I'll go and get a corpsman."

I checked over the rifle I'd taken from the wounded ammo humper and called over to Gunner Holycross, "Gunner, I'm going back to get a corpsman." He yelled back, "Okay. I'll cover you."

Chief Warrant Officer RICHARD HOLYCROSS
3/26, 81mm Mortar Platoon—Commanding Officer
Silver Star Citation (excerpt):

With full knowledge of the hazards involved, and with complete disregard for his own safety, he repeatedly exposed himself to enemy fire to reorganize and reassure his men. Moving from man to man, he personally led and directed their fire in repelling an attack which would have penetrated the battalion command post.

Staff Sergeant DAVE NUGENT
3/26, 81mm Mortar Platoon

I crawled out of the hole as quick as I could and started walking down toward the Mike Company CP. I got shot in the leg. A round creased my left leg. It just skinned me. Then I saw a Mike Company Marine coming from the direction of Mike Company. He was carrying boxes of ammo. I yelled, "Where the hell is Mike Company?" He said in a real calm voice, "We're coming." So I yelled, "Where's Captain De-Bona?" The ammo humper answered, "Oh, he's coming, too." His voice was real calm, real matter of fact.

Sure as shit, Captain DeBona ran into me. I'd been his 81s FO for a few months. When he saw I was wounded, he said, "Nugent, I can't leave you alone for five minutes." It cracked me up. "Thanks a lot," I said. He got his corpsman to fix me up a little. I told the corpsman, "You gotta get down to the 81s and fix up my radio operator." He went forward and I kept going to the rear. I found the battalion CP and got down in a big hole with the other wounded.

Captain ANDY DeBONA
Mike Company, 3/26—Commanding Officer

When I got over to the 81s position, I noticed that there were quite a few wounded Marines there, inside a little bomb crater. I also saw a lot of winks—a lot of bullets—coming from a treeline approximately 60 meters away. This was the treeline that separated my company CP and my 60mm mortars from the 81mm mortars. I stuck my head up from the bomb crater and kept it up until I had counted eight winks. Eight NVA were in the treeline firing.

I ran-crawled back to my company CP, which was about 30 meters from the 81s. I told the Mike-3 and Mike-1 platoon radiomen that the bad guys were in the area. Then I reported the news to Battalion.

Almost immediately, I received a report that Mike-3-Actual—Lieutenant John Manzi—was KIA. As near as I could ever make out, he heard the contact on his platoon's right flank and ran over there to see what the hell was going on. He ran into the gap with just his radioman, a habit my more aggressive platoon commanders unfortunately copied from me. John was shot dead and his radio operator called to tell me.

2nd Lieutenant CHAN CRANGLE
Mike Company, 3/26—1st Platoon Commander

John Manzi was killed fairly early in the fight. I was told that he left his foxhole to find out what was going on and took a round in his head almost immediately. I suspect he was killed around 1800.

Captain ANDY DeBONA
Mike Company, 3/26—Commanding Officer

John Manzi had joined Mike Company in March 1967. He was a little guy with a big hook nose. After a few months in the field, he was down to about 140 pounds with a full field marching pack on his back. He was extremely aggressive and had been with the company the longest. If I needed something done, Manzi's platoon was the one I sent to do it. The first time I ever sent him out on patrol, he saw three guys with guns on their backs rooting through a trash pile. He walked right up to them and shot them point-blank with a shotgun. He used to get big care packages from home—enough at one time, once, to throw a spaghetti dinner mess night for the battalion officers at Khe Sanh. There was even Italian wine. He was about due to make first lieutenant, and it was my intention to transfer him over to the battalion S-3 section. He'd put in his time in the field.

At the same time I heard Manzi was down, I heard that the 60s were down to five HE rounds per gun. Mike-3 reported that it was still in contact.

*

At 1832, as the battalion perimeter was struck once again by coordinated rocket, artillery, mortar, and infantry attacks, a section of two Marine F-4 fighters arrived on station.

Lance Corporal RON BURKE
Mike Company, 3/26, 2nd Platoon

We were directed to pull back because jets were going to dump napalm. They dropped it extremely close, into the trees in front of us. I could feel a lot of the heat. I was very glad we'd moved back. Then we moved forward again to our fighting holes.

Captain TOM EARLY
3/26—Communications Officer

The fixed-wing strike silenced the incoming for a moment, but only a moment.

1st Lieutenant RON ZAPPARDINO
3/26—Forward Air Controller

That one quick strike by the two fast movers was the only air support we got that night.

*

2nd Lieutenant BILL COWAN
India Company, 3/26—3rd Platoon Commander

There were a couple times the lines, to include Mike Company, flat opened up with everything. Someone would fire once or twice and then everyone got spooked and they all started firing. I went up and down the line, from position to position, trying to control the fire. I really chewed some Mike Company guys out badly for sitting down in their hole with their rifles held over their heads, firing without even looking. As far as I knew, all this was happening while there were good guys out there who were trying to get in to us.

My Marines and the NVA continued to do some shooting back and forth. After some of my men had been doing some heavy shooting, they started having trouble with their weapons. It was to be expected. At 1838, my best squad leader, Sergeant Bruce Krage, got shot in the head while he was up on the forward line trying to clear someone's M-16. He had been moving around, clearing rifles, talking to his people, and we were not receiving a barrage of fire at that time. I'm sure some NVA saw him in the light of the illumination and took a shot at him. I have no idea how many NVA were out in front of our lines; Mike Company was getting hit pretty hard from the north at that time.

I was only 10 to 15 feet from where Krage was when he was shot. I didn't see it happen, but someone called out, "Hey, Lieutenant, Sergeant Krage's been shot." He was still alive when we medevacked him later, during the night, but he died before he got to the hospital. He was the only man in the platoon who got killed that night.

Until Sergeant Krage was shot, I had been too busy or maybe too inexperienced to be scared. Maybe I was too dumb. I felt that I needed to get up and talk to all my people, and then my comm started going bad, so I had to run over to the battalion CP to see if there was anything they wanted done. I thought nothing of all that moving around. But I got real frightened when I heard about Bruce Krage. After that, I was more aware of the danger, and scared.

*

Captain ANDY DeBONA
Mike Company, 3/26—Commanding Officer

There were still eight NVA in the treeline behind Mike Company. At about 1900, I told Mike-3 and Mike-1 to stand fast. Then I formed a reaction squad composed of my two runners and the company 60mm mortar section chief. I told them the situation, that there were about 8 to 10 bad guys in the treeline. I ordered them to go in and clean them all out. The mortar sergeant took about 15 people out with him.

At that time, Mike-1 and Mike-3 reported very light contact.

2nd Lieutenant CHAN CRANGLE
Mike Company, 3/26—1st Platoon Commander

My 1st Platoon was not directly attacked. Most of the fight was to my left, or southwest of my positions. What small-arms fire we took was probably the flank security elements of the NVA main attack. We took a lot of mortar and rocket incoming, but there was no ground attack.

Captain ANDY DeBONA
Mike Company, 3/26—Commanding Officer

Directly to my rear was the reaction squad. It was doing a lot of firing, and a few grenades were going off. Then everything suddenly stopped. It became extremely quiet.

The reaction squad came back to my CP about 10 minutes after it left. The 60s section chief had a bullet wound through his shoulder. His report to me was, "We got them all, sir." I reported this to Battalion, then I told Mike-1 and Mike-3 to start pulling way back where they joined in the center of the company position. We had too much front to cover, and I wanted to consolidate my positions. I had to make sure that Mike-1 still maintained contact with Kilo, on its right, and Mike-3 maintained contact with Mike-2, on its left. We had to create a big salient in our line.

Lance Corporal RON BURKE
Mike Company, 3/26, 2nd Platoon

Right about dark, they told us to move back a little. I had everything just right by then—my ammo was where it was supposed to be and my hole was just right—so I was not excited about the order. Some illumination started before we moved. We weren't about to move while the illumination was up. It seemed to last a long time. We eventually did move.

2nd Lieutenant CHAN CRANGLE
Mike Company, 3/26—1st Platoon Commander

Andy reshuffled the platoons to tighten up the perimeter. What was formerly the company commander's position became the front line. I'm not sure how big the battalion perimeter was, but Mike Company was pulled in tight!

Captain ANDY DeBONA
Mike Company, 3/26—Commanding Officer

When we finished reorganizing our line, it was about 20 meters in front of the 81s and within spitting distance of the company CP. There was no need to tell the individual Marines to dig in deep; it looked like they were playing prairie dog.

More artillery started coming from the bad guys. They kept firing four to six rounds without shifting fires; they kept hitting the same spot. I received word on the battalion tac net to attend a meeting at the battalion CP. On the way to this meeting, my invincibility was shattered. The bad guys threw one round out of the way and I felt some warm stuff on my leg.

Once we got into the battalion CP, I heard a voice from the bottom of a hole. I'll never forget the words: "Spread out so one round will not get us all."

This was my first introduction to the new battalion commander. After the artillery stopped, he stood up in his hole. It was the first time I had seen Harry Alderman since 1962, when we both had served in the same battalion at Camp Lejeune. The gist of the conversation was that there were a lot of bad guys in the area.

Captain TOM EARLY
3/26—Communications Officer

When that incoming fire was in vogue, nervousness persisted. The battalion commander was erect and mobile, but he was not enthusiastic. I don't think any of us were much different except that we were callous and positive we would succeed.

*

Captain ANDY DeBONA
Mike Company, 3/26—Commanding Officer

After the meeting at Battalion, I went back to the company area and called up Lieutenants Crangle and Gall and the staff sergeant who had assumed command of Mike-3. I asked the staff sergeant where John Manzi's body was. He said that John was still out where he had fallen. I was furious. In a low, calm tone, I said, "Go get him now." I also ordered the staff sergeant to make sure that he and his men policed up all their trash in the grass out there. The mission was accomplished quickly.

*

2nd Lieutenant BILL COWAN
India Company, 3/26—3rd Platoon Commander

One of my positions reported there were some grenades coming in, that they were getting some grenades thrown at them from a depression right in front of their part of our line. There were three or four grenades, but none of them went off. My guys threw one of our M-26 grenades back, resulting in screams. The next morning, we found an SKS rifle, a B-40 rocket launcher, blood, and brains. About the same time, around 1900, we saw some NVA run across a little opening in the light of the heavy-duty illume that was being fired by our supporting artillery. They were running off to the left side of our lines. We had a few Ontos with us. When we reported what we could see, one of the Ontos responded.

Staff Sergeant DAVE NUGENT
3/26, 81mm Mortar Platoon

An Ontos passed the battalion aid station in the direction of the 81s. This guy really opened up with his .50-cal on the treeline the NVA were hiding in. He shot the shit out of them.

Chief Warrant Officer RICHARD HOLYCROSS
3/26, 81mm Mortar Platoon—Commanding Officer
Silver Star Citation (Excerpt):

Chief Warrant Officer Holycross commanded an [Ontos] antitank weapon and effectively brought devastating fire on the enemy.

2nd Lieutenant BILL COWAN
India Company, 3/26—3rd Platoon Commander

The Ontos apparently killed four of them. It was very brave of the two men in the Ontos to come out, particularly since the NVA had a lot of RPG teams running around out there.

*

2nd Lieutenant BILL COWAN
India Company, 3/26—3rd Platoon Commander

My radio was not working properly and the CP was only about 35 meters from my lines, so I went over to see Captain Bill Wildprett, the S-3, and Captain Tom Early, the communications officer. I went a number of times during the early hours of the night to give them status reports and to find out what was going on.

Captain Wildprett was running the show. He had the map, the radio, and the people in the CP around him. He was talking to the people in trouble; talking to higher headquarters; getting us air and artillery support; monitoring the medevac situation; and very, very clearly providing the leadership necessary to hold the situation together. He should have been awarded a Navy Cross for what he did to save the battalion that night. He was all over the place, running the battle. Captain Early was right there with Wildprett, keeping it together, too. Wildprett and Early were doing it all. I don't recall seeing either of them in a hole or taking cover at any point. They just had too much to do.

On one of those trips to the CP, I heard that Captain Coulter had been hit and that Lieutenant Bob Stimson was in charge of the part of the company in front of our perimeter. I hadn't been with India Company very long and I didn't know Coulter real well, so I didn't have any strong feelings about him. I heard he was hit bad and maybe might die, but I didn't have feelings as strong as the ones I had for Sergeant Bruce Krage, who I thought the world of.

I had to make no major decisions that night. My responsibility was to keep my troops alert, make sure we didn't shoot any of our guys who were trying to get back through the lines (we knew they were out there), and just respond to the NVA as we could. We got penetrated and we got probed, but until Sergeant Krage was shot, I had no real reason to be scared.

*

Staff Sergeant DAVE NUGENT
3/26, 81mm Mortar Platoon

They started bringing in the helicopters for the wounded. Gunner Holy-cross showed up at the aid station, asked about my wounds, and told me, "Don't worry about it. We'll get you out of here right away. There are medevacs coming in." I told him, "Gunner, don't worry about me. Take care of the kids."

2nd Lieutenant CHAN CRANGLE
Mike Company, 3/26—1st Platoon Commander

Fairly late in the evening, I was sitting on the edge of a foxhole when a young Marine came up to me to ask for a cleaning rod to clear his jammed M-16. He was a replacement who had just joined the platoon that day. He sounded a little groggy, and I asked him if he was all right. He answered "Yes," but then I looked at his helmet and saw a bullet entry hole just about where the top of his head should have been. I told him to sit down. I held my breath while I took off his helmet, fully expecting his brains to fall out. The kid had a permanent part where the bullet had just creased his skull. One more inch and good night. I said, "Son, you've seen your war."

Captain ANDY DeBONA
Mike Company, 3/26—Commanding Officer

One of my Mike-1 Marines who had been reported wounded came back to the company CP. When I observed, "You don't look wounded," he took off his helmet and showed me where a round had gone completely through and nicked the top of his skull. It looked like a wound to me.

The medevacs started coming in to pick up the wounded. The LZ that was being used was between the battalion CP and the 81s, to the rear of the 81s. The birds reported that they were taking fire. I passed the word to Mike-3 and Mike-1 to lay down covering fire, which consisted of one magazine of M-16 fire per man. The birds managed to lift out our emergency medevacs. Our routines—our dead—did not go out. The medevac helos brought in an emergency resupply of 60mm HE rounds.

Staff Sergeant DAVE NUGENT
3/26, 81mm Mortar Platoon

I was flown out with Lance Corporal Thomas Warren, my radio operator, who had been shot in the back. They took us off at Dong Ha and ran us into the big aid station they had there. They quickly cleaned my wounds and got me ready to fly farther back to the rear. Major Mundy, the battalion exec, came by to see me and the other wounded. I was hardly in Dong Ha at all before they flew me out to the hospital ship, *Repose*. I saw Warren while I was aboard the *Repose*. A corpsman wheeled me down to see him. He was on his stomach because he'd been shot in the back, but he seemed okay. He was smiling. A corpsman told me he was going to be okay. My facial wounds were minor and quickly healed, but I lost the use of my left hand.

*

2nd Lieutenant CHAN CRANGLE
Mike Company, 3/26—1st Platoon Commander

We fired a lot of mortar and artillery H&I during the night, but, by 2300, things had pretty much settled down—except for some thoroughly frazzled nerves.

Lance Corporal RON BURKE
Mike Company, 3/26, 2nd Platoon

They kept firing stuff at us. Every once in awhile, someone would think he saw something out there. We'd lay down a little fire and wouldn't have any problems for awhile. I don't know if they were moving around or if we were picking them off.

I never slept a wink that night. I just wasn't about to go to sleep. I could sleep some other time.

2nd Lieutenant BILL COWAN
India Company, 3/26—3rd Platoon Commander

At one point, I went over toward the squad of Mike Company that was tied in with my platoon—to make sure they were still holding—and someone said there was a sniper in the church steeple. I glanced up toward the church, which was pretty far away, and tried to see through the smoke drifting through the illume. I wanted to see what a sniper looked like.

After the fighting died down and everyone was tense, they kept firing artillery illume from Con Thien and C-2. We heard them: *pop*. When the canister separated, we could hear *shwew-shwew-shwew-bomp* as they tumbled to the ground somewhere in or around the perimeter. It was very scary. Everyone was worried about getting hit by one of those things from our illume rounds. It was ludicrous when you think that we had just been through a big battle, but everyone was more worried about being hit by an illume canister than we had been about being shot.

1st Lieutenant RON ZAPPARDINO
3/26—Forward Air Controller

I finally had Puff the Magic Dragon on station beginning at 2015. All I could do was keep flares over us and direct him on targets designated by Wildprett or the grunt troop leaders on the line.

Captain ANDY DeBONA
Mike Company, 3/26—Commanding Officer

Eventually, Puff showed up on station and provided us with illumination for the rest of the night. By then, it was extremely quiet, and the night didn't produce any surprises. There was no contact.

Captain TOM EARLY
3/26—Communications Officer

The NVA dragged away their dead with meat hooks that had ropes attached. They threw the meat hooks and pulled the dead back so they wouldn't be hit with the same direct fire that had killed the dead. I think they also did it to demoralize us. We could hear the noise of the hook going into a body and the body hitting other objects as it was being dragged.

Chapter 7

Lance Corporal CHUCK BENNETT
India Company, 3/26, 1st Platoon

The last remaining member of my fire team, Lance Corporal Joseph Juaire, was hit at about twilight. He was out in front of me a ways. I crawled up to him with Doc Butsko, a little corpsman from Ohio who wore thick glasses. You wouldn't think much of Butsko just looking at him, but he was all over the place that night, doing a hell of a job. The way Juaire was hollering, "I'm hit! I'm hit! I'm hit," I thought the wound was going to be real bad. It was a shrapnel wound in the leg. It looked so bad at first—there was lots of blood—that I thought the leg was blown off, but it wasn't. In fact, there wasn't much to the wound. It was a nick. Butsko and I dragged Juaire back out of the open, back to the sick bay. Juaire wasn't hurt bad, but any leg wound was enough to keep someone from getting back into the fight.

Staff Sergeant RUSS ARMSTRONG
India Company, 3/26—1st Platoon Commander

Lieutenant Stimson got in touch with an AO sometime after sunset. The AO called a jet strike. The jets dropped napalm close enough for me to feel intense heat, even though I was down behind the berm. I had mixed thoughts: "Glad you're here; hope you're dropping accurately."

Following the air strikes early in the evening, the fight slowed down.

It was still dangerous to be there, and we were not able to even think about moving back to rejoin the main body of the battalion. But most of the early pressure was off. We continued to receive incoming, which we answered when we could pinpoint targets. I called some artillery fire from time to time, but the NVA who were facing us did not press us very hard. Nevertheless, we continued to take casualties from small-arms fire. I heard that my at first–reluctant corpsman, HM3 Albert Butsko, was shot dead while on some errand of mercy.

Lance Corporal CHUCK BENNETT
India Company, 3/26, 1st Platoon

The shooting started dying down after dark. They probed us a few times, but nothing much happened.

1st Lieutenant BOB STIMSON
India Company, 3/26—Executive Officer

At one point after full dark, I was on the radio with Captain Wildprett, telling him I thought we could break up the NVA if we could get some gunship support—Puff. He said he would see what he could do. Around that time, beginning at 1945, we could see the NVA dragging away their dead and wounded, which was a good indication that they were packing it in. But I was expecting the worst. I fully expected them to hit us again. By then the incoming small-arms fire had dwindled notice-ably, however. I didn't know what to expect.

Shortly thereafter, at 2015, we had a Puff on station, flying orbits right over our heads. After Puff was on station, things pulled our way. We could *feel* the difference.

Staff Sergeant RUSS ARMSTRONG
India Company, 3/26—1st Platoon Commander

Hope returned when, about three hours after the first rocket salvo, Puff arrived and intermittently dropped illumination over us. We also got the benefit of some H&I [harassment-and-interdiction] fire from the artil-lery batteries at Camp Carroll or C-2, maybe both and maybe other friendly bases. I don't know if the artillery hit anything of value, but it helped me no end; it was nice to know that it was ours and not the NVA's.

2nd Lieutenant PAUL DRNEC
Bravo Company, 3rd Tank Battalion—2nd Platoon Commander

We were under continuous friendly illumination all night. We were never attacked and we did not see targets in the open, but the gun tanks contributed H&I fires into the treelines with our coaxial machine guns and HE rounds from our main guns. I didn't think there was really anybody in those treelines, but it paid to be safe.

Lance Corporal CHUCK BENNETT
India Company, 3/26, 1st Platoon

The tanks sometimes fired on our own people. They were all buttoned up and couldn't see much. We lost a few people who tried to crawl up on the tank turrets to tell them to cease firing on our own people. Those Marines were shot by the NVA, who kept the tanks under fire.

1st Lieutenant BOB STIMSON
India Company, 3/26—Executive Officer

I remained concerned about our ammunition supply. It was something I harped on during every encounter I ever faced. It was important. The tendency of undisciplined troops is to spray, which really never does any good. I just kept harping on it.

Lance Corporal CHUCK BENNETT
India Company, 3/26, 1st Platoon

It was real quiet in the middle of the night. All of a sudden, there was this big explosion just a few meters from my position. Shrapnel flew over me. I could hear it going over. I don't think it was a Chicom. They made little explosions. Maybe it was one of our grenades. I went over to see what had happened and if I could help. We found a Marine from my squad, Lance Corporal Oscar Palacios. He was already dead.

Staff Sergeant RUSS ARMSTRONG
India Company, 3/26—1st Platoon Commander

Long after the fighting died off, I was able to think about getting my wounds treated. I got some help from someone and moved to the center portion of the perimeter. By that time, the mosquitoes there were absolutely atrocious. All the fresh blood from injuries was drawing them, and they were having a real heyday. My entry wound on the back of my leg was too big to be covered by the largest gauze bandage we carried, which was 4 inches by 4 inches. So the best I could do to keep the mosquitoes off was fold down my map sheet to cover the wound. There was a big ragged, jagged wound—presumably the exit wound but possibly another entry wound—on the front side of my leg. I didn't have any medical treatment because the corpsman didn't know what he could do for me.

1st Lieutenant BOB STIMSON
India Company, 3/26—Executive Officer

Things quieted down quite a bit in the hour before midnight. It seemed that we might be out of serious trouble. I called the senior corpsman over and asked him how many WIAs he had that he thought wouldn't make it through the night. He said that there were three, including Captain Coulter. It was at that point that I decided to try a medevac. I got on the radio to Captain Wildprett and made the request. He replied, "Okay, we'll give it a try."

Staff Sergeant RUSS ARMSTRONG
India Company, 3/26—1st Platoon Commander

Quite late at night, Lieutenant Stimson learned that they were going to try to get one medevac helicopter out to us to lift out the serious WIAs. They told us that the chopper had only enough room for five men. The lieutenant asked the company senior corpsman to go through the perimeter to check on all the WIAs and designate the five with the most serious wounds. I was pegged as number five. After the senior corpsman left, Lieutenant Stimson approached me and said that he was going to need some help and asked if I thought I could make it until morning. I thought about clean sheets and someone bringing me a hot meal. I didn't know how badly I had been hurt; I didn't know if I had a broken leg or whatever. I hadn't had to move around very much since I had been hit, so I didn't have a sense of the extent of my injuries. I gave some thought to both sides of the question and finally agreed to stay.

1st Lieutenant BOB STIMSON
India Company, 3/26—Executive Officer

Sometime later, we got an H-34 over us. We marked the zone—my little CP rice paddy—with flashlights and got him in without incident.

We staged the three WIAs who the corpsman thought were the worst and added two others he thought were bad enough.

Staff Sergeant RUSS ARMSTRONG
India Company, 3/26—1st Platoon Commander

The chopper set down and the wounded were loaded aboard in a matter of seconds. One of them was Captain Coulter and another was my radio-man, Lance Corporal Thomas Moore.

Lance Corporal CHUCK BENNETT
India Company, 3/26, 1st Platoon

One of the Marines flown out on the medevac was Lance Corporal Robert Pugh, the Marine from my fire team who had been hit in the back about sunset by a .51-caliber round. He was in bad shape—they thought he had spinal damage—but I heard he lived.

1st Lieutenant BOB STIMSON
India Company, 3/26—Executive Officer

The H-34 loaded the wounded, dumped a load of small-arms ammo, and left quickly, without drawing fire.

Staff Sergeant RUSS ARMSTRONG
India Company, 3/26—1st Platoon Commander

A few moments after the chopper lifted off, Lieutenant Stimson asked the corpsman who had been tabbed to go in my place. The corpsman named the man who had rated number five, but it turned out that that Marine was still with the company. Stimson called Battalion and cussed out the ALO [air liaison officer], telling him that the chopper had only four WIAs aboard. The ALO contacted the chopper and radioed back to us that, no, there were five WIAs aboard. Stimson asked for their names, which were duly reported. Captain Coulter was one, and the blinded Black Power Marine from my 1st Squad was another. It turned out that the dead artillery FO's radioman was the fifth man. As it turned out, that Marine did not have a scratch on him; he simply had jumped aboard the chopper. Of course, when the chopper's crew chief had counted up to five incoming bodies, he had given the pilot the word to go, and the pilot had gone.

1st Lieutenant BOB STIMSON
India Company, 3/26—Executive Officer

After the medevac and ammunition resupply, we were able to take the time to sort out squads and platoons by shuffling people to various sectors. That gave us our first chance to count noses, and we came up 13 short. I reported the short count to Battalion and they eventually came back with news that six of them had somehow followed Kilo Company back to the main perimeter. The six had been absorbed into Bill Cowan's 3rd Platoon. So, we stood at seven of our Marines missing and unaccounted for.

Staff Sergeant RUSS ARMSTRONG
India Company, 3/26—1st Platoon Commander

We learned late at night that Kilo Company and a squad of the 2nd Platoon that was supposed to maintain contact had kept moving back the 500 meters to the battalion main perimeter. Kilo Company and half of the India Company squad made it back safely. The NVA main thrust, after it passed through us, apparently overtook and overran the tail half of the 2nd Platoon's link-up squad and then hit the battalion main body.

1st Lieutenant BOB STIMSON
India Company, 3/26—Executive Officer

There were a few NVA probes during the night after the medevac, but we had the upper hand in all of them and easily drove them off. We were on top of the situation.

At sunrise, when we could see, there were dead people all over the place. The situation was appalling, worse than I thought it would be. It was a bad scene.

*

1st Lieutenant RON ZAPPARDINO
3/26—Forward Air Controller

In the morning, I went out with Kilo Company to help bring back the India Company patrol. There was no contact. We joined up quickly because they were not far away.

Staff Sergeant CHARLES OWENS
Kilo Company, 3/26—Company Gunny

We set up and told India to move back inside our perimeter. They told us the same thing they'd told us the night before, that they'd follow us out. This time, our captain told them, "No, I said get in here, and do it now!" So they came on in with some of their dead and wounded. When they came in, we went out to bring in the rest.

The India dead and wounded were all spread out—a little patch of people here and a little patch of people there, killed or wounded. I found one guy who had been bayoneted two or three times. He was still alive. Most of the wounded we found had stayed awake and fought most of the night, alone.

Staff Sergeant RUSS ARMSTRONG
India Company, 3/26—1st Platoon Commander

We had seven men missing. When Kilo Company returned to our position in the morning, it retraced its route of march and found all of the missing men.

Staff Sergeant CHARLES OWENS
Kilo Company, 3/26—Company Gunny

We found a group of six people, but they were all dead. They had run down to jump behind a dike, but there were NVA behind them. In fact, it looked like the Marines jumped right in with the NVA.

Staff Sergeant RUSS ARMSTRONG
India Company, 3/26—1st Platoon Commander

The six dead Marines were all shot and bayoneted. One of the dead Marines had been stripped of all his belongings except his trousers. The seventh missing Marine was found alive, though he was seriously wounded.

1st Lieutenant RON ZAPPARDINO
3/26—Forward Air Controller

There were dead people all over the ground. No one wanted to pick them up. Everyone was just stunned. When the tanks cranked up, some of the sergeants started yelling, "Pick up the dead. We gotta get outta here; we gotta get moving.'' But almost everyone was standing there, in shock. There were so many of them, and most of them were so young. Finally, the troops started moving—lifting the dead Marines onto the tanks. Then I started looking around, seeing who was left. It was a relief to see people I knew who were still alive. I asked about people I knew and they asked about people they knew. The shock wore off pretty quickly, and it became a matter of getting the job done and trying to get back to the battalion perimeter before the NVA started throwing artillery and mortars at us.

Lance Corporal CHUCK BENNETT
India Company, 3/26, 1st Platoon

We had to police up our dead and wounded. I didn't want to do it. We were tired and it was very hot. Some of the dead guys were already decomposing. They smelled terrible and some were blown all to hell. But we had to get them out of there.

I helped load Staff Sergeant Armstrong on one of the tanks. He was a little delirious then. He kept yelling, "Let's get outta here! Get me outta here!" He was in a lot of pain.

1st Lieutenant BOB STIMSON
India Company, 3/26—Executive Officer

One of the things I had learned in Vietnam was that leaders could not get too wrapped up in the casualties. You had to see that the wounded were treated and the dead received proper treatment, but it was too important to stay alert to ongoing danger to spend any time on remorse or might-have-beens or even good-byes. I had learned to get them the hell out of there and move on to the next job. My concerns that morning were for security, getting the wounded patched and evacuated, getting the dead gathered up, and getting all the rest of us the hell out of there. Only after I had done as much as I could in other areas, I went around to each of the wounded men, thanked him for serving with India Company, and wished him well.

While Kilo Company searched the area for wounded NVA and intelligence matter, my Marines loaded the dead and wounded on the tanks and searched the area of the contact for anyone we might have missed.

One of the dead Marines was Sergeant Larry Flora, whom I had encountered on my way to join Captain Coulter in the rice paddy at the start of the battle. I was too wrapped up in my work that morning to do more than acknowledge Sergeant Flora's loss, but in all the time since I have regretted not taking him with me.

2nd Lieutenant PAUL DRNEC
Bravo Company, 3rd Tank Battalion—2nd Platoon Commander

When Kilo Company arrived at about 0800 and swept through the area, I inspected the damaged B-21 tank and found that it was towable. In fact, with the transmission out, it would roll easier than it would have otherwise. We backed the B-25 tank up to it and connected a cross-cable hookup and rigid tow bars because B-21's brakes also were out.

We had wounded and dead Marines on the tanks when we left, and more dead Marines were added as they were found during our slow march across the paddies and on into the trees.

Staff Sergeant RUSS ARMSTRONG
India Company, 3/26—1st Platoon Commander

The sun was shining and the metal surface of the tank on which I was riding was very hot. I was feeling the blood loss and the result of hours of adrenaline flow. As I looked down, I saw three NVA corpses that had been tossed headfirst into a hole beside the trail. They were wearing good-quality green uniforms, squared away right down to bloused trousers. I clearly knew that I hated the bastards, but at that moment I conceded to myself that I felt a lot of respect for them. I had no respect for the sneak-around, hide-in-the-bushes Viet Cong guerrilla, but I knew the NVA were good. I thought about how we had met, as adversaries, but as men equally determined to kill the enemy, to come out ahead. Everything I had seen of them in the waning light as I had been flickering in and out of possession of my faculties had convinced me that my enemies that night had been professional soldiers, equals who were worthy of my respect.

I wondered then and wonder now if their families ever learned what happened to them, ever learned that they died bravely. I know the families never saw their men, their loved ones, again, never had an opportunity to bury them at home. But I wonder if anyone told them how bravely their men died.

*

2nd Lieutenant BILL COWAN
India Company, 3/26—3rd Platoon Commander

In the morning, when I went out and looked, one of our positions had laying around it three or four Chicom grenades that had not gone off. In contrast, the Marines in that position had thrown some M-26 grenades. When we went forward of that position, we found blood and guts all over the place, and picked up some weapons.

We also found that some 140mm rockets had landed within 2 feet of several of our fighting holes. The ground was so hard—shale—that the rockets hit and exploded upwards. The only damage my men suffered were some blown eardrums. They didn't even want to be medevacked.

I walked over by the church—I'm not sure why—and found a little North Vietnamese coin on the ground. I picked it up and kept it as a souvenir of my first battle.

Lance Corporal RON BURKE
Mike Company, 3/26, 2nd Platoon

We went out early in the morning to sweep the area. The detail my squad was on meant carrying the bodies back toward the perimeter. It seemed like we were on that tasteless detail forever. We also saw many signs of enemy killed—scraps of clothing, drag marks, blood pools. Someone was hurt bad. My buddy found a payroll. It was in a canvas sack—a double-stitched canvas sack full of North Vietnamese money. It was just laying there, on the ground. There was blood around it. One of the sergeants took it up to Battalion.

Captain ANDY DeBONA
Mike Company, 3/26—Commanding Officer

I assigned Mike-2 to conduct a platoon-size sweep back through our old positions and to come back in down the treeline where my company's reaction squad had made the contact during the evening.

The Mike-2 commander was 2nd Lieutenant Bob Gall. He was not a very aggressive kid. He had been knocking around the battalion for months, getting moved from company to company and finally to the 106 Platoon. Finally, our former battalion commander asked me if I would take Gall on to straighten him out. I said I'd give it a try. I stayed right on top of Gall from then on, checking on him and letting him know I was checking on him. Something changed for Gall that night. He came around. When I ordered him to fill the gap between Mike and India-3, he went right at it. I heard something new in his voice when he reported. When I sent him out to sweep through the treeline in front of the 81s' position in the morning, I saw he had the fire in his eye. Even his voice was stronger. I knew he was going to be a good leader after all. He knew he was in charge of that platoon.

In its sweep through the trees, Mike-2 found a total of seven dead bad guys and a live one who was shot through the ankle. There was no shooting.

The POW was a young kid who was just scared to shit. He was crying and sniveling and, I guess, begging for mercy. I could imagine how he felt. Of all the men he had been with the night before, he was the only one he knew was alive. At least the seven others he was with in the treeline were dead, and he was wounded in the ankle and immobilized.

2nd Lieutenant BILL COWAN
India Company, 3/26—3rd Platoon Commander

I went over to the prisoner and interrogated him in the rudimentary Vietnamese I had learned in a 12-week course at the Defense Language Institute, in Monterey, California. It was my first attempt ever at using my language training, and I didn't talk to him much. He was quite obviously scared and disoriented. I kept asking him what his unit was and where his headquarters was and he kept saying, *"Nui Tan Than, Nui Tan Than."* That means Hill 88 or Mountain 88. I tried looking it up, but there was no Hill 88 on our map.

*

Captain ANDY DeBONA
Mike Company, 3/26—Commanding Officer

At around the time Gall's 2nd Platoon was sweeping the treeline with Mike-2, we started evacuating our routines—our dead—and nonserious wounded. We also had another meeting at Battalion. I heard that Lima Company was coming out and that we were going to move to a new position.

2nd Lieutenant CHAN CRANGLE
Mike Company, 3/26—1st Platoon Commander

One of the medevac helos managed to fly into a tree. He turned his blades into corkscrews and thumped back down to ground.

Captain ANDY DeBONA
Mike Company, 3/26—Commanding Officer

The H-34 had the POW aboard. The crew chief of the bird gingerly picked up the POW—gentle as a baby—and carried him about 15 meters. It looked like the crew chief was carrying his bride over the threshold. Then he unceremoniously dumped the POW on the deck—just dropped him. Plop!

2nd Lieutenant CHAN CRANGLE
Mike Company, 3/26—1st Platoon Commander

Andy DeBona damn near killed the pilot on the spot! He handed him a rifle and told him in no uncertain terms to take a position on the perimeter as a rifleman. The helo presented a real problem. We were all very itchy to get out of there before the NVA got more artillery or rockets on us.

*

1st Lieutenant BOB STIMSON
India Company, 3/26—Executive Officer

I did not realize the extent of the battalion main body's battle until I got back to their perimeter. We came in through India Company's own sector of the line and I ran right into Bill Cowan, who gave me a good overview. Then I reported to Lieutenant Colonel Alderman and told him what our situation was—how many Marines we had lost, how many we had left, and how much we were still capable of doing.

Staff Sergeant RUSS ARMSTRONG
India Company, 3/26—1st Platoon Commander

The tanks took us back to the battalion perimeter. I was mildly surprised to realize that we had been fighting our battle only 500 meters from where the battalion main body had been under attack. As far as I had been concerned that night, we might as well have been a thousand miles away.

As the tanks rolled into the battalion perimeter, I realized that I couldn't remember the last time I had had a cigarette. Of course, I started longing for one. Just then, one of the tankers asked if anyone wanted a smoke. I said I did, and most of the other wounded Marines said they did. The tanker took his own pack from his pocket and lit a cigarette for each of us in turn. He didn't know us from Adam and he wasn't going to see any of us again because we were all going to be going places that he hoped he wouldn't ever see. It was a small incident, but one of those things that stays with you forever, part of the bond between men who have faced battle together.

2nd Lieutenant BILL COWAN
India Company, 3/26—3rd Platoon Commander

The totality of the battle did not hit me until I saw the two tanks coming in with India Company's dead and wounded on them. That's when it really hit me—what was going on. I started finding out who was there, who wasn't, who had been medevacked, hearing some of the things that had happened out there, finding out what had happened elsewhere within our own perimeter.

Bob Stimson came over and led me over to the tanks to see three old-time 3/26 Marines—originals. After all the fighting Bob had seen in Vietnam and on September 7, he was really shaken because the three guys, with only weeks to go before going home, had all been killed, probably by one mortar round. I couldn't see why they were dead. I couldn't see any marks on them, but they were all dead. That really hurt Bob quite a bit. One was a corporal Bob was really close to; they had talked a lot about what they were going to do when they got back to the States. That was the hard thing about that night. When you look at all the guys who had been with 3/26 for 12 months—less than a month away from going home—who wound up casualties in that action, that was hard to take.

*

Captain ANDY DeBONA
Mike Company, 3/26—Commanding Officer

When the battalion was ready to move, the crashed medevac bird was still in the zone. Mike Company received the dubious distinction of staying behind to protect it.

The battalion pulled out at 1120 and I immediately set up a 360-degree perimeter. As I went around the bird to check out my 360, I ran into some engineers who had set up a 180 inside of my 360. When the engineer sergeant told me that it was his mission to protect the downed bird, I informed him, "There's a company out in front of you, so kindly don't do anything dumb."

About the same time, some of the little booby traps that were set up in front of Mike-3's old position went off. I had my 60s set up and they immediately started firing at Mike-3's old positions. I wanted to deter any bad guys out there in case they had any ideas of coming on down. The 60s fired about a hundred rounds and got down to about 10 rounds of HE per tube, so I started shooting illume at them. I figured, if nothing else, I'd at least get their attention.

2nd Lieutenant CHAN CRANGLE
Mike Company, 3/26—1st Platoon Commander

The battalion, less Mike Company, departed while we waited for the retrieval helicopter. It got quite lonely waiting for the recovery crew. The feeling of isolation—one lone company in the middle of a lot of bad guys, and on terrain that had been thoroughly registered by NVA rockets, mortars, et cetera—was most unsettling.

Altogether at The Churchyard, 3/26 sustained 20 Marines and corpsmen killed and 70 wounded. Based on a count of bodies actually located and an estimate based on evidence such as drag marks and blood trails, 3/26 claimed 108 NVA killed. About two-thirds of that number were probables. One NVA was taken prisoner.

It is now known that the NVA units that attacked 3/26 on September 7, 1967, were elements of the 324B Division's 812th Regiment, a crack veteran unit that had been living and fighting just south of the DMZ for over a year. Based on the body counts, Marine casualties, and eyewitness estimates, it is probable that no more than two 250-man battalions of the 812th Regiment took part in the late afternoon and evening assaults. That the assaults were supported by regimental heavy-weapons units such as .51-caliber antiaircraft machine guns, is obvious. It is also obvious that heavy rocket and artillery units belonging to the 324B Division and higher-level units north of the DMZ were employed in support of the infantry assaults.

It is not known why the 812th Regiment launched its attacks against 3/26 on September 7—it had had ample opportunity to attack the smaller contingent of 1/9 that had occupied and patrolled out of The Churchyard for days prior to the September 6 turnover.

PART II

Staked Bait

Chapter 8

Captain DICK CAMP
Lima Company, 3/26—Commanding Officer

Lima Company was serving as a Rough Rider convoy escort when we happened to arrive at Dong Ha late in the afternoon of September 7. After escorting the convoy inside the base gate, we made our way straight to the brand-new battalion rear encampment to engage in the usual ritual of showering, getting clean clothes, and catching up with our mail from home. As I jumped from my jeep in front of my tent, I yelled across to my company gunny, Staff Sergeant Marvin Bailey, "Okay, get 'em billeted and let's see if we can't get some chow." Normally, the mess-hall hours were not that long and they might not have been expecting us, so I wanted to get the troops fed before we did anything else.

Corporal FRANK GARCIA
Lima Company, 3/26—2nd Platoon Squad Leader

When we got into Dong Ha from Rough Riders on September 7, the first thing they wanted us to do was unload our weapons, shower, shave, and put on clean clothes. I thought it was ridiculous, but it happened every time we got into a base. I'd heard a congressman had once greeted the battalion when it got into a base, and the battalion was looking dirty from being in the field. So, after that, every time we got into a base, we had to clean up.

Lance Corporal MIKE HEFFLIN
Lima Company, 3/26, 2nd Platoon

We got into Dong Ha from Rough Riders, and for once, they had chow waiting for us—lime Kool-Aid and peanut-butter-and-jelly sandwiches. They put us in hooches over by the depot and got us hot showers. They also had mail for us that had been tracking behind us for a month.

2nd Lieutenant JOHN PRINCE
Lima Company, 3/26—2nd Platoon Commander

Prior to riding Rough Riders for about a week, Lima Company had been attached out to 2/9 in an operation east of the Con Thien–Cam Lo MSR. Just Lima Company. The CO of 2/9 always gave us the shitty details. Every time we were assigned to somebody else, our company was always point. Then, after there was contact, instead of changing companies or platoons, they would make us point again. Since Captain Camp and I had joined Lima Company at the end of June, the company had very seldom operated with the rest of our own battalion. Someone always needed just one company to do a job, to reinforce another unit, and they always came to 3/26 to get the company. It seemed like the company that got opconned [attached out] to another unit was always Lima Company. We were always attached out.

*

Major CARL MUNDY
3/26—Executive Officer

I was monitoring the battalion's initial contact on the radio. As the various staff officers stood around listening to all the contact, people were hollering in the radios and we could hear the crack of gunfire. As such things go, when your unit is in contact and you're sitting back in the Combat Operations Center or the Radio Watch Center listening to this go on, you experience a very helpless feeling of unmanliness.

Captain DICK CAMP
Lima Company, 3/26—Commanding Officer

As the gunny was getting the troops down to chow, I went over to the battalion rear CP, which was set up in a big tent. When I got inside, I could tell right off that there was some action going on. There was quite a flurry of activity, unusual in that the main body of the battalion was in the field, up near Con Thien.

I asked a lieutenant I collared what was going on. "Jesus, sir," he responded, "the battalion's in action."

"Well, what the hell's going on, Lieutenant?"

"Well, sir, we don't know. It's kind of confusing out there, but we do know that we got a lot of casualties and they're coming into Delta-Med [the Delta Company, 3rd Medical Battalion, aid station] down by the runway." As I was chomping that tidbit, I heard the lieutenant say in a very distinct voice, "Yeah, India-Six has been wounded. He was hit in the head. They got a lot of casualties down there, sir."

"Jesus," I exploded, "what's going to happen?"

"Well, sir, we don't have any word, but it looks like you're going to go out in the morning."

Without waiting around to get more information from the busy staff, I ran down to the mess hall and located Gunny Bailey and called a meeting of the platoon commanders and the key staff. It was a motley crew because the only officer besides me was Lieutenant John Prince, my 2nd Platoon commander. My old 1st Platoon commander had been wounded on September 1. He had not been replaced by another officer, so the 1st Platoon was commanded by Sergeant Wendell Mullins. Gunnery Sergeant Juan Almanza was the 3rd Platoon commander; I didn't want an officer to replace him. My exec was on R&R and not due back for several days. I never had had an officer commanding Weapons Platoon. So, the meeting consisted of me, Prince, 1st Sergeant Edward Miller, Gunny Almanza, Gunny Bailey, Sergeant Mullins, several other sergeants, and a few corporals.

"Okay," I said after telling them about the battalion's fight, "it looks like we're going to go out in the morning. Make sure that we get an ammunition resupply and that all the troops are well fed. Be prepared to move out at first light."

Next, I trotted back over to the battalion rear CP and said to the senior officer present, an assistant S-3, "Give me more scoop. Where the hell is the battalion?" The lieutenant couldn't tell me exactly where the battalion was, except that it was somewhere northwest of C-2, out toward Con Thien. The news was vague. Clearly, India Company, whose skipper had been wounded, had been hit hard and had taken numerous casualties. Beyond that, there was no hard information. As the afternoon wore on, repeated trips to the CP produced vague reports that mainly sounded like "Things are not going well out there," or "It's not looking good." It was obvious that the battalion was getting hit harder and harder, without letup. By the late evening, the entire battalion was up to its ears in NVA, who were trying to overrun the battalion perimeter. It appeared that all or part of India Company was fighting a separate, isolated battle for its life somewhere beyond the battalion main perimeter. The outpouring of disjointed, incoherent bad news got me to the point where I found myself thinking in terms of taking Lima Company out there to *rescue* the rest of the battalion, that we would be the cavalry going to the rescue.

I told Top Miller and Gunny Bailey to round up every Marine they could find, and Bailey later reported that they had scouted the battalion area and had come up with a list of about 30 men who had come out of the field because they each had less than six days left to do in-country. At the time, there was a policy that if a Marine had about a week left in Vietnam, he would be pulled into a rear area to turn in his gear and get himself ready to go home. A week might not seem like a big deal, but I knew that it was a very big deal to men who had put in 13 months less a week in Vietnam. I felt extremely bad popping the question, but 30 combat-experienced Marines represented a significant group of reinforcements, virtually a platoon.

I stalked through the battalion area, list in hand, and discussed the situation with each of the short-timers. I did not feel right *ordering* any of them back into the field, but I made sure each man knew how important his personal presence might be to the outcome. I told them that the battalion was getting hit hard and that it looked like we were going out the next morning. I said the battalion needed help and I needed volunteers.

Every one of them volunteered to go back out, so I sent them down to Supply to redraw their gear, which had already been turned in. I had always felt that being a Marine carried with it certain obligations, but the performance I witnessed on the afternoon and evening of September 7, 1967, was something special. A few of those Marines had been counting on leaving for Danang and the Big Bird home with our scheduled return convoy in the morning. They didn't have to go out with us, but they all did.

Before I went to work on the short-timers, I had directed Gunny Bailey to round up every cook, baker, and bottlewasher he could find and get them saddled up so we could take them with us. In this case, I was empowered to issue orders, and I did. We also dragged in a few new men who had just arrived in-country and who had not been assigned out to the companies. Gunny Bailey had to see that they drew combat gear and Top Miller saw that the S-1 accounted for their arrivals and quick departure.

*

1st Lieutenant HARRY DOLAN
Mike Company, 3/26—Executive Officer

I had not left Khe Sanh with Mike and India companies when they flew to Camp Carroll on September 5. Andy DeBona felt that I had had enough time in the field, and he had arranged for me to complete paperwork on awards for the troops.

The rear echelon arrived in Dong Ha on September 7. During the day, we were told that the battalion main body had contact with a significant NVA force, but I heard no specifics. That evening, I was sitting by a trench with my helmet and flak jacket on, listening to a big firefight off to the northwest. I had my map out, and I figured the fight was just beyond C-2. I assumed that 3/26 was into something. Some rockets were fired at the airstrip at Dong Ha and Captain Bill Dabney, the brand-new battalion headquarters commandant, came through yelling for everyone to get in trenches or a hole. The warning seemed like an overreaction at the time, probably because the rounds were impacting at least 500 meters away and I was experiencing some guilt feelings about not being with my unit. At any rate, we all complied with the order.

Later that evening, I received word from Andy DeBona to round up all the Mike Company troops at Dong Ha and bring them out to the field the next day with Lima Company.

Captain DICK CAMP
Lima Company, 3/26—Commanding Officer

The cooks we were leaving behind kept the mess hall open so we could grab coffee and chow as we worked into the night to get Lima Company up to snuff and the reinforcements squared away. I kept making passes through the CP tent to follow the battalion's progress, which, if anything, appeared more serious with each new report. The main body appeared to be fighting for its life and had suffered heavy casualties.

Major CARL MUNDY
3/26—Executive Officer

At about 2300 or so, the first of the casualties began to be medevacked and were brought into Delta-Med. Among those casualties was Captain Wayne Coulter, the India Company commander. Under such circumstances, the company first sergeants went down to the aid station to collect the equipment and weapons that were brought back in with the casualties. I went down to survey what was coming in. It was not a very happy sight.

Wayne Coulter had been clipped with a shell fragment across the back of his head, and it had peeled away a chunk of his scalp. That had given him a concussion and he was a little bit out of his head. Wayne grabbed me by the lapel and said, "Don't notify my dad. Don't notify my dad." His dad had a heart condition and Wayne did not want to alarm him. Of course, we had to send some notification, but I made sure they didn't notify his father.

Captain DICK CAMP
Lima Company, 3/26—Commanding Officer

I managed to get a few hours sleep, but I was up well before sunrise, at least an hour before the relief force was to form on the road beside the rear CP area. As I was checking in with the operations duty officer to get the latest dope on the battalion—nothing new—I was waylaid by the operations chief, Master Gunnery Sergeant Thomas McHugh.

Top McHugh was Old Corps. By the time he joined 3/26, I suppose, he'd had 26 years in the Corps—as many years as I had been alive. He had served in World War II and, no doubt, in Korea. He was one of those old-time senior enlisted Marines who rarely condescended to speak with somebody who wasn't a field-grade officer, a major or above, except on official business. As I was leaving the CP tent, Top McHugh looked kind of sideways at me and said, "Hey, Skipper, you got a minute?"

"Sure, Master Guns, what do you need?" I was really surprised that he had initiated the conversation, but I was bowled over by how friendly he sounded.

"Come on over to the tent, sir. I want to talk to you."

I thought, "Jesus, what the hell could he want?" I followed him over to his tent and he sat down, looked at me, and said, "Well, you know, sir, it's going to be tough out there."

"Yeah, I imagine it is, Master Guns."

"Well," he said, "I want to wish you the best of luck."

I thought, "Jesus!" and said, "Thanks, Master Guns, I appreciate that." I turned to leave.

"Hey wait a minute, sir." He held up his hand. "Here's something I want you to take with you." He handed me a canteen.

"Thanks, Top. What's in it?" I had a pretty good idea, after the big buildup.

"There's something in it, Captain, that you may need. It's just a little medicinal alcohol, but if it really gets tough, I mean, you can have this and maybe it'll help you out."

I thought, "My God, I have *arrived!*" I mean, here was a master gunnery sergeant who had not only condescended to speak with me off the record but who had given me his best go-win-one-for-the-Gipper speech. I was authentically touched by the depth of feeling behind this normally reticent man's heartfelt display. I thanked him from the bottom of my heart and went off to complete arrangements to leave Dong Ha.

*

Lance Corporal MIKE HEFFLIN
Lima Company, 3/26, 2nd Platoon

I graduated high school in 1965 at 18, got married, and went to work at McDonnell Douglas. I had considered going into the Marine Corps because an older brother was in. When a lot of guys in southern California started getting drafted in early 1966, I received my notice. They asked for 10 out of every 100 to go into the Marine Corps, so I opted for it.

I went to Vietnam in late 1966 and was assigned to 2/9. In the spring of 1967, when they were trying to stagger 3/26's rotations, which all would have come up in September, a bunch of us were transferred to 3/26. I and several of my boot-camp buddies were assigned to Lima Company.

When we got into Dong Ha, my squad, which was down to bare minimum, picked up a couple of new guys to replace casualties we'd taken in late August and early September. I was a short-timer by then, so I never bothered to learn the new guys' names. I had only two weeks left to do in the field; I didn't want to know anyone anymore. In fact, I didn't want to go back out. A letter from my wife told me my son, a newborn baby, was going to have surgery. I wanted to get the hell out of there and see my family, so I went over to the Red Cross to see if they could help. We had a few guys in the squad who were so short they got pulled from the company and sent home as soon as we reached Dong Ha. I had no luck getting home early, but I gave one of the guys who was going home a message to deliver to my mom and dad—that I'd be seeing them in two weeks. He delivered the message the same day my folks heard I was Missing in Action.

Chapter 9

1st Lieutenant HARRY DOLAN
Mike Company, 3/26—Executive Officer

Sometime during the night, I received a message from Andy DeBona to gather up all hands from the company rear echelon at Dong Ha and, along with any replacements we rated, join the company in the field. Additionally, I needed to pass on to Lima Company's commander, Captain Dick Camp, an urgent message from Andy that wherever we stopped and debarked troops along the MSR through C-2 to Con Thien, we must do it in a hurry because the NVA had the whole road zeroed-in.

Captain DICK CAMP
Lima Company, 3/26—Commanding Officer

Bright and early on the morning of September 8, I ordered Gunny Bailey to get Lima Company fed and on the road. It was SOP to put about 20 Marines on each truck, so a 130- to 140-man company needed seven trucks. When I went out to take charge of the company that morning, I counted about six supply trucks for the battalion and the seven troop trucks for Lima Company. However, there must have been 270 Marines standing on the roadway, geared up and ready to go.

It was the biggest formation of Marines I had ever taken over. I was dumbstruck. Sure, we had told many of these men, "Get your ass in formation; you're going out with us," but the majority of the extras were volunteers, many of whom had turned up on their own, without any appeal from me or my sergeants. A tremendous feeling of pride came over me as I gave "Right face" and 270 men responded with nearly parade-ground precision. It was very emotional.

Corporal FRANK GARCIA
Lima Company, 3/26—2nd Platoon Squad Leader

While we were at Dong Ha, I heard there was shit going on with the rest of the battalion, but no one in authority told us anything. When we left Dong Ha on the morning of September 8, I thought we were going out on a search-and-destroy mission in the hills.

Lance Corporal MIKE HEFFLIN
Lima Company, 3/26, 2nd Platoon

No one told us what was going on, but we knew it was something bad. We had heard shells going off all night. The way we rode out was strange. Generally, when we went up into an area like that in trucks, we didn't load guys in the trucks the way we were loaded that morning. Usually, we had sandbags in the truck beds, but not all the trucks were loaded with sandbags for this trip. My squad got into an open truck with an open bed. We were standing up behind the cab with no sandbags. A lot of us short-timers were leery. Whenever I caught anyone's eye— any of the old-timers—we exchanged glances. We knew something was up.

Captain DICK CAMP
Lima Company, 3/26—Commanding Officer

The drive down Highway 9 to Cam Lo was uneventful. From there, we turned north and then ran the short distance into C-2.

Lance Corporal MIKE HEFFLIN
Lima Company, 3/26, 2nd Platoon

After we took the corner in Cam Lo, we could see Con Thien right in front of us—the big hill.

1st Lieutenant HARRY DOLAN
Mike Company, 3/26—Executive Officer

I don't recall anybody being along the side of the road trying to sell us bread or Coca-Cola or anything else. It was a very, very solemn kind of ride. It was even more solemn when we turned off Highway 9 toward Con Thien. It got very quiet.

Lance Corporal MIKE HEFFLIN
Lima Company, 3/26, 2nd Platoon

Usually, the Vietnamese knew ahead of time when something was going to happen. Then they'd stay away from us.

Captain DICK CAMP
Lima Company, 3/26—Commanding Officer

When we arrived at the artillery position, I halted the column and stepped down to try to get directions from someone in the base CP. I still didn't know where the battalion was. The fire-base commander wasn't sure either, so I radioed the battalion CP and spoke with Lieutenant Colonel Alderman, the new CO. He told me to follow the road out from C-2 about 750 meters and that he would send an officer back to guide me in.

I had given the troops a break, so it took several minutes and the usual amount of yelling to get them back aboard the trucks. While I was waiting, I ran into an old friend, Captain Bob Johnston. His battalion, 3/9, which was stopped at C-2, was on its way to relieve the Marine battalion then holding Con Thien. As soon as Bob told me where he was going, I blurted out, "That's too bad." Then, catching myself, I laughed and asked, "Hey, Bob, can I have your watch?"—reassuring banter like that. Then I found myself repeating, "Jeez, Bob, good luck," over and over, as if to say good-bye to him for the last time. Bob was very calm, very stoic. He kept saying, "Oh, it's going to be okay."

We left C-2 as soon as everyone was back aboard the trucks and proceeded up the Con Thien road, which was nothing more than an all-weather dirt lane that probably wouldn't have shown up on most local road maps in the United States. As narrow and crude as the road was, it was the combat base's main supply route and, as such, heavily used by jeeps, tanks, amtracs, and trucks. My convoy of about 20 trucks, including resupply vehicles, moved out into the traffic and ground forward less than 1,000 meters, to the spot at which I was to meet the officer from the battalion main body. We pulled over as far as we could to give other traffic sufficient clearance, but we created quite a bottleneck because the roadway was so narrow. Bottlenecks are targets, so I immediately ordered the troop leaders to "get the troops off the trucks" and "spread 'em out."

1st Lieutenant HARRY DOLAN
Mike Company, 3/26—Executive Officer

The trucks rolled north of C-2 some distance and halted along a curve in the road.

The area on each side of the road had been bulldozed and they had dug a trench alongside the road, big enough for a man to get his head down. There were piles of stumps and roots and logs around there, too.

Captain DICK CAMP
Lima Company, 3/26—Commanding Officer

There was no end of confusion. We had nearly 270 men on and around the roadway, the trucks, and all the vehicles trying to pass in both directions. Confusion? It was sheer chaos.

The more I looked around, the less I liked where we were. There were shallow drainage ditches on both sides of the roadway, maybe 8 to 10 inches deep, and the brush had been bulldozed clear to a distance of a few hundred meters on both sides, to lessen the likelihood of ambushes. The place at which we had stopped was on a little knoll, with a clear view in every direction—and which could be observed from cover extending virtually in every direction. Except to drive by on Rough Rider convoys, I had never been in the area and no one at C-2 or Battalion had warned me of any danger. But I didn't like what I was seeing, so I got on everybody's case about spreading the troops out, getting them off the roadway, away from the traffic jam.

I was standing tall on the roadway with my command group, waiting to find out what was going on, when I spotted a line of troops coming through the scrub growth. I could see that they had tanks with them. I figured it was the group the CO had said would come back to guide me to the battalion main body. I pointed it out to the others and we rubbernecked as they got closer. The word spread among the troops, who, on their own, started getting ready to move out, they were that motivated to help their comrades.

As the column closed on us, I could see that it was most of an infantry company accompanied by four tanks—something a great deal more than the expected officer guide the battalion CO had spoken of. As the tanks got closer still, I could make out bundles on their rear decks, and the bundles slowly resolved themselves into bodies. The tanks were covered with Marines who had been killed or wounded in the previous night's battle royal. There were a lot of them. The effect of those bodies on my troops was mixed; they wanted revenge, but they were sobered.

Captain TOM EARLY
3/26—Communications Officer

1st Lieutenant Bob Dobies, the Kilo exec, and I took the WIAs and KIAs on the tanks to the MSR to link up with Lima Company.

2nd Lieutenant PAUL DRNEC
Bravo Company, 3rd Tank Battalion—2nd Platoon Commander

The 3/26 battalion S-3 came up on my radio and ordered me to stop on the road so the dead and wounded could be loaded aboard the trucks. He wanted us to accompany Kilo and Lima companies back to the battalion main body immediately. I told him that the gun tanks were very low on fuel and ammunition and that I wanted to go straight back to C-2 and refurbish. In any case, we had to tow the dead tank back; we couldn't just leave it on the roadway. However, the big factor in my mind was that C-2 was a covered position, that we could do our work under cover.

Staff Sergeant RUSS ARMSTRONG
India Company, 3/26

The tanks stopped near a gravel road on which many trucks were lined up in two columns, on the shoulders of the road.

Staff Sergeant CHARLES OWENS
Kilo Company, 3/26—Company Gunny

There was a civilian photographer out there, taking pictures of the dead and wounded as they were being loaded. We'd had news of a family in the States seeing their dead son on the television before they received word he was dead, so I ran over and told the photographer to stop taking pictures and give me the film out of the camera. He said he wasn't going to give me the film. I grabbed the camera out of his hands and told him I was going to bust it. 1st Sergeant Goddard came running over and took the camera from me.

Staff Sergeant RUSS ARMSTRONG
India Company, 3/26

When you'd been in-country for between six and nine months, the personnel officer started hitting on you to extend your one-year tour for an extra six months. They routinely offered a 30-day home leave as incentive. My experience was that a lot of rear-area types took the offer, or guys who wangled rear-area jobs as an extra incentive. We had very few extensions among the guys who were slogging through the mud. An exception was Kilo Company's 1st Sergeant Bernard Goddard. He said he would stay an extra year. When the personnel officer told him he only needed to stay six months, Goddard said, "I said 'a year,' Lieutenant." And when the lieutenant asked him when he wanted his 30-day leave, Goddard said, "I don't want any leave." Even more exceptional was the fact that, unlike most first sergeants, Goddard spent almost all his time with the company, in the field. He had a way with officers. Kilo Company once had a lieutenant who was something less than sharp. I heard Goddard tell him, "It's a good thing you're not a Pfc because I wouldn't recommend you for lance corporal." Quite a guy—a Marine's Marine.

Staff Sergeant CHARLES OWENS
Kilo Company, 3/26—Company Gunny

Goddard asked for the film, but the photographer said he couldn't have it, so Goddard wrapped the camera strap around his own hand. He told the photographer he was going to smash the camera against the side of a tank if he didn't give the film up. It was an expensive camera. The photographer took the film out, but he put it in his pocket. Then I told one of my sergeants to take every roll of film the man had, used or unused. The sergeant and a few of his Marines wrestled the photographer to the ground and took all the film he had out of his pockets and his camera bag. I told him I'd give it to him next time I saw him. I put the film rolls in my pack and me and Goddard left to rejoin the company. I didn't mind that he took the pictures; I just didn't want them in the newspapers before the next of kin were notified.

*

Captain DICK CAMP
Lima Company, 3/26—Commanding Officer

As soon as the tanks stopped, and without a word, some of the Kilo Company infantrymen started pulling the KIAs off the tanks to put them on our trucks. Also without a word, some of my Lima Company Marines pitched in to help. It was downright eerie, particularly as the normal traffic flowed past us in both directions.

2nd Lieutenant JOHN PRINCE
Lima Company, 3/26—2nd Platoon Commander

One of the casualties on one of the tanks had his hand out from under the poncho, and I could see a wedding ring on it. I thought about the wailing and the gnashing of teeth. Somebody back home was going to be mourning.

Captain TOM EARLY
3/26—Communications Officer

The Lima Company Marines were standing about in clusters, and I frantically told them to spread out. I guess they thought I was just fanatically overwrought because they ignored me.

Captain DICK CAMP
Lima Company, 3/26—Commanding Officer

As I was standing there, with my mouth agape, watching the dead and wounded being lifted from the tanks to the trucks, my good friend, Captain Tom Early, the battalion communicator, walked right up to me. Obviously, he was the officer-guide. As Tom approached, his eyes got real wide and he glanced around at my troops. Then he kept repeating, "Spread 'em out, Dick, spread 'em out!"

Tom was usually very calm, very collected, but he was nearly hysterical when he reached me. By then, he was yelling: "Spread 'em out, Dick, spread 'em out! They're gonna get you."

I was flustered, but I managed to say, "Hey, Tom, take it easy. Jesus, we're all right. What the hell's going on here?"

As I was trying to get Tom under control, I happened to glance over at the nearest tank. There, I focused on a dead Marine whose body was frozen in a grotesque attitude of death. This kid's whole face was just blown out. His head was there, but his face was gone. As I watched, the men were trying to get him off the tank and onto one of the trucks, but things kept falling out of his head. It was a real mess. "Holy shit," I said to Tom, "What the hell is going on here?"

2nd Lieutenant PAUL DRNEC
Bravo Company, 3rd Tank Battalion—2nd Platoon Commander

As the dead and wounded were being transferred to the trucks, I jumped down to confer with the other tank commanders, to get reports and advice. Immediately, my veteran, Sergeant Vining, started jumping up and down, yelling, "Don't stay in the open! They clobbered us yesterday and they're gonna do the same thing now." I passed that concern to the S-3 by radio, but he said, "No, no, no, we have a schedule. We need you with us."

1st Lieutenant HARRY DOLAN
Mike Company, 3/26—Executive Officer

I got the eight Mike Company Marines I was responsible for off the trucks and moved them to the edge of the bulldozed area of the MSR. We were about midway back in the column of trucks. I could see that several trucks had gotten their front wheels caught in the trench beside the road as they tried to pull off into the bulldozed area. Men were dropping off everything aboard the trucks so the trucks would be light enough to push out of the trench. I also saw that tanks and infantry had arrived, and wounded and dead Marines were being loaded aboard trucks near the head of the column.

Getting the trucks unloaded and turned around was taking too long. I had an urgent message from Andy DeBona to tell Dick Camp to get the trucks unloaded and the men off the exposed roadway as quickly as possible. I got my Mike Company Marines under cover in the trench and ran forward to deliver my message to Captain Camp. He told me he had things under control. Captain Early was there also, telling Captain Camp the same thing I was trying to tell him. I delivered my message and ran back to rejoin my men in the trench. As I was running, I heard several rockets being launched from the north.

*

Staff Sergeant RUSS ARMSTRONG
India Company, 3/26

Marines unloaded the dead and wounded off the tanks and put us on the trucks. They had about completed the transfer when, from the near distance, I heard the telltale *boom-boom-boom* of artillery being fired. "Oh no," I thought, "it's incoming!" Clearly, they were aiming at the convoy, and there wasn't anything I could do about it. The cargo areas on the trucks were open, exposed, and filled with wounded, and there were no drivers around.

2nd Lieutenant CHAN CRANGLE
Mike Company, 3/26—1st Platoon Commander

While we were cooling our heels at The Churchyard, waiting for the recovery helo, a volley of rockets and a barrage of artillery came over our heads. We heard the firing and the rounds coming overhead. For a second, we thought it was going to be our turn again!

Captain DICK CAMP
Lima Company, 3/26—Commanding Officer

I heard the distinctive *boom-boom-boom* of artillery being fired from a distance. Just what I needed! "Incoming! Incoming," I screamed, a cry that was taken up before it actually left my mouth. I just dropped, right into the ditch beside the roadway, which was all of about 8 inches deep and 2 feet wide.

2nd Lieutenant PAUL DRNEC
Bravo Company, 3rd Tank Battalion—2nd Platoon Commander

I dove under one of the tanks.

2nd Lieutenant JOHN PRINCE
Lima Company, 3/26—2nd Platoon Commander

Everybody was running for cover, but there was no cover because the entire area had been bladed flat and clean.

1st Lieutenant HARRY DOLAN
Mile Company, 3/26—Executive Officer

The road had a curve in it. It was my impression from the message from Andy DeBona that the NVA had every inch of the road registered. All they had to do was fire their artillery, throw in minor adjustments, and walk it around the curve.

Captain DICK CAMP
Lima Company, 3/26—Commanding Officer

I heard more and more guns being fired as I went into overdrive, trying to pull my helmet right around my ankles, trying to dig deeper with the buttons on my shirt. I thought the first round was going to hit me right in the back. I cringed. The adrenaline was coursing through me as—*boom-boom-BOOM-BOOM-BOOM*—the rounds started impacting around me. The noise of the detonations was overlapping and continuous. I quickly lost count and I damn near lost control of my bodily functions as the ground heaved and buckled beneath my body. Close, very close. Too close.

Staff Sergeant RUSS ARMSTRONG
India Company, 3/26

The stuff started falling in around the trucks and I experienced the most totally helpless feeling I have ever had. Guys around me started screaming for help.

Despite the fall of the rockets, my platoon's surviving corpsman, HN Robert Davis, who was moderately injured himself, got up and started tending to the injured men. As I looked on in admiration, I saw most of Doc Davis's left arm blown off by a chunk of shrapnel.

Staff Sergeant CHARLES OWENS
Kilo Company, 3/26—Company Gunny

I saw the corpsman get his arm blown off. He was a brave man. When the rockets were falling, he kept helping the wounded.

1st Lieutenant HARRY DOLAN
Mike Company, 3/26—Executive Officer

Rockets and artillery rounds were impacting at the front of the convoy. They were just busting shit up. Some troops were hit and trucks were destroyed. It occurred to me that many of these young Marines were replacements and already had been wounded before firing a round. As the shells and rockets hit at the front of the column, Marines continued to load wounded aboard the trucks at the rear of the column, and those trucks continued to try to turn back toward C-2. I cannot begin to describe the confusion and chaos created by the shelling. The rockets and artillery walked right down along the road, along the entire column.

Lima Company was my original company. I knew a lot of the kids out on that road, so I ran back toward the front of the column and tried to help some of them get under cover, to tell them where the trench was. It was really bad at that point. I knew the NVA were going to burn the trucks.

Captain TOM EARLY
3/26—Communications Officer

Even in this petrifying situation there can be humor. I dove under a tank as the artillery rounds were airborne, but just before they fell, the tank drove away, leaving me totally exposed.

Captain DICK CAMP
Lima Company, 3/26—Commanding Officer

There was a little break in the roar of the detonations, so I chanced a quick peek over the lip of the drainage ditch. As I had been falling flat seconds earlier, I had noticed Tom Early jumping underneath the nearest tank, which was sitting in the middle of the roadway. As I lay cringing during the first salvo, I found myself wishing that I had been as sane as Tom, that I had thought of it first. Well, when I looked up, the tank was long gone. Its driver was even saner; he was racing to get clear of the large gaggle of people that was attracting the artillery. What I saw was Tom, alone and exposed, out in the middle of the roadway, a human version of an ostrich, with his head approximately invisible and the rest of him trying to crawl into his helmet. It would have been as funny then as it seems now if I had been watching from a klick or two away.

*

Corporal FRANK GARCIA
Lima Company, 3/26—2nd Platoon Squad Leader

My squad was on the left side of the road, but the rest of the company went to the right.

Lance Corporal MIKE HEFFLIN
Lima Company, 3/26, 2nd Platoon

I don't know what the hell was going on to the right, why everyone else went that way. When we heard *boom-boom-boom*—rockets being fired—some of the guys in the 3rd Squad looked at each other. We headed toward the base of a little mound that had some brush on it.

The first rounds hit right where we were running and we went right through them. I took a little shrapnel in the hand.

We all fell down by the base of the mound as the rockets walked across the road toward the rest of the company. I heard screaming. We all started looking at each other, waiting to see what the next guy would do. We were all on line. Corporal Frank Garcia, myself, and another fire-team leader told everyone to keep their heads down and spread out. Then we just laid there and waited to see if anything was coming our way. We were the only Marines out there, less than a squad.

Corporal FRANK GARCIA
Lima Company, 3/26—2nd Platoon Squad Leader

We tried to shovel ourselves deeper with our helmets. The rocket fire was going over us, hitting the guys on the other side of the road.

Lance Corporal MIKE HEFFLIN
Lima Company, 3/26, 2nd Platoon

A short round hit close to us.

Corporal FRANK GARCIA
Lima Company, 3/26—2nd Platoon Squad Leader

I got minor fragments in the back. They went through my pack and cut into a can of C-rations, which also cut my back. I didn't feel the wounds, and they didn't slow me down at all.

Lance Corporal MIKE HEFFLIN
Lima Company, 3/26, 2nd Platoon

When a second short round came in on us, there was hot shrapnel flying around. I was carrying a pouch that was full of extra M-79 rounds and plastic explosive, which I threw as far away as I could. Everyone else who was carrying explosives did the same.

*

Staff Sergeant CHARLES OWENS
Kilo Company, 3/26—Company Gunny

I had kept my people spread apart and very few of them were near the road. There was a big pile of roots and stumps and tree trunks left from when they'd cleared the verges of the road, so, when the rockets stopped falling in, I went and motioned my troops to go and hide in there. We all started running just as we heard the second volley leaving the launchers. Getting into those stumps and things saved a lot of my men getting wounded when the second volley came in. We had only two wounded in Kilo Company.

Captain DICK CAMP
Lima Company, 3/26—Commanding Officer

The second salvo arrested all thoughts about the future. Then there was dead silence for several long beats of my heart.

I found myself laying head-to-head with my company radioman, Corporal David Johnson, who was yelling, "God, I'm hit, I'm hit!" He was writhing, so I said, "John, take it easy. You're all right, you're all right. Stay down, just stay down." But he kept writhing and yelling, "I'm hit, I'm hit!" I wasn't ready yet to get up and take a look, so I kept repeating, "Just take it easy, John. Take it easy."

2nd Lieutenant JOHN PRINCE
Lima Company, 3/26—2nd Platoon Commander

I had hopped in a little low place right near the road. I was cramped for space, so I laid down on top of one of Captain Camp's radiomen, Corporal Johnson. A piece of hot shrapnel fell on the back of his legs. He was kicking me in the hip. When he turned around and apologized to me, I said, "Go ahead, no problem."

Captain DICK CAMP
Lima Company, 3/26—Commanding Officer

When I was sure the barrage was over, I got up on my knees and checked Corporal Johnson over. I found a gigantic jagged piece of shrapnel—probably 8 to 10 inches long by 3 inches wide—resting on his leg. It had just fallen on him, obviously with some force, but it had not penetrated. It bruised his leg and was so hot it had burned right through his utility trousers. He felt a terrific thump and terrible burning. No wonder he thought he was hit.

I knocked the shrapnel off him and told him what it was, adding, "Jesus Christ, John, now how about taking it easy." We started kidding about it, but the humor was flat. It had been a close one; we both knew how close.

We must have been hit by two batteries, at least. The shell holes indicated that they had been firing 130mm guns at us, very effective. I was sure they had been on us with the first round, without adjusting. They must have had that knoll zeroed-in, the fire was so accurate.

As soon as I finished getting Corporal Johnson back on track, I jumped up to resume command of the company. By then, dozens of Marines were jumping up and running around, counting up the number of men who had been hit and helping to treat them. I ran over to a young Marine I found laying out on the roadway. He had a grisly arm wound. I was sure the doctors would never be able to save his arm. I didn't recognize him, but he had definitely come out with Lima Company because the Kilo people were well off to the side, in their own area. I felt dumb asking, but I had to know who he was. "Marine," I said in his ear, "Who are you? Who are you with?" He was in a lot of pain and going into shock, but he managed to tell me that he was a brand-new Marine, had just arrived in-country, and that he hadn't even been assigned to a unit yet. The S-1 had sent him out to pick up any company that could use him. It was very sad. He hadn't been in-country a week yet and there he was, severely wounded, probably going to lose his arm. All that training, all that personal pain, all the good and bad dreams— for nothing. I held his good hand and promised, "Okay, Marine, we're gonna get you out of here. You did a good job." But it was bullshit. I just felt so damn sorry for the kid.

After the new man was carried off, I came across another casualty, one of my 60mm mortarmen. He had been laying on the deck when one of the rockets landed right in front of him. The force of the blast had cut his helmet right across the top and forced the jagged edges into his scalp. He had a pretty nasty scalp wound, a deep gash from ear to ear. When I found him, he was just standing there, off beside the road, holding the top of his head while blood cascaded down his face. He looked terrible, like he was going to keel over and die at any second. I was shocked when I saw him. "My God," I blurted out, "Sit down, sit down." I thought he was going to die right there. I grabbed a corpsman and he immediately wrapped a bandage around the Marine's head. The bandage was dripping blood almost as soon as the doc tied it off. In the end, not only did the Marine survive, he rejoined Lima Company within a month, complete with a great big scar that ran from ear to ear across the top of his head.

2nd Lieutenant JOHN PRINCE
Lima Company, 3/26—2nd Platoon Commander

This kid later put on a hell of a show. He blew smoke out of his ear because his eardrum was burst by the rocket blast.

1st Lieutenant HARRY DOLAN
Mike Company, 3/26—Executive Officer

Lima Company got shot up to a fare-thee-well, but my little group of Mike Company people wasn't touched.

Corporal FRANK GARCIA
Lima Company, 3/26—2nd Platoon Squad Leader

When the rocket attack was over, I spread my squad on line on the left side of the road while the rest of the company took care of the wounded and sorted itself out. No one told me to do that, but it seemed the right thing to do. We were facing outboard to the left, waiting to see if we were going to get attacked.

Staff Sergeant CHARLES OWENS
Kilo Company, 3/26—Company Gunny

After the second volley fell, we all jumped up and started running out of the area. I went back to check on my two wounded, to see how many there were and how bad they were. 1st Sergeant Goddard had come up from behind and gotten into a drainage ditch alongside the road. I took my wounded over to him and we loaded them aboard a truck. Meantime, the other Marines out there were pulling passing trucks and jeeps over and loading wounded aboard them.

Staff Sergeant RUSS ARMSTRONG
India Company, 3/26

Suddenly, Marines appeared from nowhere and leaped into the cabs of the trucks. I don't know if they were the drivers, and I sure didn't care if the guy who was driving my truck had a valid license.

2nd Lieutenant PAUL DRNEC
Bravo Company, 3rd Tank Battalion—2nd Platoon Commander

As soon as the shelling lifted, the forward trucks moved out, down the road toward C-2. As the other trucks started turning around to follow them, I told my tankers, "We're going back to Charlie Two. Button up and follow the lead trucks." This was against the orders the 3/26 battalion S-3 had given me before the shelling, but I knew I needed fuel and ammo or the tanks would have been useless.

Staff Sergeant RUSS ARMSTRONG
India Company, 3/26

We bounced along the roadway for only 10 to 15 minutes and pulled up to the helo pad at Fire Base C-2. There were lots of people waiting there to get us off the trucks. I was eased down onto a litter and carried away. As I was being carried, I looked up at the silhouette of a large Marine whose face I could not see because the sun was directly over his head. I have no idea who he was, but he knew me. I heard him say, "That's Staff Sergeant Armstrong. Get him outta here." Before I could ask him who he was, I was on the deck of a chopper. Then we flew away.

Captain DICK CAMP
Lima Company, 3/26—Commanding Officer

We had 28 Marines and corpsmen wounded and one Marine killed. As we gathered them in, my sergeants were stopping jeeps and trucks trying to pass us on the MSR. Who could blame the drivers for not stopping? The troop leaders were commandeering the vehicles to rush our WIAs to C-2. Most of the WIAs were thrown aboard any passing vehicle, without even getting any first aid—anything to get them off the exposed roadway and into the artillery fire base, which had a medical bunker. Gunny Bailey was moving like a madman, trying to get the names of the WIAs so he could keep the company roster up to date and have the radiomen report names and probable destinations to Battalion Rear. It was pandemonium. Meantime, we didn't know if the NVA were finished clobbering us, so everyone had an ear cocked to detect more incoming. All the motion, emotion, responsibility, and concentration kept the adrenaline flowing until I nearly keeled over.

Lance Corporal MIKE HEFFLIN
Lima Company, 3/26, 2nd Platoon

Our squad stayed on the left side of the road until after the rockets stopped. A couple Marines came over from the other side of the road to find out where we were, but we stayed there, covering the whole company in case anyone tried to attack us on the ground. The guys who came over to us told us one guy had had his arm cut off by shrapnel and that there were lots of other wounded. Someone told us to stay where we were, but we went out a little farther from the road, to near the top of the mound we had been using for cover, so we could see out in front of us. Con Thien was way up to our right, and in front of us was a gully with a little stream in it. We just stayed there and made observations, played lookout. There was all kinds of activity going on behind us, but we kept our attention to our front, toward the west. I was aware of the trucks running down the highway, back toward Cam Lo, but I didn't pay much attention. We were scared shitless since we were the only ones out there.

Captain DICK CAMP
Lima Company, 3/26—Commanding Officer

We finally got the KIA and the last of the WIAs evacuated and finished sorting ourselves out. Kilo Company formed up ahead of us and we started humping our tired bodies and all the fresh ammunition and supplies cross-country, out toward the battalion area.

*

Staff Sergeant RUSS ARMSTRONG
India Company, 3/26

The medevac chopper I was on landed at Dong Ha, which was only a few miles up National Route 9 from C-2. They pulled us off the choppers and carried us straight into the Delta-Med triage ward, to have our wounds assessed and prioritized for treatment.

As I lay in the aid station waiting to have my wounds treated, I chatted a little with some of the others and thought back over the battle.

When the doctors got to me, I overheard them talking and figured out that one was an old hand showing the other, a new guy, the ropes. The old hand looked at the two wounds in my leg and said, "Let's see if the wound goes all the way through.'' He got a steel rod about the diameter of my thumb and 15 to 18 inches long and inserted it in the back of my leg, pushing it through, and pulling it out the front. I had not been sedated at all. I screamed the whole time.

Captain BILL DABNEY
H&S Company, 3/26—Commanding Officer

When the casualties started coming in, I went down to Delta-Med to see if I could help with anything. The triage center was swamped with badly wounded Marines, but the doctors and corpsmen waded right in.

I was standing over one Marine on a litter when the corpsman said he couldn't find a pulse and the Marine wasn't breathing. The Marine was dead. But, 15 minutes later, as I was passing through one of the wards, I saw the same Marine sitting up on a cot, puffing away on a cigarette. The doctors just wouldn't give up.

Major CARL MUNDY
3/26—Executive Officer

Delta-Med was a gory place, a gory scene, with rifles and helmets being thrown over into a pile. I picked up one of the helmets. It had a bullet hole right through the side of it, and a great deal of brain matter on the inside.

Chapter 10

2nd Lieutenant PAUL DRNEC
Bravo Company, 3rd Tank Battalion—2nd Platoon Commander

After the bombardment on the MSR, my platoon drove to C-2 to refuel. I called my company CP, at Camp Carroll, and asked them to send a retriever for the dead tank. Then I told the crew of the B-25 tank that I was sending them back, too. They were pretty upset about missing more action, but there wasn't any choice. Sergeant Vining's crew and I took over the B-22 tank and my platoon sergeant and his crew transferred into the B-25 tank. We stripped the dead B-21 tank of its working radios and all its remaining ammunition. Then we shifted around whatever ammunition B-22 and B-25 had left to even out the loads. We had it all done in under 45 minutes and drove out to rejoin 3/26. By then, they were on the move to a new position south of The Churchyard. We linked up with them in the open. I never heard anything from the S-3 about my unauthorized side trip to C-2. I was sure I had done the right thing.

1st Lieutenant BOB STIMSON
India Company, 3/26—Executive Officer

The new battalion position on September 8 was on a hilltop. In India's sector, part of our line had a hell of a problem with fields of fire. The vegetation was very high and thick in there. If we had been at full strength, we would have tried to move around to the outside of the growth so we could get a better view than we did have. But we were

143

well understrength and had to consolidate inside the foliage and make the best of it. I was very worried about that position if we had to sustain another enemy attack, which seemed very probable to me as long as we remained in that area.

2nd Lieutenant BILL COWAN
India Company, 3/26—3rd Platoon Commander

By the time we moved out to the new position, we had put the trauma of the night behind us and had no expectations of getting into contact again. We weren't out there watching every movement, afraid we were going to run into something. Fear wasn't there; we felt confident.

1st Lieutenant RON ZAPPARDINO
3/26—Forward Air Controller

While I went out on patrol and the battalion main body moved to the new position, my radiomen stayed back to dig my hole. They were the happiest people in the world. They were so happy, they dug my hole 5 feet down and 3 feet in. They were scared after what had hit us the previous night. The whole perimeter was like that. Everyone who could dig dug for hours.

*

Corporal FRANK GARCIA
Lima Company, 3/26—2nd Platoon Squad Leader

I didn't hear any details about the night action of September 7—just that there had been a lot of activity and that there were lots of dead gooks. There were rumors that there was a battalion or regiment or division of NVA out there—Regular Army. I was scared to shit.

Captain DICK CAMP
Lima Company, 3/26—Commanding Officer

The remainder of our journey to rejoin the battalion was blessedly uneventful. The battalion had moved about a klick south, closer to C-2, from The Churchyard. It turned out that the move had been programmed in advance as part of the battalion's mission, which, as I heard it later, was to try to flush out the headquarters of the NVA regiment that was reputedly operating in the area south of Con Thien.

When we reached the new battalion area, India Company and the battalion CP were digging in. Mike Company was still back at The Churchyard, waiting for a damaged helo to be recovered.

Lieutenant Colonel Alderman greeted me and showed me where he wanted Lima Company to deploy along the perimeter line. I passed the word to my troop leaders, and they instantly shook out their Marines and got down to business. Meantime, Gunny Bailey went to work feeding the few replacements and volunteers we rated into the two dozen fresh gaps that had been inflicted by the artillery barrage.

Captain ANDY DeBONA
Mike Company, 3/26—Commanding Officer

We moved over to our new position and set up for the night. They had left a hole for Mike. Kilo Company was on my left and India Company was on my right. As we started digging in, I requested a resupply of 60mm ammunition.

2nd Lieutenant CHAN CRANGLE
Mike Company, 3/26—1st Platoon Commander

I was so tired, I couldn't stay awake more than an hour or so. Fortunately, my platoon was placed in battalion reserve, off the perimeter.

Captain ANDY DeBONA
Mike Company, 3/26—Commanding Officer

The Mike Company exec, 1st Lieutenant Harry "Zero Fingers" Dolan, joined us that afternoon. I had sent word back to Dong Ha in the morning that I wanted everybody from Mike Company forward, including the supply sergeant. The supply sergeant, who had the distinction of being in the Marine Corps for 18 years and 9 months and getting only to the rank of sergeant, broke his glasses as he was getting off the truck. He whimpered and went back to Dong Ha. I was so mad I wanted to put him up on charges.

1st Lieutenant HARRY DOLAN
Mike Company, 3/26—Executive Officer

I returned to Mike Company and Andy DeBona told me that Lieutenant John Manzi had been killed. John had been an exceptional platoon commander. His platoon was probably the most aggressive in the company. Andy thought the world of John, and there was a unique bond between them. Andy sent me down to take over John's 3rd Platoon. Now I would finish my tour as it had begun, as a platoon commander.

Captain ANDY DeBONA
Mike Company, 3/26—Commanding Officer

Zero Fingers Dolan was an original member of the battalion. He had been with Lima Company and kept getting into trouble with his skipper. One night at Khe Sanh, I'd had to step in when he got into a little fight with John Manzi and Chan Crangle. Four days later, the battalion commander told me I was getting Dolan.

I called him Zero Fingers because he had lost the tips of two fingers of his right hand when they got caught in the fan belt of a car he had been restoring when he was a kid.

1st Lieutenant BOB STIMSON
India Company, 3/26—Executive Officer

Harry Dolan and I were the same age and, like me, he was from Detroit, though I didn't know him then. We went through The Basic School together and were both assigned to 3/26 when it was being formed at Camp Pendleton. He had an irreverent sense of humor. He was a good officer.

*

2nd Lieutenant BILL COWAN
India Company, 3/26—3rd Platoon Commander

We got some replacements after Lima Company arrived, all new men. A new man who made an impression right off was Lance Corporal Howard Chamberlin. That was because of a story he told on himself as soon as he joined the platoon. He had come in-country through Danang, and Danang got shelled. Then he had moved up to Phu Bai, and Phu Bai got shelled. Then he had been at Dong Ha, and Dong Ha got shelled. Finally, he had been on the convoy coming up to us, and the convoy got shelled.

1st Lieutenant BOB STIMSON
India Company, 3/26—Executive Officer

There was nothing I could do to replace the casualties India Company had sustained the night before. There were only a few replacements for us that day. I spoke with the platoon commanders, and we reallocated a few men and made sure that men had been appointed to fill vacant squad- and fire-team–leader billets—no matter how junior they were. We wound up with Pfcs and lance corporals filling corporals' and sergeants' jobs, and I had two of three rifle platoons under the command of buck sergeants. We had to stand down several fire teams to make it work.

Lance Corporal CHUCK BENNETT
India Company, 3/26, 1st Platoon

I didn't have a fire team left to command. They put what was left of the 3rd Squad all together. There were only four of us.

There had been all kinds of weapons and gear lying around the paddyfield in which India Company had been attacked. I'd taken an M-79 from a dead Marine and someone had told me to pack a loose radio. That was a bit much—my own M-16, the M-79, *and* a radio! I damn sure didn't want that radio because radiomen were about the first to go. I didn't know a hell of a lot about radios, besides pushing the button in to talk. I made up my mind to ditch it as soon as I could.

One of the new guys we got was Sergeant Bruce Huntington, who was new in-country. He joined the 3rd Squad as the new squad leader. Maybe they even made him the 1st Platoon commander. I had a radio and my M-16 and an M-79. I wanted to get rid of the radio, but Sergeant Huntington made me his radioman. I passed the M-79 along to someone else and put the radio in my pack and bent down the whip antenna. I didn't want the NVA to see I had a radio.

*

Captain DICK CAMP
Lima Company, 3/26—Commanding Officer

About an hour before dark, a runner arrived to escort me to the battalion CP for a command meeting. As I approached the CP, which was all dug in and below ground, I nearly ran into a huge mound of equipment—packs, rifles, helmets, field gear, boots, parts of uniforms—that was sitting on the ground. The mound was maybe 6 feet high and about 12 feet around. It was all castoffs from the casualties the battalion had suffered the night before. I looked at it, trying to evaluate it in terms my mind could comprehend, but all I could think was, ''Holy shit, they really got hit hard!'' I figured there was enough gear in there to equip 70 to 80 combat Marines. My mouth dropped open as the extent of what had happened the previous day and night started hitting me.

1st Lieutenant BOB STIMSON
India Company, 3/26—Executive Officer

As the acting India Company commander, I attended the command brief on the evening of September 8. Until that point, I had not known why we were out there, so I was looking forward to the briefing. However, Lieutenant Colonel Alderman did not have anything new to tell us, just that he expected word to come down from higher authority in the morning. Then we would know what we were supposed to do next. He tried to reassure everybody, but I was very concerned about why we were still out there and whether we could continue a battalion mission. My main concern was whether India Company could carry out a company mission, as badly whittled down as we had been. It was obvious to me that we had been involved in a rather heavy action and that our casualties were extensive. As I knew well by then, the Marine Corps in general did not react quickly to incidents like that in terms of committing reserves, reinforcing units that had taken casualties, resupplying, and so forth, so there was no telling what higher headquarters might ask us to do. As far as they were concerned, a battalion was a battalion, no matter what shape it was in.

2nd Lieutenant PAUL DRNEC
Bravo Company, 3rd Tank Battalion—2nd Platoon Commander

While the command meeting was under way, the flame tank, which was parked right next to the battalion CP, cranked up its engine so it could move into its night position.

Captain DICK CAMP
Lima Company, 3/26—Commanding Officer

I had just been hit by artillery, my company had lost 15 to 20 percent of its strength without getting a chance to shoot back, and my battalion had been hit harder than I ever thought possible. Everybody attending the command meeting was nervous—not outwardly, but I could feel it. We were listening to what was being said, but our attention was directed outward. Our antennae were up and we were extremely alert. As the battalion commander was droning on, the tank cranked up its engine. There was the familiar initial whiny crank-up noise, but for some reason it sounded a little like the start of incoming rounds. Without anybody saying anything, without missing a beat, everybody was suddenly laying on the deck. One second we were standing there, listening to Lieutenant Colonel Alderman, and a half second later everybody was on the deck.

1st Lieutenant BOB STIMSON
India Company, 3/26—Executive Officer

Everyone was pretty spooked at that point. When the tank fired up its engine, I was one of the guys who suddenly found himself on the ground.

2nd Lieutenant PAUL DRNEC
Bravo Company, 3rd Tank Battalion—2nd Platoon Commander

Everyone was very jumpy. Any loud noise was enough to set them all off. People were ducking and flinching for cover all over the place. All of them had one thought: "Incoming!" It took 15 to 20 seconds before they all started realizing it was just a tank starting up.

Captain DICK CAMP
Lima Company, 3/26—Commanding Officer

Typical of Marine officers, we all started restoring our individual macho images. Suddenly we were all on our feet again. To a man, we were flicking dust off of our utilities, saying dumb things like "Aw, I tripped," or whatever nonsense came to mind.

The meeting ended and we all split up to return to our troops or other duties. As I left the CP, which was just a bunch of holes in the ground, I started feeling sick. I got sicker with every step. I was really sick—sick to my stomach. Then I was throwing up. I became incapacitated. I was so sick, I hurt so bad, that I was bent over. I didn't know what had hit me, but I'm sure now it was the result of everything that had happened that day. It might have been some bad water, but I'm sure it was from the strain. I finally turned to John Prince, my only officer, and said, "You've got it. I can't do anything. I'm just going to curl up in my poncho liner. You got the helm tonight."

I was shivering and shaking, sick as a dog, but I finally fell asleep.

*

Captain ANDY DeBONA
Mike Company, 3/26—Commanding Officer

About the only thing that happened that evening was H&I fires. I wasn't worried. It all sounded like our own artillery. Suddenly, though, I heard *bang-shhhhm-boom*s come in nearby. It sounded like it was coming from the direction of Camp Carroll, so I reported to Battalion that we were receiving friendly H&I fire. It was only one gun at a time and it was spaced well apart. Camp Carroll denied that they were shooting anywhere near the location we reported, but the *bang-shhhhm-boom*s continued.

I got out my compass and shot an azimuth to the next *boom*. It definitely was coming from Camp Carroll. I requested Battalion again to tell them that we were receiving friendly incoming, but Battalion came back and said again, "No, Camp Carroll denied it."

2nd Lieutenant PAUL DRNEC
Bravo Company, 3rd Tank Battalion—2nd Platoon Commander

I was standing by my gun tank when the first artillery round landed nearby. Right away, I got my ass chewed royally. One of the senior infantry officers wanted to know, "What the hell are you doing shooting with the goddamn tanks?" I said, "We didn't shoot," but he said, "Goddammit, I saw you!" We had a big flap until more shells started hitting.

2nd Lieutenant BILL COWAN
India Company, 3/26—3rd Platoon Commander

My platoon wound up in a very dense thicket. I tried to move some of my people out and clear some fields of fire, then I went to work trying to help get everyone set in. As a result, I didn't get my own hole dug that afternoon. It got pretty dark before I started trying to work on my hole, but I found a little spider hole some NVA had already dug. I decided to expand it a little and I got out my shovel. I have never hit anything as hard as that ground with a shovel. It was like granite. Every time that shovel hit the ground it bounced back. I was exhausted and I finally gave up. The hole wasn't any bigger than a little end table, so I stretched out alongside of it so I could get in there if something happened. I fell asleep, but sometime in the middle of the night, without any warning, there was a tremendous explosion. That scared the shit out of me, so I started trying to dig like mad. I wasn't able to dig any better than I had before. By then, of course, everyone was up and alert. Suddenly, there was another explosion.

1st Lieutenant BOB STIMSON
India Company, 3/26—Executive Officer

It was a relatively quiet night. There was a hell of a lot of air and artillery going into the general area all the time—as I had seen from Camp Carroll on the afternoon of September 5—but none of it was directed at us. I had finally fallen asleep—my first since the night of September 6—when a large-caliber air-burst round detonated right over our position. It was right over me.

Lance Corporal RON BURKE
Mike Company, 3/26, 2nd Platoon

That night, I was awake on the perimeter. I'd had a nap that afternoon. There was a little artillery fire going off in the area. All of a sudden, there was a flash and a *BOOM* almost overhead.

1st Lieutenant BOB STIMSON
India Company, 3/26—Executive Officer

It was very intense. The rifleman right next to me cried out. It was so close that I thought we must have lost half the company. I called for a corpsman to see to the rifleman who had yelled, and then I started moving around the perimeter to see what else might have happened and how many men we had lost. It turned out that the only man hit was the Marine next to me. By the time I got back to my CP position, he was dead. I have no idea how we got by with only the one casualty.

Captain ANDY DeBONA
Mike Company, 3/26—Commanding Officer

I became a little bit hostile. I called Battalion again and told them to stop the artillery. They replied that Camp Carroll denied it was theirs.

2nd Lieutenant PAUL DRNEC
Bravo Company, 3rd Tank Battalion—2nd Platoon Commander

I hopped up on the flame tank and tried to get in. The tank commander, Corporal Wolfberger, said, "There's not enough room in here," but I said, "Bullshit," and stuffed myself down the hatch. A flame tank's turret, which contained a 450-gallon napalm tank and 9 or 10 gas cylinders, was a pretty crowded place, but I got in and closed the hatch over me.

2nd Lieutenant CHAN CRANGLE
Mike Company, 3/26—1st Platoon Commander

My radioman and corpsman attempted to wake me and get me into a hole. No luck; I slept on. They told me about it in the morning.

Lance Corporal RON BURKE
Mike Company, 3/26, 2nd Platoon

I thought we were being attacked. Everyone was up, ready to repel an attack.

Captain DICK CAMP
Lima Company, 3/26—Commanding Officer

I was sicker than a dog and fast asleep, but I thought I heard Lieutenant Prince saying, "Goddammit, they just hit India Company. They killed a Marine." In the background, on an open radio channel, I could hear Andy DeBona cursing up a storm.

Captain ANDY DeBONA
Mike Company, 3/26 —Commanding Officer

I waited until the next *bang* and had Battalion get hold of Camp Carroll to see if they had just fired. I was told they had just as the next *shhhhm-boom* sounded. Artillery fire then was stopped in that area for the rest of the night. It was a very quiet night after that.

Corporal FRANK GARCIA
Lima Company, 3/26—2nd Platoon Squad Leader

When we heard the incoming that night, we all got scared and prepared for an attack, but after it happened word came around that it was friendly fire. Nobody knew why our own guns were shooting at us.

2nd Lieutenant PAUL DRNEC
Bravo Company, 3rd Tank Battalion—2nd Platoon Commander

When the shelling lifted, I flipped open the flame tank's turret hatch to look out and see if it was all clear. Unbeknownst to me, the catch on the spring mechanism that was supposed to stop that 250-pound clamshell hatch was broken. When I threw the hatch open, I expected it to catch, but the hatch came back and hit me just as I was lifting my head. The weight jammed me into the edge of the hatchway, and I cut my whole lower lip open. I asked one of the grunt corpsmen to throw a couple of stitches in, but he sort of moaned, "I can't do that; I'm not a surgeon." I decided, to hell with it, I couldn't take the time to get medevacked back to some fancy place to have my face stitched up. I threw on a dressing and laid myself out on the back of the tank because I was very groggy from the hit in the head.

Lance Corporal MIKE HEFFLIN
Lima Company, 3/26, 2nd Platoon

The hill was a terrible place to dig in and very crowded. There were rocks and sagebrush and weeds 3 to 4 feet high. We hadn't really dug in. We were tired and a little strung out. But after the short rounds came in and we heard that a Marine was killed, everyone started digging at least a little hole.

2nd Lieutenant BILL COWAN
India Company, 3/26—3rd Platoon Commander

I spent the rest of the night sitting scrunched up in the little NVA spider hole. I tried to get a little sleep, but even after they checked fire, I was too wide awake to doze off. Someone fired illume from time to time. The next morning, when I got out of the spider hole, I found that all of my gear was peppered with shrapnel. My poncho liner was melted together where hot shrapnel had landed on it and burned through.

Captain DICK CAMP
Lima Company, 3/26—Commanding Officer

Other than the short rounds, it was an uneventful night, for which I am eternally thankful because I would have been too sick to defend myself. Next morning, I woke up and there was nothing wrong with me. I had had a great night's sleep and I felt great; there was nothing wrong.

Chapter 11

Major CARL MUNDY
3/26—Executive Officer

There was not a great deal of excitement in what I did at the rear. That was mainly getting the tents up, getting the company CPs established, preparing for any casualty evacuation, getting the mess hall going so that we could occasionally fly some hot chow out into the field if the opportunity presented itself. I had to be concerned with such things as mail, administration, replacements who were coming in, and Marines who were returning—Marines whose year in Vietnam was up and who had to be processed out of the battalion.

Two new officers reported in to the battalion rear the evening of September 8. One of them was Major Joe Loughran and the other was Captain Matt Caulfield. Both were just out of the Amphibious Warfare School, in Quantico. Joe, a very red-headed, hard-charging Irishman, had been in Dong Ha for a couple of hours when he said to me, "I'm your new S-3." I began by saying, "What's your date of rank?" It turned out that he was significantly senior to me because I was at that time a very junior major, having only four or five months in grade, which was unusual for battalion execs. When we established our dates of rank, I said, "No, I'm the S-3 and you're the exec." We quickly established the precedence, and he had no trouble at all taking over as exec.

After Joe Loughran relieved me as exec, I began showing him the ropes and getting ready to move down to the battalion main body to take over as S-3 from Bill Wildprett, who would become my assistant. At that time, we put the other new arrival, Captain Matt Caulfield, out in a little command tent to sleep. I was up at various odd hours of the night, and as I walked by Matt's tent, I noticed that he was pacing back and forth. It turned out that he was rehearsing his pitch.

The next morning, September 9, at about 0530, Matt came out of the tent, approached me, and laid out this really moving appeal to go out and be a company commander.

The battalion S-4 had been promised a rifle company, and India Company had opened up when Wayne Coulter was wounded and medevacked. I had been getting set to send the S-4 out to be the new India Company commander when Joe Loughran and Matt Caulfield arrived. Before I could dispatch him, however, Matt played to tender heartstrings while talking his way into India Company.

First, he was a very senior captain, about to come into the promotion zone for major. He knew that if he didn't command a company now, he probably wouldn't. When I had received my orders to Vietnam, I had been in the same boat. My orders directed me to III MAF headquarters, and I made considerable effort to seek relief. I explained that, if I didn't go to a division before going to III MAF, I would have no opportunity to command in combat. I even wrote a letter to the commanding general, Fleet Marine Force, Pacific. My efforts had no effect. I was, therefore, sensitive, as a "fellow traveler," to Matt's argument. Second, Matt had a child with scoliosis, curvature of the spine. He put forth a moving testimonial that his child's situation could result in his being recalled home early and in not having a chance to come back to Vietnam. Thus, he saw this as his only opportunity for live combat. Third, Matt—like me—had been ordered to III MAF headquarters. Before reporting there, he had gone directly to see Colonel Kenny Houghton, who was then G-2. Matt believed Houghton to be a genuine Marine, and Matt had given him the same pitch he gave me. Houghton had gone to the mat for him at III MAF, arranging his transfer out.

Caulfield was one of the most influential people you would ever want to know. I was moved by his request and by the fact that Kenny Houghton had also been moved to the point of getting him out of III MAF. I figured he rated the chance at being a company commander and that the S-4 still had time for another opportunity. Matt left Dong Ha to assume command of India Company about mid morning, September 9.

1st Lieutenant BOB STIMSON
India Company, 3/26—Executive Officer

I was summoned from my position with India Company back to the battalion CP, where Captain Matt Caulfield was being introduced by Lieutenant Colonel Alderman. The battalion commander told me that Captain Caulfield was superseding me as commander of India Company. Almost immediately, I walked with Captain Caulfield to the company CP, where I introduced him to the platoon commanders.

The captain was very frank. He told us he was brand-new in Vietnam, that he had just completed the course at the Amphibious Warfare School, that he had been briefed and was aware of what had happened over the past several days, and that he knew that most of the men had had a fair amount of combat experience. He said he would appreciate all the help we could give him. He impressed me immediately as being a very professional officer who seemed to know what to do and who was willing to ask for our opinions. I immediately felt very comfortable with him.

2nd Lieutenant BILL COWAN
India Company, 3/26—3rd Platoon Commander

When Captain Caulfield checked in as the new India Company commander, I found him to be very cool, very methodical. Rather than coming in and taking over, wanting to get things done his way, he let it be known that Bob Stimson and I had the reins for the moment, that for the next few days he wanted us to do things as we had been doing them, until he saw what was what. It was very impressive.

1st Lieutenant BOB STIMSON
India Company, 3/26—Executive Officer

In addition to Captain Caulfield, India Company received about 20 replacements. That did not begin to make good our September 7 battle losses, but we were glad to have as many as they gave us. Like the captain, they all had just recently arrived in Vietnam, though we got a sergeant who had had a previous tour. I still wasn't certain about what we were going to do next out there, but I felt that we were better prepared to face it with the additional men. I felt better; things were looking up a little.

*

Lance Corporal MIKE HEFFLIN
Lima Company, 3/26, 2nd Platoon

On the morning of September 9, they took a survey of everyone who had been wounded in the rocket attack on the MSR; we did a head count. We also regrouped our squad, which had lost old-timers and gained new people in Dong Ha. A lot of guys were disoriented from the day before because the company had not fully reorganized before nightfall. We had to sort everyone out in the morning.

Corporal FRANK GARCIA
Lima Company, 3/26—2nd Platoon Squad Leader

On September 9, we went out on a water detail and found blood in a pool of water. It looked like somebody had gotten killed, but they'd taken the bodies away. We started looking around for other signs of the enemy, but there wasn't anybody there. We couldn't get the water because it had blood in it, but someone drank out of it anyway. He later got sick.

We kept searching. We saw signs—drag marks and a lot of fresh trails—but we couldn't find anybody in the thick brush. We started following one of the trails, but I began thinking, "Hey, enough of this shit; they're out here," and I turned around and led the detail back to the company.

1st Lieutenant BOB STIMSON
India Company, 3/26—Executive Officer

The patrols we sent out during the morning of September 9 were security- and reconnaissance-type movements in the general area to see if we could see or make contact with the enemy. The patrols did not go very far out.

Lance Corporal MIKE HEFFLIN
Lima Company, 3/26, 2nd Platoon

I stayed in the company area all morning and afternoon. We sat around on ponchos on the ground—laying in the sun, waiting for the water run to come back in to us. I had the shrapnel wounds in my hand rebandaged. There was no firing. It was peaceful and quiet, but I started getting very nervous. I must have picked up something from the guys who made the water run. We all started moving around a little more cautiously, pushing our senses out.

Lance Corporal CHUCK BENNETT
India Company, 3/26, 1st Platoon

It was hot and we ran low on water. We were getting water out of the rice paddies, from rain puddles. We had to use our halazone tablets.

Captain ANDY DeBONA
Mike Company, 3/26—Commanding Officer

Mike Company did not move outside the perimeter during the morning or early afternoon. Then we were told we were going to move to another position—Hill 48—about a klick away, generally to our southwest.

*

1st Lieutenant BOB STIMSON
India Company, 3/26—Executive Officer

When India Company received the plan of the day from Battalion, we learned that we had the point again.

2nd Lieutenant BILL COWAN
India Company, 3/26—3rd Platoon Commander

I was standing under some trees with Bob Stimson and Captain Caulfield, trying to get acquainted a little bit, talking about things that had happened. When it was time to move out, Caulfield, Stimson, and I walked out to lead the company. Hill 48, the battalion objective, was about 500 meters away, across an open field and up a little hill to the knoll. There was a lot of brush to the left of our route of march and an opening leading to the knoll. We were going to work our way along the brush on the left.

1st Lieutenant BOB STIMSON
India Company, 3/26—Executive Officer

As usual, while we were waiting for word from Battalion to begin the move to a new position, there were smaller patrols moving around. Since we were going to be leading, Captain Caulfield directed that certain intermediate objectives be reconnoitered. It was by the book, exactly what I would have done.

2nd Lieutenant BILL COWAN
India Company, 3/26—3rd Platoon Commander

I was very concerned about sending such small patrols, because of the chance we would get into another engagement.

Following the death of Sergeant Bruce Krage on the night of September 7, my number one squad leader was Corporal Frank Hazzard—appropriately named. Hazzard was a good man, about my best. He had just taken over his squad from Sergeant Krage. I wanted to impress the new company commander, to do the move right—I wanted to get up on the objective, do a good job. So I said to Corporal Hazzard, "Corporal, see that little clump of trees down there about 50 meters out?"

"Oh, yes, sir," he replied.

"You take your squad down there, get 'em down there, and stand by 'til I give you the word to move out on the objective. You understand?"

"Oh, yes, sir. No problem."

I should have known better.

1st Lieutenant BOB STIMSON
India Company, 3/26—Executive Officer

As Bill Cowan and I were scanning the area through field glasses, trying to keep an eye on our people out there, someone said, "Look out there on that hill. There's movement!" It was the battalion's final objective. Then we realized to our horror that we were seeing *Marines* on the objective.

2nd Lieutenant BILL COWAN
India Company, 3/26—3rd Platoon Commander

I said, "Oh shit! Goddamn! We're gonna get in trouble!"

Corporal Hazzard had taken his squad all the way to the battalion objective and was almost on top of it! Captain Caulfield's mouth dropped open. The rest of the battalion couldn't see; they were back in the trees. I screamed so loud—"Hazzard, you fucking idiot, get your goddamned people back here!"—that he heard me. The squad was almost up to the top, but it turned around and came on back. I moved the rest of my people up to support Hazzard and his squad in case something happened, but it didn't.

So there it was, my first chance to impress the new company commander.

1st Lieutenant BOB STIMSON
India Company, 3/26—Executive Officer

It was very embarrassing, especially for Bill, who had just fleeted Hazzard up to fill a vacant squad-leader billet. Hazzard was a problem child; he was regularly involved in missteps over the course of the year, but this was classic. Aside from how funny it seemed even at the time, it was a miracle the patrol wasn't annihilated. There was no way we could have effectively supported it if it had been engaged by the enemy.

Captain Caulfield did not make a commotion about Corporal Hazzard's gaffe. He already was learning very quickly that things did not go according to recipe, the way they went at a Quantico field exercise.

2nd Lieutenant BILL COWAN
India Company, 3/26—3rd Platoon Commander

Of course, India Company marched up to the objective without any trouble.

2nd Lieutenant CHAN CRANGLE
Mike Company, 3/26—1st Platoon Commander

En route to Hill 48, the tanks were a real problem. First of all, we had to form up on the base of the hill and wait for the damned tanks to get in position. Then, as we swept across the open fields in a very open line, one of the tanks did its damnedest to drive into a ditch or stream in the middle of the open area. The tank-infantry phone on the tank's rear fender wasn't working. The only way I could stop the tank was to run in front of it and wave my arms. So much for mobility and communications. Once we got across that "obstacle," we swept up on Hill 48, but the tank closest to me promptly threw a track in the underbrush. Given the NVA proclivity to fire artillery or rockets or mortars at every opportunity, being immobilized while somebody repaired a mechanical widget got to be a real pain, a real pucker factor. Infantry survives on mobility—even just foot mobility—but it dies on immobility.

*

1st Lieutenant BOB STIMSON
India Company, 3/26—Executive Officer

The day's move was unusual in that it was to a hill very close to the one on which we had spent the night of September 8. They were within sight of one another. It bothered me that we were still very much in the neighborhood of the NVA regiment that had nearly overrun us on the night of September 7. I assumed, however, that it was all being run with a purpose from higher levels and that we would know what we were supposed to be accomplishing out there whenever they deemed it time for us to know.

The fields of fire on Hill 48 were wonderful. The whole position was quite different from the positions we had occupied on previous nights.

Lance Corporal MIKE HEFFLIN
Lima Company, 3/26, 2nd Platoon

When we got to the new hill, Hill 48, they told us to dig in, but we couldn't. The ground was too hard. A few guys got a little way into the ground - little shallow trenches. It was a crying goddamn shame. The next day, we found Vietnamese graves on the next hill over. We would have been able to set in there with all the cover in the world already there for us.

Captain ANDY DeBONA
Mike Company, 3/26—Commanding Officer

When we pulled up on Hill 48, there were a lot of old fighting holes there, obviously Marine-made from their shape. We registered in our fires, got our fire plans from the platoons, and spent an uneventful afternoon.

Lance Corporal MIKE HEFFLIN
Lima Company, 3/26, 2nd Platoon

Late in the afternoon, Captain Camp, the gunny, and the platoon commanders had their maps out, trying to figure out what we were doing next. Then they called all the squad leaders and fire-team leaders together and mapped out the next day's move. They told us we would be advancing along the top of a ridge, set up the sequence of the platoons and squads, and assigned out the machine guns. They gave our 3rd Squad two of the M-60 teams.

2nd Lieutenant CHAN CRANGLE
Mike Company, 3/26—1st Platoon Commander

We had no contact that afternoon or night.

Staff Sergeant Russ Armstrong, India Company platoon commander. (*Compliments of Russell Armstrong*)

Staff Sergeant Marvin Bailey, Lima Company gunnery sergeant. (*Compliments of Michael Heffline*)

Captain Dick Camp, Lima Company commander. (*Compliments of Richard Camp*)

Lance Corporal Chuck Bennett, India Company rifleman. (*Compliments of Charles Bennett*)

2nd Lieutenant Bill Cowan, India Company platoon commander. (*Compliments of William Cowan*)

Captain Andy DeBona, Mike Company commander. (*Compliments of Andrew DeBona*)

1st Lieutenant Harry Dolan, Mike Company executive officer. (*Compliments of Harry Dolan*)

2nd Lieutenant Paul Drnec, tank platoon commander. (*Compliments of Paul Drnec*)

Captain Tom Early, 3/26 communications officer. (*Compliments of Thomas Early*)

Corporal Frank Garcia, Lima Company squad leader. (*Compliments of Francis Garcia*)

Staff Sergeant Edward Gayton (on left), Mike Company platoon sergeant killed in action on September 10, 1967. (*Compliments of Andrew De-Bona*)

Lance Corporal Mike Hefflin, Lima Company grenadier. (*Compliments of Michael Hefflin*)

Chief Warrant Officer Dick Holycross, 81mm Mortar Platoon commander killed in action on September 10, 1967. (*Compliments of Dr. Allan Millett*)

Sergeant Marshall Jesperson (on left), Lima Company squad leader. (*Compliments of Ricky Bender*)

2nd Lieutenant John Manzi (on left), Mike Company platoon commander killed in action on September 7, 1967. (*Compliments of Andrew DeBona*)

Master Gunnery Sergeant Thomas McHugh, 3/26 operations chief. (*Compliments of Andrew DeBona*)

Major Carl Mundy (on right), 3/26 executive officer. (*Compliments of Carl Mundy*)

Staff Sergeant David Nugent, 81mm mortar section chief. (*Compliments of David Nugent*)

Staff Sergeant Charles Owens, Kilo Company gunnery sergeant. (*Compliments of Charles Owens*)

2nd Lieutenant John Prince, Lima Company platoon commander. (*Compliments of John Prince*)

Lance Corporal Terry Smith (seated, left), Lima Company tactical air control operator. (*Compliments of Richard Camp*)

1st Lieutenant Ron Zappardino (l.), 3/26 forward air controller, and 1st Lieutenant Bob Stimson, India Company executive officer, just before the main body of 3/26 lifted off from the Khe Sanh helipad, September 5, 1967. (*Compliments of Robert Stimson*)

2nd Lieutenant Paul Drnec waves from the commander's cupola as his only surviving M-48 gun tank enters Fire Base C-2, September 11, 1967. (*Compliments of Paul Drnec*)

The Lima Company, 3/26 command group, in the Cam Lo-Con Thien area, late August 1967. (*Compliments of Richard Camp*)

Some Lima Company survivors at Fire Base C-2, September 11, 1967. At lower right, with M-60 machine gun, is Corporal Frank Garcia. (*Compliments of Richard Camp*)

Puff the Magic Dragon, an Air Force AC-47 gunship. (*Compliments of David Steinberg*)

PART III

Ambush Valley

Chapter 12

2nd Lieutenant CHAN CRANGLE
Mike Company, 3/26—1st Platoon Commander

Very early on the morning of September 10, my platoon was ordered to make a reconnaissance along the streambed just west of Hill 48. Since the purpose of the patrol was to find stream crossings for the tanks, I had some tankers with me, but no tanks. We patrolled southwest along the stream for some distance, as far as the road crossing.

To put it mildly, I was apprehensive about being so far out in front of the battalion. This neck of the woods was definitely not guerrilla-warfare country; the bad guys were NVA Regulars. At the stream-road intersection, my pointman crossed the stream and found a Ho Chi Minh sandalprint still filling with water.

I suspected that we were within a very few meters of an NVA force. The hair was distinctly standing up on my neck. One very frightened platoon went to ground without a sound. I reported to Battalion and asked if I was to follow the road or come home. I was praying that I could come home!

I won't argue the point that my mission was to find a crossing for the tanks, other than the road. I could have told Battalion that I was going to go up the trail (west) rather than ask for instructions. But, at that point, I was one infantry platoon 1,000 to 1,500 meters in front of the battalion. The experience the India Company patrol had had on September 7 was quite fresh in my mind. Bottom line: I didn't volunteer to follow the trail. I reported what we had found and Battalion told me to come home. I have no regrets over that decision.

As we turned for Hill 48, we were moving backwards with all firepower focused on the streambed and the low ridge on the opposite side. It was a very touchy situation.

My platoon patrol found no stream crossings, and that led to the decision to follow the high ground in a horseshoe direction to the southwest, rather than move the battalion across the open ground to the west.

*

Captain DICK CAMP
Lima Company, 3/26—Commanding Officer

As soon as we got up before dawn on September 10, we went through our usual morning ritual—making sure our weapons were clean, eating a C-ration breakfast, and undertaking little housekeeping chores to prepare for the day.

Lima Company was going to patrol along the low ridgeline on the left, the south side of the V-shaped valley Hill 48 overlooked to the west. Later, the rest of the battalion would follow us to a new position overlooking the next valley to the west.

Lima Company saddled up and started moving at about 0730. We humped right out toward the first, lower hill on the ridgeline that defined the left side of the valley. The hill was 200 to 300 meters from the battalion perimeter. The previous afternoon, Captain Bill Wildprett, the S-3, had told me to climb the ridge and advance, to see if I could find any signs of NVA in that direction.

It was an extremely hot day and the brush was extremely thick.

2nd Lieutenant JOHN PRINCE
Lima Company, 3/26—2nd Platoon Commander

My platoon had point. The brush was just unbelievably thick. In four hours we probably walked 300 yards, snaking along back and forth because we were walking in between the thick brush.

Captain DICK CAMP
Lima Company, 3/26—Commanding Officer

It took us three to four hours to reach the top of the first hill. As soon as we got there, I ordered the company to close up and told everyone to take a break. I reported to Battalion and they told us to hold up there.

I expected to be moving out again soon, so I made no arrangements to dig in. There was some scrub growing throughout our position, so it was marginally shady, though extremely hot. We stayed there for 30 minutes without orders.

Lance Corporal MIKE HEFFLIN
Lima Company, 3/26, 2nd Platoon

They told us to dig in there and have lunch. I always carried extra food. Most of the guys knew enough to do that. I also always carried three canteens of water. My squad leader, Corporal Frank Garcia, always carried extra canned tortillas he got from home. We ate lunch right by some Vietnamese graves at the top of the hill, on the right side, overlooking the rice paddies.

Captain DICK CAMP
Lima Company, 3/26—Commanding Officer

The soil was tough, very rocky. The troops were sure we were going to move again soon, so, when I ordered everyone to dig in, the effort was halfhearted. I took out my E-tool to set an example, moved one shovelful of rocks, and said "Screw it, we're probably going to move out anyway."

Then an hour had passed. No orders.

It was hot. I believe someone measured the temperature at around noon and it was up to 107 degrees. The heat was so bad that it sapped our strength and our will. I wanted to do something, but I wound up just sitting there, sort of panting in the shade of a little bush. As hot as it was, we all kept on our helmets and flak jackets, so we were all sweating like dogs. We had to watch our water supply, so there was no relief from the heat. We were simply debilitated, baking in the heat, apathetic. I didn't know what the hell was going on, what Battalion had in mind, why they were keeping us up there for no discernible reason. I didn't know what to do, so I just sat and panted.

Yet another half hour crept by. Nothing. I called back and asked, "What's going on?" Battalion replied, "You're going to hold there."

The word from the troops was that they were running out of water. Small wonder. I got out my map and saw that there was a little blue line running through the area at the base of our hill—a stream of some sort. I looked down at the base of the hill to check. I could not see a stream, but, sure enough, there were overgrown rice paddies stretching across the valley floor. As I peered into the waist-high scrub within the regularly shaped diked paddies, I could see an irregular break that probably was the stream marked on my map. If we were halfway lucky, there would be water down there.

I immediately announced that we were going to send down a water detail. I grabbed Sergeant Albert Peck, the platoon sergeant of John Prince's 2nd Platoon, and told him he was going to lead the detail. Peck formed a mixed squad of 10 or 12 Marines from all the platoons, added a radioman, and began collecting canteens. Within a minute or two, the dozen Marines were festooned with canteens. When they moved down off the top of the hill, I sort of half-watched them, but I was so apathetic from the heat that I really didn't pay much attention.

Lance Corporal MIKE HEFFLIN
Lima Company, 3/26, 2nd Platoon

My squad was in front of the rest of the company, overlooking the rice paddy to our front and a gully between our hill and the hills to our left. When the water detail went out, our squad, with two attached M-60s, was the lookout for them.

The water detail went down off the hill and into the rice paddies. There was foliage down there and the detail disappeared into it.

Captain DICK CAMP
Lima Company, 3/26—Commanding Officer

Nothing happened. When the water detail returned about an hour later, Sergeant Peck marched right up to me and announced, "Skipper, I smell gooks in that rice paddy."

I thought, "Jesus! Gooks in the rice paddy!" and asked, "What do you mean?"

"I can smell them in that rice paddy," Peck insisted.

So there I was. I had been sitting on that damn hill for hours. The company was beat to hell by the heat. I looked down at the rice paddy, but I couldn't see anything out of the ordinary. "Screw it," I said, "your nose is out of joint or something. Whatever you're drinking, get me a case of it." Peck shrugged, nodded, and left to help distribute the water.

*

Captain ANDY DeBONA
Mike Company, 3/26—Commanding Officer

The plan of the day on September 10 was for the entire battalion to move out to a new position with India on the point, Mike on the right flank, Lima on the left flank, and Kilo in the rear.

2nd Lieutenant PAUL DRNEC
Bravo Company, 3rd Tank Battalion—2nd Platoon Commander

As I was given to understand it, this was an administrative move. Lima Company reached its objective without incident, and the remainder of the battalion started its displacement. The order of march was Lima Company, India Company, Mike Company, the two gun tanks and the flame tank, the battalion command group, and Kilo Company with the two Ontos as rear security.

2nd Lieutenant BILL COWAN
India Company, 3/26—3rd Platoon Commander

First thing on the morning of September 10, one of the kids in one of the other companies shot himself in the knee cleaning his rifle. He had to be medevacked from the hill, from a little pagoda up there.

1st Lieutenant BOB STIMSON
India Company, 3/26—Executive Officer

A couple of days had elapsed since the action of September 7, but everybody was still very tired and very wary. These factors probably combined by September 10 to make everyone a little less alert, a little less aggressive than would have been the case if we had been fresh troops.

2nd Lieutenant BILL COWAN
India Company, 3/26—3rd Platoon Commander

I didn't think anything of it at the time, but I always have had a nagging feeling since then that we gave something away by standing up by the pagoda and pointing here and there in full view of whoever was looking at us.

*

Captain ANDY DeBONA
Mike Company, 3/26—Commanding Officer

When Mike-1 returned from its dawn patrol, I passed the word to all my platoons to be ready to move out early in a company wedge to cover the battalion right flank. About the time Lima Company had moved out to take up high overlook positions on the ridgeline to the left, I decided to move about 300 meters out of the battalion lines and slightly to the right so that we would not be part of one big battalion gaggle streaming from the same position. We moved forward after we were resupplied. We got the two gun tanks and one zippo tank when we moved out on the flank.

1st Lieutenant HARRY DOLAN
Mike Company, 3/26—3rd Platoon Commander

We moved out in a westerly direction. Chan Crangle's 1st Platoon was on the right flank, Bob Gall's 2nd Platoon was in the center, and my 3rd Platoon was on the left flank—in something like a company wedge. The company didn't move far, perhaps 300 meters. We moved down a trail made by a tank. My platoon was deployed in echelon right and linked to Bob Gall's platoon.

Forward movement stalled for some reason. As soon as our movement stopped, I told my squad leaders to have their men dig hasty holes.

The troops never asked questions. I said, "Advance!" and the men advanced. I said "Stop!" and they stopped. I said, "Dig in!" and they dug in. They were great troops. They never questioned a single order that I gave them. I—and they—owe that to John Manzi, who had been a great platoon leader. Thanks to John, those troops trusted their leader even though they didn't know much about him. They were good troops.

Captain ANDY DeBONA
Mike Company, 3/26—Commanding Officer

We had rice paddies about 100 meters to our right and the hills were about 100 meters to our left. In a straight line, Lima Company stopped 300 to 400 meters ahead of our forwardmost position. There was waist-high scrub brush and one small tank trail right about in the trace of Mike-2. The Mike-2 point was the point of my company wedge. It was on a little high spot with one of the gun tanks. My CP was about 30 meters directly behind that tank.

I do not consider myself a superstitious individual, but when the CP group stopped along the side of the trail, I saw flowers. There were very few blooming things in Vietnam, and inevitably in the past, when I had seen flowers we had made contact.

We stayed put for hours.

*

Major CARL MUNDY
3/26—Operations Officer

On September 10, I flew out to the field on a resupply helicopter to join the battalion main body as its new S-3. When I arrived at the landing zone, I walked up to where the battalion CP was set up more or less on top of the ridgeline. There was a lot of foliage around; it was heavy country with a lot of elephant grass and low swampy ground.

We were ¼ mile to ½ mile from the MSR that ran up to Con Thien. I could stand on the hill and look out several klicks and see the red mud hill that was Con Thien, up to the northeast of where we were.

My first thought as I got off the helicopter and started walking up to the battalion CP was that the things that you do in a training situation are exactly identical to what occurs in combat. On the way up to the CP, I had to hail a couple of NCOs who were cleaning weapons in one of the fighting holes and say, "Go up and tell the Marines on the line to get their flak jackets on." There were a couple of Marines who were standing up passing their helmets back and forth like a football. It was a bright, sunny day. Nobody was shooting at anybody, but the lesson to be learned for anyone in command in a situation like this is that the same fundamentals that you have to stress when you're on the three-day war exercise at The Basic School are the ones you find yourself reemphasizing right in the middle of the combat zone.

Staff Sergeant CHARLES OWENS
Kilo Company, 3/26—Company Gunny

I had ordered some fresh peaches that were available, and they brought me a Sunday pack, with candy and cigars and things like that. We passed out the peaches, new uniforms, and the stuff from the Sunday pack while we were getting ready to move out. We were going to be rearguard, behind the 81mm mortars and the battalion CP.

Major CARL MUNDY
3/26—Operations Officer

I arrived in the battalion CP's small perimeter, which was a few small fighting holes. The battalion commander greeted me. Lieutenant Colonel Harry Alderman was a very outgoing, personable man, very friendly. He thought the world of those of us who worked for him. When he came out, he was genuinely warmly welcoming. Captain Bill Wildprett, who was to stay on as the assistant S-3, briefed me that the movement of the battalion was then under way. He indicated that the battalion was moving to the west to new and perhaps more defensible terrain as a base of operations from which to operate for the next day or so. He explained his intent to minimize the time we occupied terrain because the NVA either had it zeroed or quickly got it zeroed. The move was not an attack, but, rather, a tactical relocation of the battalion to new terrain.

Bill Wildprett was quite distraught. He had been without sleep for a few days and he was just on that ragged-edge point where he was getting a little bit shaky. I think he was glad to see some help coming out. After Bill briefed me, I told him to go get some rest, that I'd pick it up from there.

At that particular time, India Company was on the move. Lima Company had moved out, but on a little bit of a different course. Kilo Company was in the perimeter, around the battalion CP, and Mike Company was just in front of Hill 48.

*

2nd Lieutenant BILL COWAN
India Company, 3/26—3rd Platoon Commander

True to form, India Company didn't start moving off Hill 48 until around 1300. Moving late in the day was something the battalion was getting good at. I have heard a lot of people over the years register the same complaint about their battalions in Vietnam. I don't know what it was that made us unable to get up in the morning and get moving. Every time we made contact, we made it late. If it was starting to get dark, it was hard to get resupplied, hard to get organized, and hard to dig in while under fire.

Captain ANDY DeBONA
Mike Company, 3/26—Commanding Officer

The point of India Company moved past us to our left, between our position on the tank trail and Lima's position on the ridgeline. My plan was to wait until India Company uncovered Mike Company. Then I was going to start moving on out.

As India Company moved through Mike Company, I felt that India-Six must have changed routes. When I had talked to India-Six before the move, he had said he wasn't going to be on the trail or anywhere near it, that he was going to be to the left of the trail. But, somehow or other, India's rear elements got over to the trail. I figured maybe they were trying to close up the column and were using the trail because it was the path of least resistance. A company column can get really spread out in high grass and brush. It would have been nothing for the India column of platoons to be a klick from point to tail.

1st Lieutenant BOB STIMSON
India Company, 3/26—Executive Officer

The terrain was much easier than what we had been experiencing since September 7. We were able to move pretty rapidly as those things go.

2nd Lieutenant BILL COWAN
India Company, 3/26—3rd Platoon Commander

My platoon was the company vanguard.

1st Lieutenant BOB STIMSON
India Company, 3/26—Executive Officer

Bill Cowan had come to us from Lima Company sometime in August. He was a first-rate officer, the only Naval Academy grad in the battalion, as far as I know, but Annapolis never came up. Bill was not there punching tickets; he was in there doing his job, just commanding a rifle platoon.

I was pretty far up in the column, closer to Captain Caulfield than I usually was to a company commander during a company movement. This was because he was new.

Cowan's platoon passed close to Lima Company, which was on the top of a low hill. We moved along the side of the hill, across a draw, and up over the top of the next hill to the west. The hill was covered with fairly low grass. I could see very well as we went up and over and began an oblique right turn to begin mounting the next hill in line. The next hill in front of us ran roughly from southwest, where we were, to northeast, toward the new battalion objective.

2nd Lieutenant BILL COWAN
India Company, 3/26—3rd Platoon Commander

As we moved out ahead of everyone else in the battalion, India Company was just a long line of troops; we were really strung out.

An AO was up ahead of us, and he reported seeing some fresh bunkers and firing positions, but he didn't see anyone around them.

Captain DICK CAMP
Lima Company, 3/26—Commanding Officer

India Company hiked to the base of the hill we were on. At about 1430, India's point platoon started up the next hill ahead of ours, a few hundred meters ahead of us. We had nothing to do except watch India moving. Right off, I was struck by how small India Company looked, how roughly it had been treated two nights earlier. The only reason I was watching India was because its movement was the only distraction from the heat and my bored misery. I'm sure I could hear exchanges on the battalion tactical net, but my mind was fried; I really didn't have the foggiest idea what the hell was going on, what the point of our move and India's was.

2nd Lieutenant BILL COWAN
India Company, 3/26—3rd Platoon Commander

We passed Lima Company and cut over the side of a small hill—not over the top, but around on the side of it—and dropped down to a little watercourse.

1st Lieutenant BOB STIMSON
India Company, 3/26—Executive Officer

As the lead element of Bill Cowan's 3rd Platoon and most of the company CP group went down into the draw between the hills, most of India

Company was back behind or on top of the hill the lead element had already crossed.

The vegetation in the draw was thicker than on the top of the hill we had just crossed, but it wasn't bad—not as bad as anything we had faced on our patrol on September 7. We had a good view of the side of the hill ahead of us, beyond the draw, and the large area of rice paddies to our right, our north.

2nd Lieutenant BILL COWAN
India Company, 3/26—3rd Platoon Commander

Everything to the south of us was very bushy; everything to the northeast of us was rice paddies with a couple little fingers of vegetation shooting out into them.

We crossed the low spot and made our way along an old tank trail with very thick scrub vegetation on both sides. We were moving in a column. The foliage was very thick on both sides of the trail—scrub 4 to 8 feet high. There was a little clearing up ahead followed by more high brush along the top.

1st Lieutenant BOB STIMSON
India Company, 3/26—Executive Officer

We halted in the draw and a squad from the 3rd Platoon advanced on the next hill, to look it over.

2nd Lieutenant BILL COWAN
India Company, 3/26—3rd Platoon Commander

One squad was out in front of me, then there was my radioman and me.

As the point was moving through the open area, which was about 10 meters wide, there was a burst of AK-47 fire, followed by several more little bursts. I asked someone, "What was that?" and someone else answered, "We're taking fire."

Chapter 13

1st Lieutenant RON ZAPPARDINO
3/26—Forward Air Controller

I was two or three people behind Bill Cowan. I glanced ahead, up the hill, and saw what I took to be a Marine company. Everyone I saw up there was wearing helmets and flak jackets. I was just starting to wonder what Marines were doing in front of India Company when everything broke loose from the top of the hill, from in front of us.

1st Lieutenant BOB STIMSON
India Company, 3/26—Executive Officer

Almost simultaneously, as the squad from 3rd Platoon took fire, an AO overhead reported that there was an NVA squad on the hill ahead, overlooking our position.

Captain ANDY DeBONA
Mike Company, 3/26—Commanding Officer

The India rearguard was still going through Mike Company when their point platoon, India-3, reported contact. I could hear quite a bit of fire to the front.

Captain DICK CAMP
Lima Company, 3/26—Commanding Officer

I was watching one of the India platoons as it reached the top of the hill and half-listening to the chatter on the battalion tactical net when, all of a sudden, I was brought bolt upright by the sudden onset of heavy fire at long range. It was all small-arms fire, and it broke out all at once, in a great, distant roar. I was sniffing the air like a bird dog and immediately realized that there was something going on with India Company. Fully alert, without a shred of my former apathy, I picked up Captain Matt Caulfield's New York City accent on the open tactical net: "My lead platoon has been shot down."

Wow! Electrifying! The adrenaline hit my bloodstream like a superconductor. The hours of heat and thirst I had endured that day meant nothing. "My lead platoon has been shot down" sent everyone in Lima Company scrambling for their weapons, got everyone searching outboard for NVA. Before we had fully reacted, the fire-support request nets were starting to come up strong while, on our flank, the heavy volume of fire rose as M-79s and M-60s added their voices to the roar of M-16s and AK-47s.

*

1st Lieutenant RON ZAPPARDINO
3/26—Forward Air Controller

The next thing I knew, Cowan and the three or four other India Company Marines slammed into me and I was backing down the way I had come, firing my M-16 with one hand and my .45-caliber pistol with the other. John Wayne Zappardino! Every hand was needed, every bullet counted. We were toe-to-toe, punching it out.

2nd Lieutenant BILL COWAN
India Company, 3/26—3rd Platoon Commander

I immediately rushed forward and saw that one of the Marines in the point squad was down. He was about 5 feet in front of everyone else. It was Lance Corporal Howard Chamberlin, the new man who had been shelled every step of the way out to us, including his arrival on the road from C-2. He had not been hit in any of the shellings, but he was shot in the stomach by the first burst of fire that afternoon.

As Chamberlin had fallen, everyone else had pulled back. When I went forward, they were all bunched up in a small group. I told them to spread out some and, as I did, a Chicom grenade came flying out of the bushes and landed 5 to 6 feet in front of us. None of us really had time to react. I simply ducked my head so that the bill of my helmet protected my face. The grenade exploded and only one Marine received a shrapnel wound—it was minor, in the top part of his chest. After the grenade went off, Sergeant Richard Hamilton, my platoon sergeant, moved up and joined us.

1st Lieutenant RON ZAPPARDINO
3/26—Forward Air Controller

We were all bunched up, in the worst possible spot: in the trough between the two hills. They were over our heads and the only way for us to go was back up the face of the hill at our backs. The guys behind us were still trying to get forward. I don't think they realized yet that we had run into something. In no time, there were about 15 people all bunched together, unable to keep backing up, in the worst place imaginable.

2nd Lieutenant BILL COWAN
India Company, 3/26—3rd Platoon Commander

It seemed like everyone in the platoon was right there looking at me, as if to say, "What do we do now, Lieutenant?" That was the one question the instructors at The Basic School had asked over and over and over again: "What do we do now, Lieutenant?"

I ordered the lead squad to spread out and prepare to assault. Everybody immediately fell back and we got the lead squad up on line. As they moved, we took another burst of fire, which wounded another one of my Marines. We were getting hit from only one position, so we put all our fire on it. Concurrently, my radioman reported that the AO was over us and that he was reporting a lot of movement in front of us, on the objective. The AO knew more about what was happening than I did.

Sergeant Hamilton was still getting the men ready to assault the enemy position when we started receiving very heavy AK-47 fire. Our point, who had fallen back on the platoon when the shooting started, was hit in the arm.

Lance Corporal Matthew Guilfoyle—everyone called him Gunny Guilfoyle because he looked like he should have been a gunny—fired his M-79 up in the air like a mortar, so the rounds would fall only 15 to 20 meters away. I had never thought about doing something like that, nor even heard of someone doing that. But Guilfoyle was doing it, very effectively. He later told me he did it that way because the brush was too thick to fire directly into and also to confuse the enemy into thinking we had locked onto them with mortars.

I had no idea if we had inflicted any casualties on the bad guys. We had done a lot of shooting up there, but I never saw any of them. They were in the bushes the whole time, in spider holes, I'm sure.

Captain MATT CAULFIELD
India Company, 3/26—Commanding Officer

I thought we had only 15 enemy to deal with. I intended to maneuver another platoon around to the left.

Major CARL MUNDY
3/26—Operations Officer

I got on the radio with Captain Caulfield, who at this point had been in command of India Company for only two days. I asked him what he was receiving. He was not certain. He estimated initially that he was facing a small, perhaps squad-size, unit. But then, as I stood there listening, I could hear the staccato of firing pick up steadily. More weapons were being brought to bear.

Captain ANDY DeBONA
Mike Company, 3/26—Commanding Officer

India-Six came up on the radio and said he estimated that he had run into a squad of bad guys. He said he was going to attempt to find them. About this same time, in the crescendo of firing, I recognized the sound of a few .51-cals that were firing. A squad of bad guys didn't have .51-cals.

Captain DICK CAMP
Lima Company, 3/26—Commanding Officer

I grabbed the radio handset from my battalion radioman and called India-Six: "Let me fire—let me seal off your flank. I can see your flanks. Let me take my machine guns and fire along your flank." To which Caulfield replied, "They're coming in on me, they're coming in on me!"

Captain MATT CAULFIELD
India Company, 3/26—Commanding Officer

Lima-Six came up on the radio: "If you mark the extreme left of that platoon, I can support you with fire." We marked the flank.

Captain DICK CAMP
Lima Company, 3/26—Commanding Officer

I grabbed one of the M-60 gunners and pointed toward India Company. He and his assistant got the message, flopped down on the ground, and prepared to open fire. When I looked up, all the M-60s in Lima Company were being readied to support India by fire. In less time than it takes to tell it, my M-60s were firing along India's flank.

Lance Corporal MIKE HEFFLIN
Lima Company, 3/26, 2nd Platoon

The two M-60s that were on the left face of Lima's hill opened fire at something to our left front, around the side of the hill to our left.

Captain MATT CAULFIELD
India Company, 3/26—Commanding Officer

The firing became so heavy it was impossible to distinguish between ours and the enemy's. However, we had no .50-caliber machine guns, and I could hear two firing.

Captain DICK CAMP
Lima Company, 3/26—Commanding Officer

I thought we were doing okay, but India-Six came up on the net: "Lima-Six, cease firing. I can't tell whose fire is whose." My M-60s instantly shut off. The worst thing in the world is to shoot fellow Marines.

I called Battalion and said, "Lookit, give me your tanks, give me your tanks, and I'll go up on the flank to try to take some of the pressure off India." Carl Mundy came up on the net and replied, "Yes, we'll send them up."

1st Lieutenant BOB STIMSON
India Company, 3/26—Executive Officer

Battalion told us that we would be attacking the hill with two companies abreast, us and Lima. We were to hold where we were until Lima arrived from over the hill to our rear. The line of departure for the two-company attack was the line held by the bulk of Bill Cowan's 3rd Platoon—that is, the bottom of the draw facing the NVA-held hill.

Captain ANDY DeBONA
Mike Company, 3/26—Commanding Officer

The rearguard of India Company finally passed through Mike. I told my platoon commanders to prepare to move out behind India. Then I reported to Battalion that India's rearguard had cleared our position and that I was getting ready to move out. Battalion told me to hold fast. I passed the word via my radio operator and the platoon radio operators for my platoons to hold fast. I heard on the battalion tac net that Lima was moving up to support India. I asked Battalion if they wanted me to move up, too, but they told me again to stand fast.

*

1st Lieutenant BOB STIMSON
India Company, 3/26—Executive Officer

While Lima was getting ready to move up abreast of us, Captain Caulfield was issuing orders down through our company chain of command, to the platoon commanders and, from them, down to the squads and fire teams. At the same time, we were beginning to try to acquire the means to run some tactical air down on the NVA-held hill.

Captain MATT CAULFIELD
India Company, 3/26—Commanding Officer

Friends at Amphibious Warfare School had told me never to move unless the FAC and the FO were no more than 15 meters away. It was good advice. I turned to the FAC and asked, "Lieutenant, where is the air?" He replied, "It's on the way." I interpreted "on the way" as "commencing a run."

I was screaming for air and artillery. I must have asked the FAC a hundred times, "Where in the hell is the air?" He kept saying, "It's on the way."

We had artillery, but, as the FO and AO were adjusting it, the FO told me, "A check fire is in effect because of air." I almost hit him with a rifle. But it was true. Some idiot had checked fire because the AO was in the area.

1st Lieutenant BOB STIMSON
India Company, 3/26—Executive Officer

Ron Zappardino was different from all the other air liaison officers and forward air controllers who had served with 3/26. He fit right in, like one of the boys. He never winced. Most aviators just wanted to fly, but Zap was always out there with us. He was a very colorful fellow— very funny and irreverent. And very competent.

1st Lieutenant RON ZAPPARDINO
3/26—Forward Air Controller

I had gotten right on the radio to try to find some air support. I couldn't believe it when, in the middle of all that chaos, Captain Caulfield was screaming in my ear, "Why don't we have air? Hurry up and get air." I just turned and looked at him. It was incredible that he would think we had air right on station. I started to laugh. I couldn't believe he would say that! I'd known him for only five minutes, and my first impression was that he was kind of pudgy—a new guy, fresh from the States, with no physical conditioning. That and his unreasonable expectation that we had air hovering overhead, *waiting* for something like this to happen, caused my confidence in him—the benefit of the doubt—to disappear immediately, completely.

1st Lieutenant BOB STIMSON
India Company, 3/26—Executive Officer

I thought that Captain Caulfield's demand for *immediate* air support was pretty humorous, but he was new; he didn't know what to expect. Zappardino, myself, and others who had been there always figured, as a rule of thumb, that we could depend on at least 30 minutes to get air. We had to assume that it was going to come from Danang and that it would take some real scrambling to be on station in as little as 30 minutes, if nothing went wrong.

1st Lieutenant RON ZAPPARDINO
3/26—Forward Air Controller

I was about to yell, "I don't have any air up here. Are you crazy? This doesn't happen!" But it *was* there; I had air coming on station in just 90 seconds—not the usual half-hour minimum. Of course, Captain Caulfield thought that was normal; it was the way he had been taught it was supposed to be, and he was too inexperienced to know it *never* worked that way—except this once. Air in 90 seconds! I couldn't believe it!

1st Lieutenant BOB STIMSON
India Company, 3/26—Executive Officer

Things seemed to be going reasonably well. The air was there in record time, and Zappardino was already setting up the first runs on the objective.

Lance Corporal CHUCK BENNETT
India Company, 3/26, 1st Platoon

India-1 was near the rear of the company. We were on flat ground when the shooting started. We advanced directly toward the sound of the firing to lend the lead platoons our support. As we were working forward, the jets came over.

2nd Lieutenant BILL COWAN
India Company, 3/26—3rd Platoon Commander

The fixed wing started rolling in on the positions with which we were in contact.

1st Lieutenant BOB STIMSON
India Company, 3/26—Executive Officer

Rather than coming in down the long axis of the objective, for reasons of cloud cover the jets had to come in from right behind us, perpendicular to the objective.

1st Lieutenant RON ZAPPARDINO
3/26—Forward Air Controller

The first flights were F-4s. They had 250-pound bombs aboard. The pilots said they could see the engagement because there were so many troops moving around. When the first guy rolled in, he dropped everything he had. I don't know how many bombs he had. After that, the air guys took care of it themselves. They told me they could see what was going on so clearly that they didn't need me. I knew we were in serious trouble, and they did, too. I told them to do what they thought they had to do to help get us out of there. It was wild. I wanted them to drop anything they had, just to show the bad guys we could get them. I wanted the NVA to balk so we could get back up the hill to our rear.

As the first F-4 pulled out, he drew fire from NVA .51-caliber heavy antiaircraft machine guns. The second F-4 pilot decided to go hit them.

As he came in at a 60-degree angle, the world opened up on him. I never saw a pilot pull back on the stick so hard. He went from a 60-degree down position to almost a 60-degree up position. He must have popped every rivet in the aircraft and pulled 20 Gs, but he would have been dead if he had continued his dive.

Captain DICK CAMP
Lima Company, 3/26—Commanding Officer

For some reason, the jets were all coming in the wrong way. Usually, they run parallel to the front lines so, if they're short or long, it doesn't make any difference. In this case, they were being called perpendicular to—right over—India's hill. The F-4s were trying to snap into their runs, into their final heading, just off our hill.

2nd Lieutenant BILL COWAN
India Company, 3/26—3rd Platoon Commander

I started getting a bad feeling, thinking that they better keep their eyes on the enemy-held hill and not on the one to our rear. Just as I said—aloud, I think—"God, I hope they're paying attention up there," I looked up and saw an F-4 going through a little cloud, coming right at us. It was like the Keystone Kops. All the guys on top of the hill were running off in every direction as fast as they could.

Captain DICK CAMP
Lima Company, 3/26—Commanding Officer

I looked up in time to see one F-4 just as he snapped out to make his final run-in through a little cloud. I could see him wiggle a little to get through the cloud, a move that set him up on the wrong hill. I could see that he was going to drop short. He pickled three or four bombs right between India Company and my company. Long before the bombs hit, I screamed, "Get down, get down! He's bombing wrong!" There were assholes and elbows everywhere as everybody ran to get under cover.

The concussion from the bombs rolled over us in huge overlapping waves, but nobody was hurt. I went right up on the tac-air net, yelling, "Goddammit, he's bringing them in the wrong way, he's bringing them in the wrong way."

1st Lieutenant BOB STIMSON
India Company, 3/26—Executive Officer

When that ordnance let go, I was standing there with Zappardino. I saw that the bombs were going to land right on top of the hill behind us, right in the middle of the 2nd Platoon. Why the company wasn't wiped out has to do with a miracle. In fact, nobody was hurt.

Lance Corporal CHUCK BENNETT
India Company, 3/26, 1st Platoon

We were cheering the jets until they dropped their bombs right in front of my platoon. I heard someone on the radio yelling at someone else to tell the pilots they were dropping short.

2nd Lieutenant BILL COWAN
India Company, 3/26—3rd Platoon Commander

That F-4 dropped six to eight bombs right smack on top of our hill. There were tremendous explosions and all the Keystone Kops ran back to the top of the hill. The AO started screaming at the pilot: "You stupid son of a bitch. You dropped those bombs on Marines." I couldn't blame the pilot. There wasn't 100 meters between the hills. And when he rolled out of that cloud, he didn't have time to figure out which hill he was bombing. It was an honest error, and it wasn't bad. We had one guy hurt by the concussion, but what that aircraft really did was set us up some nice fighting holes on top of the hill.

The air strike stopped the NVA who were after us, and things seemed to quiet down.

1st Lieutenant BOB STIMSON
India Company, 3/26—Executive Officer

It was a sharp encounter, and then it ended. Those of us in the draw had not taken any fire; just the squad in front of the 3rd Platoon had.

I wasn't crazy about being in that draw. But, by the same token, the AO, who had a pretty good look, said there was only a squad up on the hill facing us.

As the bombs fell in behind us, I saw 10 to 15 troops coming off the hill in front of us, at eleven o'clock from our route of march. They were wearing Marine helmets and flak jackets. I thought to myself, "Oh my God, part of the point squad was still up there during the air strikes!'' My first reaction was that it was great so many were still alive. Almost immediately, as they continued to move our way, I looked closer and saw that they weren't Americans. I noticed that the helmets looked very big on their heads and the flak jackets looked very big on their bodies. I could tell they weren't Americans. They were North Vietnamese!

The engagement resumed when the NVA wearing Marine gear opened fire on us.

I don't know what Captain Caulfield was thinking, but it certainly was very clear to me that we had to get the hell out of that draw. There was likely more NVA on the hill in front of us than a squad. Just as the captain started to order a withdrawal, I said to him, ''We better get the hell out of here.''

Captain ANDY DeBONA
Mike Company, 3/26—Commanding Officer

At about 1515, India-Six came back up on the battalion net and reported that he was falling back to a defensive position because there were too many bad guys out there.

1st Lieutenant BOB STIMSON
India Company, 3/26—Executive Officer

The company CP group were the first people in the draw to start back up the face of the hill to our rear. Marines over our heads—behind us—were firing at the NVA-held hill, covering our withdrawal.

Things were happening very quickly. Heavy rifle and machine-gun fire was flying, and I knew we were under very heavy pressure—under attack—from the North Vietnamese. The withdrawal up that hill was not picture-perfect; it was much less than orderly, to say the least. There was a lot of confusion in our ranks.

2nd Lieutenant BILL COWAN
India Company, 3/26—3rd Platoon Commander

A draftee in my platoon, Lance Corporal Lee Pate, stayed behind and covered everybody while we pulled up the hill. Pate was the last in line, firing as we withdrew. We were carrying Lance Corporal Chamberlin, who was hurting bad, yelling, in real pain. He was crying for water, but the doc wouldn't let him have any because of his stomach wound.

The guy with the arm wound was being escorted. Behind me were only three people—Lance Corporal Guilfoyle, Sergeant Hamilton, and Lance Corporal Pate. We were not taking any fire then, but Pate kept firing back at the enemy, firing quite a bit.

As we made our way back along the tank trail, I heard the AO say on the radio, "There's people following you."

We pulled back across the draw and on up the next hill to wait for the rest of the battalion to join us. As we were moving, Zappardino was still calling in jet strikes. He ran three or four planes on the hill on which we had been in contact.

Chapter 14

2nd Lieutenant PAUL DRNEC
Bravo Company, 3rd Tank Battalion—2nd Platoon Commander

While we were stopped in front of the battalion position with Mike Company, my tank, B-22, had a track separation, which forced us to stop to prevent further damage. The two other tanks—B-25 and the flame tank, F-23—continued to move up the column to deliver C-rations and ammunition to Lima Company. My crew was out on the ground, getting ready to replace the separated track, which the platoon mechanic said would be a lengthy operation. Rather than holding up the whole battalion's movement, I decided to have the other two tanks pull back to my position and tow B-22 to the new defense perimeter so the repairs could be made there.

Captain ANDY DeBONA
Mike Company, 3/26—Commanding Officer

When Battalion granted Lima-Six permission to join India Company, I dispatched my tanks over to Lima Company, with the exception of the one that was on the point with Mike-2's point. It wouldn't move. The thing had broken down.

2nd Lieutenant PAUL DRNEC
Bravo Company, 3rd Tank Battalion—2nd Platoon Commander

On request of the Lima Company commander, I ordered the two operable tanks to engage the enemy under his direction.

188

Captain DICK CAMP
Lima Company, 3/26—Commanding Officer

Medevacs were on the way to pick up the two wounded Marines, and a gun tank and a flame tank were on the way out from the battalion main body to support Lima Company's advance to link up with India.

I got the company up so we would be ready—rarin'—to go by the time the two tanks showed. In fact, we jumped the gun a little and began an early move down to the nearest rice paddy to link up with the tanks.

By the time the lead platoons were forming up at the bottom of our hill, the bombing had pretty much abated and the sound of firing from India's hill was merely a dull roar.

Captain ANDY DeBONA
Mike Company, 3/26—Commanding Officer

At the time Lima was moving out, there was still heavy firing to my left front, from around the India Company point.

*

1st Lieutenant BOB STIMSON
India Company, 3/26—Executive Officer

The top of the hill we occupied was longer than it was wide—about 25 meters at its maximum width and maybe 40 meters along its long axis. There was a distinct high point on top, and there were some big rocks up there.

Following our withdrawal up the hill from the draw, the men went too far back up the hill. I didn't know what Captain Caulfield was thinking or doing then, but I was afraid the men wouldn't know when to stop, that they didn't know how far we meant for them to withdraw. I was afraid they were going to run right back over that hill. As soon as I got out of the draw, I tried to stop the men. I booted a few of them in the seat of their pants to get them forward, but I thought right away I could have done the job without going to that extreme. I can't fault them; it wasn't clear what we wanted them to do. Anyway, I started grabbing men, turning them around, facing them toward the enemy.

1st Lieutenant RON ZAPPARDINO
3/26—Forward Air Controller

Some of the young Marines broke. They just broke. Bob Stimson was on them right away, shaking the shit out of them, grabbing them, throwing them around. While the rest of us just stood there and watched, Stimson got one kid by the shirt collar and almost shook his skin off his bones. Bob was a good leader, but very mild mannered. I couldn't believe how strongly he reacted. Boom, Stimson straightened their heads right out. When he was done, he talked to me for a minute, very calmly.

1st Lieutenant BOB STIMSON
India Company, 3/26—Executive Officer

I was doing anything I could to get that line stabilized along the forward brow of that hill, where we would have good fields of fire on the attacking NVA and on the hill they were coming from.

*

Captain DICK CAMP
Lima Company, 3/26—Commanding Officer

An H-34 helo passed us like a bat out of hell, coming in low and fast. It disappeared from view for a few moments, then roared back the way it had come, well below the tops of the hills. I presume it had picked up India's casualties.

2nd Lieutenant BILL COWAN
India Company, 3/26—3rd Platoon Commander

We got our people evacuated and set up our perimeter on the hill. Unfortunately, Lance Corporal Howard Chamberlin, who had been shot in the stomach during the initial encounter, later died.

My platoon started out being on the forward—northwest—edge of the hill, where we had pulled back to after our firefight. For whatever reason, Captain Caulfield wanted us to shift our people around a little bit. My people shifted around to the east. India Company's half of the perimeter ran on the north side, from 270 degrees right to 90 degrees. I had been over on the northwest quadrant, but the captain had us move to the northeast quadrant. That put us facing back more or less toward the battalion main body, which was to our right. I could see the paddyfields off to my left front. We were a little higher than the rice paddies, but not much. The only thing that obscured our vistas was shrubbery.

*

Captain DICK CAMP
Lima Company, 3/26—Commanding Officer

As the medevac helo passed us again—at about 1545—Gunnery Sergeant Juan Almanza's 3rd Platoon was leading Lima Company along the southern edge of the big paddyfield on the valley floor. The troops were alert to danger, but their brains were still a little fried; they were missing a few of the finer points I had tried to drive home during the past two months. They were slow getting organized, slow spreading out, and slow deploying flankers. Really, all attention was in the direction of India's hill, from which the sounds of battle emanated.

Almanza's platoon crossed an overgrown rice paddy, then another, then mounted the eastern end of India's hill. I radioed India-Six to let him know that we were starting to come up on his flank, and his radioman acknowledged.

2nd Lieutenant JOHN PRINCE
Lima Company, 3/26—2nd Platoon Commander

We got the order to go ahead and move out. We got in line. My platoon was on the right flank.

Lance Corporal MIKE HEFFLIN
Lima Company, 3/26, 2nd Platoon

We saw two tanks come flying by across our front, from our right to our left.

Captain DICK CAMP
Lima Company, 3/26—Commanding Officer

I looked back at our former position and saw that my rearguard—Prince's 2nd Platoon—had started down off the top. Just as I was about to redirect my gaze forward, the whole ridgeline that we had been sitting on disappeared under towering detonations—140mm rockets. The whole hill was being dusted off.

2nd Lieutenant JOHN PRINCE
Lima Company, 3/26—2nd Platoon Commander

As we started moving up, as we moved off our hill into the rice paddy, we got rocketed. I lay right down in a tank track—an impression in the ground one of the tanks had just made. The tank track was probably an inch deep, but I had an advantage: I was an inch lower than everybody else. I was feeling pretty good at that one second.

*

Lance Corporal MIKE HEFFLIN
Lima Company, 3/26, 2nd Platoon

Our squad and two M-60 machine guns were on the left side of Lima Company's hill, overlooking the rice paddies. We were the company rearguard. After all the rest of Lima Company passed behind us, across the gully to our left, the first volley of rockets fell in on the 3rd Squad. Frank Garcia and I told everyone to take cover, and we all ducked down in the Vietnamese graves up there.

Corporal FRANK GARCIA
Lima Company, 3/26—2nd Platoon Squad Leader

When the rockets started hitting, four of us jumped into a circular grave that had a mound in the center. It was me, Lance Corporal Mike Hefflin, Corporal Jack Sims, and Lance Corporal Chuck Holland. We were all hunkered down when a rocket hit right in the center, right on the mound.

Lance Corporal MIKE HEFFLIN
Lima Company, 3/26, 2nd Platoon

A rocket from the second volley hit the rim of the grave and collapsed the mound. If it had hit 2 to 3 feet over, Frank and me would have bought the farm. It hit so damn close to us, my ears were buzzing for quite a while.

Corporal FRANK GARCIA
Lima Company, 3/26—2nd Platoon Squad Leader

I felt I went unconscious; it was dark. I pushed up and there was a lot of dirt and pressure on my back.

Lance Corporal MIKE HEFFLIN
Lima Company, 3/26, 2nd Platoon

The blast flipped me over onto my back. I didn't feel a thing; I was just numb from the waist down.

Corporal FRANK GARCIA
Lima Company, 3/26—2nd Platoon Squad Leader

I started checking on everyone else and crawled over to Hefflin. He smiled and said, "I'm hit."

Lance Corporal MIKE HEFFLIN
Lima Company, 3/26, 2nd Platoon

I looked up and saw Frank looking down at me. I said, "Something's wrong. I'm going home."

Corporal FRANK GARCIA
Lima Company, 3/26—2nd Platoon Squad Leader

He was happy; he knew he was going home. "I got one," he said. He was still smiling. He didn't think it was a bad wound.

Lance Corporal MIKE HEFFLIN
Lima Company, 3/26, 2nd Platoon

I looked down and saw a steel sliver 10 to 12 inches long stuck through my right foot. I didn't feel anything, so I didn't really think about what I was seeing. My trousers were all shredded to shit.

Corporal FRANK GARCIA
Lima Company, 3/26—2nd Platoon Squad Leader

The fragment had screwed up his foot. He felt good; he was high, he was happy. Of the four of us, he was the only one who got hurt.

Lance Corporal MIKE HEFFLIN
Lima Company, 3/26, 2nd Platoon

Frank cut my right boot off and yanked my left boot off and he and Lance Corporal Tom Hawkins, my boot-camp buddy, put a pressure bandage on the wound in my right foot. They pulled off my pack and the bag with all my M-79 rounds. I kept my .45 and pistol belt, but that was it; everything else had gone flying or was taken from me. My shirt was gone, too, but I still had my trousers on.

Corporal FRANK GARCIA
Lima Company, 3/26—2nd Platoon Squad Leader

Holland helped Hefflin. Sims had a radio. I grabbed Hefflin's pack and covered the others while they started up the hill.

Lance Corporal MIKE HEFFLIN
Lima Company, 3/26, 2nd Platoon

Lieutenant Prince came running up from the gully and said, "Hef, you been hit?" I said, "Hell, yeah." He reached down, picked me up, and threw me over his shoulder. I felt something cold running down my leg and grabbed my nuts to make sure I was all there. I was, so I reached back with my left hand and pulled it back to see. It was covered with blood. That's when Frank Garcia said, "Aw shit! You been hit!" I looked at the blood again and said, "Yeah, but how bad?" The shrapnel had cut off the left cheek of my ass—had cut the meat right off. Frank and Hawkins pulled my trousers off and put a pressure bandage on, and Lieutenant Prince carried me down into the gully and up the next ridge, to where Lima Company had a perimeter thrown up.

Corporal FRANK GARCIA
Lima Company, 3/26—2nd Platoon Squad Leader

As I started walking up the hill behind them, one of the sergeants—it might have been Peck—stopped me and asked if anyone was carrying Hefflin's M-79. I said, "I didn't see anybody pick it up," so the sergeant told me to go back and get it. We were still getting blasted. I handed Hefflin's pack to somebody and went back down to the grave mound to get Hefflin's 79 and the ammo. Hefflin had dropped everything down there—his pack and all his stuff—but nobody thought to pick up the 79 and the ammo. I picked it up and ran after everyone.

*

Captain DICK CAMP
Lima Company, 3/26—Commanding Officer

As the rockets were detonating, we went into overdrive, right up the hill toward India Company. I couldn't have held the troops back if I had wanted to; no one wanted to be caught in the open by a barrage for the second time in 48 hours. As I humped up the hill just ahead of Sergeant Wendell Mullins's 1st Platoon, Gunny Almanza's 3rd Platoon halted at the top. I had no idea why Almanza stopped, but it was easier to keep going than to try to call him on the company net. All of a sudden, as I neared the top of the hill, I found myself in an old Marine position. That's why the gunny had stopped. There was more than enough cover for the whole company, plenty of holes in which to weather the rocket barrage. As I checked the place out, I found what had obviously served as the company CP.

Almanza's 3rd Platoon was all secure, completely emplaced on the southwest end of the hill. A platoon of India Company was to Almanza's right, just on the other side of a bunch of big boulders, but out of sight. About half of Mullins's 1st Platoon Marines had already reached the crest, and they were going into position on Almanza's left flank without even having to be told. Prince's 2nd Platoon was coming up on Mullins's left. On its left, Prince's platoon was tying back into India's right flank.

2nd Lieutenant JOHN PRINCE
Lima Company, 3/26—2nd Platoon Commander

My platoon was on line. We made contact with India Company up there and started taking small-arms fire.

India Company was basically ahead and on our left. On our right was a rice paddy. We just moved up the hill on line, leaving the right flank exposed because we had visual coverage of it.

Corporal FRANK GARCIA
Lima Company, 3/26—2nd Platoon Squad Leader

By the time I was moving up to the company position on top of the hill, there was a line being set up. The men were spread out, dispersed over a lot of ground. I couldn't see many Marines; most of them were in the bushes or down in the grass. I looked for my squad, but I couldn't find it. The first of my guys I ran into was badly shaken; he was vibrating right off the ground. Another guy and I held him down until he cooled off. Then I started moving along the line to find the rest of my squad, which must have been the last one up the hill. I might have been the very last Marine to get up the hill.

*

2nd Lieutenant BILL COWAN
India Company, 3/26—3rd Platoon Commander

I saw a squad of what looked to be Marines. They were crossing one of the paddies below us. They looked exactly like Marines. The only thing that caught my attention was that they were short and taking choppy steps. Other than that, looking at them at a quick glance, they could have been Marines, but they were in fact NVA wearing our helmets and flak jackets.

2nd Lieutenant JOHN PRINCE
Lima Company, 3/26—2nd Platoon Commander

I knelt down to look around, to try to find out what the hell was going on. As I did, I saw a group of men jogging or double-timing probably 30 yards in front of my platoon's line. They were dressed in green uniforms, so I thought they were Marines. I was wondering, "What in the hell are Marines doing out there?" Then I noticed that they had clean clothes on, so I figured they couldn't be Marines.

The leader of those jogging people was moving across my front. I was in a kneeling position. I fired one round into his chest area as he trotted behind a bush. Then I did the same to the second man as he went behind the bush. I fired at four men and then my M-16 jammed. I got down, out of sight, so if they realized someone was shooting at them, they wouldn't spot me. I called for an M-60 machine-gun team to move up, in the general direction those people were moving. As soon as the gunners got up there, a hand grenade hit them. One of the gunners got shot and the other guy got wounded by the hand grenade.

I moved up to see what was going on with the M-60 team and something landed on the ground about 10 feet away from me. It exploded. My mind was moving a million miles an hour. I could see the piece of shrapnel heading directly toward my right eye. As fast as I could, I hit the ground.

I looked down at my rifle and there was blood streaming down the barrel. The rifle barrel was so hot the drops of blood boiled away as they fell on it. I put my hand up against the side of my head. My head was numb to the touch; I couldn't feel my hand as it touched my head. I turned to the Marine next to me and asked, "Do I still have an ear?" He looked at me a little funny and said, "Yes, Lieutenant." I was embarrassed. Here I was, worrying about myself when I had a job to do. I quickly forgot about my ear and got down to business.

I noticed that I was soaking wet. I was perspiring so heavily, it was as if I'd just come through a torrential storm.

Corporal FRANK GARCIA
Lima Company, 3/26—2nd Platoon Squad Leader

I saw the NVA—just a lot of green uniforms—charging right at me. I started shooting. I saw them going down and then I couldn't see them anymore.

My rifle jammed.

Chapter 15

No one who was there *really* believes so much time passed between milestone events. It all seemed to have been a continuous ordeal compressed into only a few minutes. However, only a few weeks after the battle, Lieutenant Bill Cowan painstakingly reconstructed the time line so he could write the official after-action report. Cowan's research in late September 1967 indicated that the NVA rockets fell in on Lima-2's rearguard at 1555. At 1630, Cowan and others saw NVA soldiers dressed in Marine helmets and flak jackets. Those NVA and others applied unremitting but not overwhelming pressure on the portions of India and Lima companies that were facing north, across the large paddyfield, until 1655. Then, according to Cowan's research, the next milestone event occurred.

Captain DICK CAMP
Lima Company, 3/26—Commanding Officer

Sergeant Albert Peck, who had smelled NVA while he was leading the water detail, later told me he was right behind John Prince when he happened to turn around in time to see something really awesome. In Peck's words, "The rice paddy stood up." Just so. As Peck looked on, at least a company of NVA—and most likely one of their little 250-man battalions—stood up in unison from hiding places in one of the rice paddies. The NVA launched an immediate running assault down the valley toward the 3/26 main battalion position, at the base of the valley. At that very instant, many NVA on the heights and in other rice paddies opened up on the various parts of Lima Company with a renewed gunfire assault.

Captain MATT CAULFIELD
India Company, 3/26—Commanding Officer

A young corporal jumped up, pointed, and screamed, "God, the whole mountain is coming." I ran to his position. Two columns of the enemy—between 200 and 400 of them—started on a direct diagonal toward us.

1st Lieutenant RON ZAPPARDINO
3/26—Forward Air Controller

I glanced over toward the rice paddies there. I saw the NVA in lines—in waves. There had to be a thousand men out there, a regiment. They had the battalion split. They were coming right toward us. They had us by the balls.

1st Lieutenant BOB STIMSON
India Company, 3/26—Executive Officer

At the moment I felt we were getting our line stabilized, it became clear to me that there were a *hell* of a lot of North Vietnamese in the open rice paddies to our immediate north. I could see them all over, in front of us and off our right front—from about my eleven o'clock around to my two o'clock. That arc became greater in size—from two o'clock to three, and on to four—as I watched it advance across the rice paddies below our hill. We were being engaged by this huge force to our right as well as by the NVA attacking our hill from the draw from which we had just withdrawn. We got fire on both NVA forces, especially the one in the open.

Captain MATT CAULFIELD
India Company, 3/26—Commanding Officer

I had perfect fields of fire; they were in an open rice field. It reminded me of bears in a shooting gallery. The only problem was that as soon as we shot one, two more seemed to take his place.

1st Lieutenant RON ZAPPARDINO
3/26—Forward Air Controller

Captain Caulfield rebounded quickly from the bad first impression he had made on me. Helicopter gunship pilots are used to chaos. In the air, in combat, we keep four radios going at once *and* fly the bird.

We're more used to too much going on at once than the average grunt officer. Most grunts are lost if they have two radios going at once. But Caulfield was right on top of that day's chaos. He knew just what he wanted and he said exactly what he had to say to get it done. He just took that company over and made it run the way he wanted it to run. Just like that. Of course, typical of every infantry fight I ever saw or experienced, radio discipline went straight to hell right away. Everyone with a radio was yelling into it. Even then, Caulfield was able to exert control. He was right next to me, so I could see that he got agitated a little, but he was able to control it, to keep his temper in check. He *looked* cool and collected, which was important right then. Everyone was bunched up at first, so he was able to get them spread out without the radios. Then he worked at getting fire suppression down. He put all the pieces together—quickly. Whether he did exactly the right thing or not didn't matter. He *appeared* to be in control, and that's what mattered just then. It all came together for him, and that got transmitted to everyone who was watching to see how the new captain was going to act. It was very impressive.

While Caulfield was winning the hearts and minds of India Company, he and I—everyone—were learning to dig with our teeth. I was firing my M-16 with my right hand at the same time I was scraping a fighting hole with my left hand. I was on the radio, too.

1st Lieutenant BOB STIMSON
India Company, 3/26—Executive Officer

We were taking small-arms fire from a 180-degree arc and indirect fire—mortars—fell on us as well. The NVA had automatic weapons up on the hill to our northwest, farther along the hill we had tried to take. Those automatic weapons were working as a base of fire for the NVA infantry that was attacking our hill. The two hills were about the same height, so they didn't overlook us, but the base of fire there provided powerful support.

*

Lance Corporal CHUCK BENNETT
India Company, 3/26, 1st Platoon

The NVA were attacking right at us in human waves. A lot of the new replacements got it then. They didn't know what to do. They froze.

They took too long getting under cover and they got it. Some hadn't been in-country more than a few days. They had no time to learn. They got in-country and ran straight into a big battle—the biggest battle I had seen in my six months in-country. It was just bad luck and lack of experience that killed so many of them.

One of the new men who was hit was my new squad leader, Sergeant Bruce Huntington. He was wounded in a big blast—peppered with shrapnel. I think it might have been a mortar round. I was his radioman, so I was right there with him. I got a little piece of shrapnel in the hand, but it was nothing. The thing that saved me was I had the radio up in front of me, and it took the blast. The shrapnel got Huntington in the face. He wasn't hit bad, but it must have hurt like hell and his face was bleeding real bad. He panicked. It was his first battle and he was scared. I ducked down, but he was still standing up. I yelled, "Get down, Sarge!" He did, and I tried to get him calmed down. Then I helped him back up the hill, to where I hoped I might find a corpsman. We crossed a little mound and ran right into Captain Caulfield. It was the first time I'd ever seen him. Lieutenant Stimson was there, too. And a radioman.

Caulfield asked me who I was with; he wanted to know if I was in India Company, or what. I told him I was from India and he asked, "What squad?" I told him, "Third Squad, First Platoon, sir." Then I said, "I'm a radioman, sir. My sergeant got hit. I'm trying to find the aid station." The captain was in control. His calm got me calmed down. Bullets started hitting around us, so I got down and pulled Sergeant Huntington down. He was still out of it. I left him with the skipper and headed back to the line.

When I got back from delivering Sergeant Huntington to the company CP, there were hundreds and hundreds of NVA coming toward us. I couldn't believe it! They were right out in the open, so we all opened up on them. I couldn't believe they were doing it out in the open. I couldn't figure out where they were all coming from. I couldn't figure out what we were getting ourselves into. I was just spraying them with my M-16. I was on semi-automatic and I was spraying. There were too many to aim at. There was just one big target out there. I knew I hit some; at least, I saw them go down. But everyone around me was firing, too, so maybe more than one of us hit those NVA. We were getting hit, too, with all kinds of stuff.

They were kind of jogging, firing from the hip, and yelling, all at the same time. Some hit the deck and fired from the prone position while others kept coming at us. I thought they were stoned.

I saw one guy running right at me. He had an RPG. He was dressed like all the other NVA, but he looked a lot bigger. I thought he might have been a Chinese advisor. We heard they were out there. He was yelling and running in my general direction. He was only 20 to 30 feet away. I didn't want to get hit by an RPG, so I put everything I had into him. I aimed for his chest—the biggest part of his body—and fired off a couple of rounds. I saw one or two tracer rounds go into that sucker's chest, but he kept coming. The bullets knocked him back for a second, but then he kept coming. I'd put about a half dozen rounds into him! I kept firing and he finally went down. I'm sure he was on dope. He sure wasn't acting right.

Corporal FRANK GARCIA
Lima Company, 3/26—2nd Platoon Squad Leader

The part that scared me the most was hearing American voices in front of me. They were coming from in front of the main line. I wanted to find them and bring them back, but I couldn't see them in the knee-high grass. The way they were yelling, I was sure they were wounded. I wasn't sure where they were. I was sure that most of them were from my squad.

I kept yelling at the guys in the grass in front of me to pull back. They were too close to the enemy. Lieutenant Prince told me to move them back, so I went forward and got a couple of guys to move back. Lance Corporal Chuck Holland was one. He was with a young new guy who had been hit in the arm. The new guy was crying, begging me to carry him. I got him around his uninjured shoulder and kind of dragged him. We had to keep low because there was lots of gunfire going by overhead. I told him he had to help me because I couldn't stand up and carry him right. I got him back up to the main line.

Corporal Jack Sims also pulled back from in front of the main line, and I gave him Hefflin's M-79 in return for his rifle. Sims fired the 79 right out in front of us, which worried me because I was sure there were still wounded Marines out there, hiding in the grass. I told Sims, "Be careful. Make sure you're hitting gooks." It was very confusing.

Sims's rifle jammed as soon as I started firing it, so I crawled back to the aid station, which was in a deep bomb crater, and asked the wounded guys for a gun that worked. They threw an M-60 at me! Good enough! To me, it was the greatest weapon I could have gotten. They threw up plenty of ammo, too.

Lance Corporal MIKE HEFFLIN
Lima Company, 3/26, 2nd Platoon

There were lots of guys laying down there, firing at the enemy coming across the rice paddies.

I was completely naked except for my pistol belt, but I still had my .45. When I saw all those NVA, I thought, "Aw shit, what am I going to do with only a .45?" I was scared shitless. The other guys were firing everything they could. Some guys were running around yelling, "Get the wounded to the crater." I was wounded, so I turned to my left to see if I could find the crater they were talking about.

I got into the crater with the wounded, but I didn't like it there. There was too much shit going on up top, outside the crater. Guys outside the crater were yelling that the enemy was penetrating the company position. I could move around okay even though I had been wounded in the foot and had had a cheek of my ass blown off. I climbed out of the crater and ran down the gully to the right. There were machine guns in the gully, firing in both directions. Our total perimeter wasn't together yet. The machine gunners yelled at me to ask if I knew what the hell was going on. Then someone asked, "What the hell are *you* doing down here?" I wasn't sure, but I knew I didn't want to be up on the hill with the rest of Lima Company. I saw a couple of NVA run through the line on the side of the hill, but the machine guns in the gully picked them off.

Lance Corporal William O'Neill, who had gotten the lobe of his left ear shot off, came and got me. He took me back up to the crater where the wounded were. He got me onto the crater and said, "I'll take care of you, Hef," and stood over me.

I found Corporal Robert Horton, a member of my boot platoon, in the crater. He had gone to India Company when a bunch of us were transferred to 3/26 from 2/9, in the spring. He'd gotten hit in the arm. Horton and I found a pack with an E-tool and dug our own hole on the slope above the crater, not quite to the top of the hill. It was slow going. He could use the shovel only one way because he'd been hit in the arm; I could use it only the other way because of the wound in my ass. He had an M-16 and I had my .45.

The rocket that had wounded me had hit so close that my bells were ringing. It was like a constant buzz in my head. I couldn't shake it out.

*

1st Lieutenant RON ZAPPARDINO
3/26—Forward Air Controller

After I ran the first F-4 passes at the very start of the action, I tried to get comm with any of the many planes I could see overhead. Nothing. I couldn't get through. I pulled my radio off my back to see what was wrong and found that the antenna had been shot off. I grabbed another radio off the India Company TACP [tactical air control party] operator and resumed contact. Right away, I was in radio contact with all the air support I ever thought I'd need.

By the time the company settled down, I had so many flights on call, I had them stacked over the battlefield. The AO was telling me what I had in the stack and some of the flight leaders were telling me what kind of ordnance they had.

2nd Lieutenant BILL COWAN
India Company, 3/26—3rd Platoon Commander

I saw an enemy FO in a little bamboo thicket about 200 meters away from our CP. I knew he was an FO because he was wearing binoculars. The captain called for a napalm strike right into that area.

1st Lieutenant RON ZAPPARDINO
3/26—Forward Air Controller

Captain Caulfield told me he had an NVA artillery FO spotted and asked for napalm. He told me how close he wanted the napalm and I called it in. It was *very* close, but I was able to direct the pilot in just the way I wanted him, so he wouldn't drop on us.

2nd Lieutenant BILL COWAN
India Company, 3/26—3rd Platoon Commander

It was pretty damn close; close enough so I could feel the heat.

*

2nd Lieutenant JOHN PRINCE
Lima Company, 3/26—2nd Platoon Commander

I called the squad leaders up. My 2nd Squad was lost. I had seen them coming up on line when the action started, but apparently they had gone to the left. It turned out that Captain Camp had grabbed on to them and used them as his CP guard. So, I had only two squads left in my platoon. One of the squad leaders was Lance Corporal Anthony Sawicki and the other was Corporal Frank Garcia.

Sawicki was from what he called "The Block" in Chicago. He was about 5 feet 3 inches tall and well built for his size. He was a hustler; he always had an angle on things. He would trade his food for two of somebody else's something or other, then trade those two for three of something else. He was the type of guy who'd have a nude photo of his girlfriend that he would show to everybody to get a favorable response.

About a month before the battle, he became my radioman. One day, when we were operating in Leatherneck Square, we had a half day off, so we were cleaning our rifles. Sawicki had an accidental discharge and just barely missed shooting Captain Camp. That got him on Captain Camp's shit list. The captain made Sawicki go for one week without any ammunition in his rifle. Fortunately, Sawicki wasn't the point then; he was my radioman, so he was in no immediate danger. But that really hurt his pride; that deflated him a little bit. A little later, after he had become the company shitbird, we had just come off a movement and were setting in a perimeter. Everybody was busy digging in. The company CP tried to reach me on the radio, but couldn't. The company exec came over to our platoon and found Sawicki asleep. The exec slapped the shit out of Sawicki then and there. I decided that Sawicki was screwing up too much as a radioman, that he should go back to being a grunt. To him, this was a demotion because being near the source of power, whatever it was, made him feel like he was working his way up in the world.

For all his problems, Sawicki was a good field Marine, a surprisingly good leader. He became a fire-team leader when I sent him back to the grunts, and he got to lead the squad because of all his field experience and because of all the people who were leaving to rotate home.

Sawicki was a gambler. In a couple of nights just before we went to Con Thien, he had won $15,000. To him, this $15,000 was two cars and some cash. He took $5,000 from one Pfc alone.

Corporal FRANK GARCIA
Lima Company, 3/26—2nd Platoon Squad Leader

After Sawicki won the 15 grand, he was all happier than shit. He had been talking nonstop about sending the money to his girl to buy a new car and about how they were going to get married as soon as he got home. Everything was going good for him; he had big bucks.

2nd Lieutenant JOHN PRINCE
Lima Company, 3/26—2nd Platoon Commander

I was getting orders on the radio from Captain Camp, and I was trying to tell Sawicki what I needed him to do.

Corporal FRANK GARCIA
Lima Company, 3/26—2nd Platoon Squad Leader

Sawicki was kneeling down, clearing a jam from his rifle. He was bent over, pushing his cleaning rod down the barrel of his rifle. He was facing toward the enemy.

2nd Lieutenant JOHN PRINCE
Lima Company, 3/26—2nd Platoon Commander

As I was speaking to Sawicki, he got shot in the forehead.

Corporal FRANK GARCIA
Lima Company, 3/26—2nd Platoon Squad Leader

He got shot right in the skull. It looked bad.

2nd Lieutenant JOHN PRINCE
Lima Company, 3/26—2nd Platoon Commander

He fell down on his back and just lay there. I saw that the bullet had knocked his forehead off. He was laying there with his brain exposed. He tried to touch his brain a few times.

Corporal FRANK GARCIA
Lima Company, 3/26—2nd Platoon Squad Leader

I didn't know what to do. I was in shock. I said, "Sawicki, I don't know what to do!" I got out one of the big bandages we all carried and put it around his head, just to cover up the hole. I wrapped it around his neck to secure it. I didn't know how to do it. I didn't know if he was alive. His eyes were just staring at me, but he wasn't moving. I got the bandage secured and said, ''I'll try to find you a corpsman. I don't know what to do.'' Later, I heard he was dead. He was probably dead the whole time I was working on him.

2nd Lieutenant JOHN PRINCE
Lima Company, 3/26—2nd Platoon Commander

Almost none of the $15,000 Sawicki had won was in real money; it was mostly in IOUs. If he hadn't died right in front of me, I would have said that one of the losers probably shot him.

*

2nd Lieutenant BILL COWAN
India Company, 3/26—3rd Platoon Commander

Lima Company called over by radio and asked for the tanks to move up. Someone in the company CP yelled at me and asked me to tell the tanks to move up to Lima's lines. Accordingly, I ran up to the tank that I thought the platoon commander was in. I pulled open the box on the rear fender, where the intercom was supposed to be. It wasn't working. Almost simultaneously, I heard a roar of gunfire from Lima Company's lines. I assumed they needed tank support *badly*, so I jumped up on the tank and banged on the turret hatch cover with my pistol. Finally, the tank commander opened up and I directed him toward Lima's lines.

2nd Lieutenant JOHN PRINCE
Lima Company, 3/26—2nd Platoon Commander

I was lying on the ground and I felt an explosion—the type of explosion where you immediately feel your throat and your nuts to see if you're still alive. I looked up and realized that a tank had moved up to my left, had swung its gun right over me, and fired a round. I looked up to see where it was firing. The main gun was aimed out toward the rice paddies. I could see two platoon-size NVA units charging across the rice paddies, straight at the battalion CP area at the base of the valley.

Corporal FRANK GARCIA
Lima Company, 3/26—2nd Platoon Squad Leader

I still had the M-60 the wounded guys had given me, but Lieutenant Prince told me to give it to one of my men because I was the squad leader. I said "Okay," but I was thinking, "The M-60 works; I'm not going to let go of it."

Then the lieutenant directed me to get the gun tank to move back, because it was drawing RPG fire. The NVA saw it and they were trying to blow it up. Prince wanted me to get it to move back from the line. I got on the little phone on the rear fender, told the commander what Prince wanted him to do, and then I walked away.

Corporal Garcia must have stated his message without waiting for an acknowledgment because, as various Marines had learned over the course of several days, the intercom phone on B-25's rear fender was not working.

1st Lieutenant RON ZAPPARDINO
3/26—Forward Air Controller

I saw a Marine tank. It was near the top of the hill, just turning back down toward the rice paddy, toward the NVA that were advancing across the rice paddy on line. At that instant, there was a little cheer from the guys around me who could see the tank. We had a tank! It was going to stop the NVA who were rushing us.

Lance Corporal MIKE HEFFLIN
Lima Company, 3/26, 2nd Platoon

The tank was on the side of the hill, between the line of grunts on the forward edge of the hill and the crater filled with our wounded.

1st Lieutenant RON ZAPPARDINO
3/26—Forward Air Controller

As soon as the tank turned down—*boom-boom*—it was history.

Lance Corporal MIKE HEFFLIN
Lima Company, 3/26, 2nd Platoon

It took a hit in the turret.

Corporal FRANK GARCIA
Lima Company, 3/26—2nd Platoon Squad Leader

I was walking away from the tank, and the next thing I knew—*boom*—it got hit. It was that quick. I saw people climbing out of the turret.

2nd Lieutenant JOHN PRINCE
Lima Company, 3/26—2nd Platoon Commander

I looked up at the tank after hearing a strange explosion, and I saw that there were people trying to get out of the turret hatch at the same time.

1st Lieutenant RON ZAPPARDINO
3/26—Forward Air Controller

One guy jumped out of the turret on fire and started rolling around on the ground. I could see other Marines run down to get him. There was enough distance between them and the enemy that they could make it back up the hill. Meantime, everything around me stopped as it dawned on us—this was for real; we were in *real* trouble.

Lance Corporal MIKE HEFFLIN
Lima Company, 3/26, 2nd Platoon

Two who jumped out of the turret were flaming. They were on fire. One guy coming out was burned on both arms and his face and chest. Grunts between him and me—it was all going on only a few feet away from me—threw him down on the ground, covered him up, rolled him around until they got the fire out, and carried him over to the crater.

2nd Lieutenant JOHN PRINCE
Lima Company, 3/26—2nd Platoon Commander

One of the tankers did not have a shirt on. His entire back was blistered—one huge blister. He knelt down on the ground beside me, lowered his ass down on his heels and sort of sat there like a praying mantis. He couldn't touch anything because he was burned. I told him to stick with me because he had no way of protecting himself. I protected him. Another tanker was killed. His buddies pulled him out of the tank and laid him out behind my platoon's line.

2nd Lieutenant PAUL DRNEC
Bravo Company, 3rd Tank Battalion—2nd Platoon Commander

The RPG that hit B-25's turret set off the ready ammunition, which killed the loader and severely wounded and burned the tank platoon sergeant and the gunner.

2nd Lieutenant JOHN PRINCE
Lima Company, 3/26—2nd Platoon Commander

Apparently, when the tank got hit, the driver put it in neutral. After the crew got out, the tank rolled down the hill, into the rice paddy.

2nd Lieutenant PAUL DRNEC
Bravo Company, 3rd Tank Battalion—2nd Platoon Commander

The driver, who was not hurt, took the time to put B-25 in reverse and shut down the engine. That allowed the tank to roll freely back down the slope so, if all the ammunition blew up, the infantry would not be endangered.

1st Lieutenant RON ZAPPARDINO
3/26—Forward Air Controller

That heavy steel weapon had represented the heart and strength of the organization to me, and it had just disappeared. It came down to him or me—the NVA or Ron Zappardino. The loss of that tank was demoralizing to whoever saw it. We were up, and then we were all the way down. At that moment, I was sure I was going to die on that hill. But, instantaneously, I also knew I was going to put up a hell of a fight for my life. I was past any feelings of patriotism or even beating the NVA. I was down to personal survival. There was no other emotion. There was no *time* for another emotion.

*

1st Lieutenant BOB STIMSON
India Company, 3/26—Executive Officer

I saw two tanks behind me, to my right rear, moving toward me. It occurred to me immediately that one of them was a flame tank. The enemy was close enough to be hit by the flame, so I ran back to try to guide both tanks forward to my position. I was vaguely aware that I was running into elements of Lima Company that were beginning to tie in with our India Company right flank. The flame tank was in the lead. The tank commander, in the turret, was firing his .50-caliber machine gun out at the NVA in the paddy.

Captain MATT CAULFIELD
India Company, 3/26—Commanding Officer

I watched it get off a burst of .50-caliber fire, and 20 to 40 enemy were knocked into the air. The gunny ran over (he had just shot his eighth NVA) and yelled, "Captain, get away from that tank." I moved.

1st Lieutenant BOB STIMSON
India Company, 3/26—Executive Officer

I thought the driver of the flame tank noticed me, so I tried to give him some hand signals he could follow. When I was sure he had seen me, I turned and started running back toward India Company's position.

I was not running like I would have down a football field; I was down and up and down and up, zigzagging all the way. I kept looking back to make sure the driver of the flame tank could see me, and I kept pointing out toward the paddy, toward where I wanted them to fire the flame. It seemed to me that he understood what I wanted and where I was directing him. The tank was moving very slowly. Finally, the gunner was swinging the turret around to bear on the paddy. It was my impression that he was positioning himself to fire. Just then, to my right, out toward where I was pointing, I saw—only 30 yards away, adjacent to some shrubbery—an NVA assault squad. I saw the man with the RPG on his shoulder and, behind him, his ammunition humper. The RPGman was lining up his sights.

In my year in Vietnam, I had never fired any personal weapon. It had never been my job to be a rifleman. In most actions I had been in, I had had to give my M-16 away to a rifleman whose own M-16 had jammed. I had already done so on that hill. Here, though, for the first and only time in my life, I was moved to fire at another human being. I tried to pull out my .45 to take a shot at that RPGman. I could see his face. As I was reaching for my holster, he let go. The RPG went flying over me and hit the tank. The flame tank never got a shot off, except with its machine gun. The tank just blew up.

2nd Lieutenant PAUL DRNEC
Bravo Company, 3rd Tank Battalion—2nd Platoon Commander

As I later learned from the flame tank commander, Corporal Guy Wolfberger, the RPG round set off the secondary fuel line, which was filled with gasoline they used to ignite the napalm. When the fuel line went up, Wolfberger and his crew—the gunner and driver—bailed out okay. In a half minute, the fire in the fuel line spread to the napalm tank, which caught fire and blew up.

Lance Corporal CHUCK BENNETT
India Company, 3/26, 1st Platoon

Someone yelled, "The tank's hit!" I didn't actually see it *get* hit, but I thought it took a direct hit from a 140mm rocket. The explosion was so big, it looked like a rocket had hit right straight down on top of it. I saw Marines all over the tank, and guys who were on fire climbing out of it. A lot of them got it because a lot of NVA were still firing on the tank even though it was shooting flames out of the turret.

Captain MATT CAULFIELD
India Company, 3/26—Commanding Officer

When the second tank was hit, word was passed that small-arms ammunition was on it. Before I had a chance to tell someone, a wounded young sergeant struggled to his feet and time and again made his way to the tank. He climbed up and threw ammo off. After the last case was on the ground and safe, he collapsed.

Lance Corporal CHUCK BENNETT
India Company, 3/26, 1st Platoon

He might have been my new squad leader, Sergeant Bruce Huntington—the sergeant I'd taken back to the company CP after he was wounded at the start of the NVA attack. When I saw Sergeant Huntington's body after the battle, he had two bullet holes in the back of his head.

I later learned that another squad leader from India-1 was killed helping the crew out of the tank. He was Sergeant Scotty Chisholm, the 2nd Squad leader. Chisholm had been an officer in the British Army before he came to America and joined the Marines to get his citizenship quicker.

2nd Lieutenant JOHN PRINCE
Lima Company, 3/26—2nd Platoon Commander

The flame tank burned and some of its .50-caliber machine-gun bullets cooked off right into our lines.

*

Corporal FRANK GARCIA
Lima Company, 3/26—2nd Platoon Squad Leader

I jumped into a bomb crater filled with a lot of Marines. They weren't doing anything, so I said, "Come on guys, you gotta fight," but they just stayed covered up. Two of the guys were short-timers; they didn't even want to put their heads up. I told them, "You get out there and start fighting or I'm going to throw a hand grenade in here with you." Then I jumped out—and they jumped out. They pissed me off.

I'd lost track of most of my squad, so I was taking charge of whoever I could find. Whenever I get mad I get a big adrenaline flow and I just do things; I don't get scared until it's over. That happened to me then. I thought I was doing the right thing. I felt confident. I thought I was being a good Marine.

2nd Lieutenant JOHN PRINCE
Lima Company, 3/26—2nd Platoon Commander

Private First Class Tyrone Watts was in the M-60 team, an ammo humper. Watts shot an NVA soldier with his rifle. The NVA soldier fell in the open and another NVA came out to pick up the wounded man, so Watts shot him, too. This kept happening until Watts shot a total of six NVA.

*

Captain MATT CAULFIELD
India Company, 3/26—Commanding Officer

The enemy paused, then made a precise left oblique turn and headed toward the battalion and Mike Company. That was a mistake. It was too good to be true—the enemy was offering me his flank.

1st Lieutenant BOB STIMSON
India Company, 3/26—Executive Officer

I could see the NVA main body moving up the paddies toward the battalion main body, but I thought they were just moving to another position from which to attack us.

Lance Corporal CHUCK BENNETT
India Company, 3/26, 1st Platoon

The NVA made a big mistake when they turned and exposed their flank to us. That's when we really put it to them. I saw them turn, but I didn't care why at the time. I kept firing at them and there was less of them firing at me. It was mad out there. There was no time to think. That was probably the turning point of the battle. They were inside of us in some places. I don't think they could have overrun us, but they could have hurt us real bad. Then they turned away from us and let us fire into them as they passed.

Chapter 16

At 1655, as two battalions of the 812th NVA Regiment launched their frontal assault against India Company and Lima-2 across the large paddy-field, several companies and perhaps a full battalion of NVA launched a separate but coordinated assault from the hill India-3 had been approaching at the start of the action. The attack went in directly against Lima-3, which was holding the southwest corner of the Marine-held hill. Lima-3 and the Lima Company CP group had not been able to tie in with India Company's right flank because they could not reach across a profusion of large boulders on the hill's western tip.

Captain DICK CAMP
Lima Company, 3/26—Commanding Officer

I turned to my company radioman, Corporal David Johnson, and was about to ask for the handset when a terrific volume of fire erupted. It was fairly peaceful one second and then there was this solid *CRACK*— like the crack of doom. I had an immediate reaction; I fell straight to the ground beside Corporal Johnson and rolled right into the nearest foxhole. *Everybody* who was up was suddenly down. Immediately, the confusion started. People were yelling and screaming, someone was yelling for a corpsman, people were blazing away at targets I couldn't see. It was chaos. And in the middle of the maelstrom, I was trying to figure out what in the hell had happened, what the hell was going on.

I was on my belly in the old fighting hole and wanted to get reports from all the platoon commanders. Corporal Johnson was in another hole about 2 feet from me. I yelled, "Hey, John, let me talk to the platoons.

Give me the handset. Throw it over here!'' It was on a rubber cord, so he flipped it to me. As I caught it, there was a tiny lull in the firing, so I sneaked a quick peek over the lip of my hole. All I had time to see was a bush right in front of my foxhole. As I looked, it was shot even with the ground.

The fire was heavy and close. It was really pouring in. As far as I could tell, Lima Company was absolutely pinned. I couldn't hear many of our weapons in action. I tried to call my platoon commanders to find out if anyone was still alive. I got Gunny Almanza, of the 3rd Platoon, and Sergeant Mullins, of the 1st Platoon. I even located a squad of the 2nd Platoon, but I couldn't raise John Prince or the rest of the 2nd Platoon. I had a searing hot lump of emotion in my chest as I tried and tried to get John on the net. I found myself yelling into the handset, as if that was going to raise the dead. The sense of foreboding was nearly debilitating. As far as I could tell, John and two-thirds of the 2nd Platoon had been disabled or wiped out. However, as it turned out, John simply was too busy to respond to my call; he was giving orders to his two squad leaders. (I had grabbed his lead squad to cover my CP group.)

My own position—the position of two-thirds of Lima Company— was tenuous during those first minutes of the NVA attack. We kept trying to establish an orderly defensive position and tie in with India Company. But, under such intense fire, it was difficult just to get a look around. Long before I had a mental picture of our initial layout, I heard the dreaded cries of "Corpsman, up!" from all around me.

From the NVA standpoint, the attack was going beautifully.

We did what we had to do. While those who were able returned fire, the rest of us tried to dig our holes deeper. The only way to do that was to scrape the dirt out from beneath our bodies and throw it up on the parapets of our holes. Progress was measured in spoonfuls. As I struggled with my hole, between garbled conversations on the company tactical net, I saw one of those little things that from time to time captured the essence of being a Marine.

Two Marines were crawling past my hole, no doubt under orders from their platoon commander to fill a gap in our line. Both had fixed bayonets, which probably seems like a small thing to most people, but the fact is that we *never* fixed bayonets. We used our bayonets only to open C-ration boxes or to play games, but we *never* attached bayonets to the ends of our rifles because we felt they were too short to use properly. So, all of a sudden, here come two Marines, crawling past me with fixed bayonets. It electrified me. All of a sudden I realized, "Hey, these Marines know how tough it is!" They were expecting hand-to-hand and they were ready to stand toe-to-toe with the enemy, to duke it out with bayonets and rifle butts.

I instinctively dropped my hand to my web belt and felt my fighting knife, which I carried instead of a bayonet. I couldn't have followed the example of those two Marines—or set one for the rest of my company—if I had wanted to. I did want to, more than anything I had ever wanted. Suddenly, I felt naked and unarmed. I had no bayonet.

The two Marines passed from sight, and I heard people yelling and screaming. I could hear my unit leaders yelling things like, "Get em, get em!" and "Get that fire out there!" and "Pass some ammunition over here"—that sort of thing. The sights and sounds were kaleidoscopic. Everything was happening faster than real life, only it *was* real life, more real than life ever had been. Everything seemed jumbled and out of order, like a poorly spliced videotape running on fast forward. There was a break now and again in the intensity of the fire, but it never really stopped. We used the breaks to move men to cover weak spots or move M-60s to engage specific targets.

The thing that really pissed me off was that we never got our 60mm mortars firing. I'm sure the gunners wanted to fire—and would have risked their lives to do so—but we had no ammunition. We had not been able to acquire any before we left Dong Ha, and we had been unable to acquire any since. We had the mortars, but they weren't even much good for braining people.

The NVA launched a direct assault on our perimeter. When I heard warning shouts from my troops and looked up to see them coming, a voice in my head said, "Dick, you're not going to make it out of here." But for the actions and examples of a few authentically brave men, that sense of resignation might have proven out.

*

A little Marine from the 3rd Platoon was manning the foxhole to my right front, 7 to 8 feet from my hole. He was a character, a kid with a wry sense of humor. He was also extremely good natured, a Marine who would do anything anyone asked of him. When he had first joined the company, other members of his squad would throw all their extra gear at him and the poor kid would carry it. It got so that he would be carrying so much extra stuff he would pass out from exhaustion and the heat. I was always on his case, advising, "Goddammit, don't let them do that to you, Marine." But he was that type of kid, so it went on.

Sometime near the start of the fight, I heard the young Marine exclaim, "Jesus Christ, I'm hit! I'm hit!" Next thing I saw, he was waving his foot over the lip of his foxhole while he yelled, "Look, look, look! They shot me in the foot, they shot me in the foot." Pretty soon, a corpsman came crawling by and dropped into the Marine's fighting hole. "Look, Doc," I heard the Marine say in a high-pitched voice, "they shot me in the foot, they shot me in the foot." A few seconds later, a boot came flying out of the foxhole. The corpsman had cut it down so he could get at the wound. As the doc worked, the Marine kept saying things like, "Look, Doc, they shot me. It hurts. The goddamn foot hurts!" Next thing I knew, the Marine, who was crawling past me, stopped to say, "Skipper, they shot me in the foot!"—as if I was his dad and was going to maybe kiss it to make it better. A short time later, I noticed that he was back in his original fighting hole, just to my right front. He had been shot, he had to say "Goddamn this hurts," but he was back in his position, doing his job.

*

One of the bravest of the brave was Sergeant David Brown, the platoon sergeant of the 3rd Platoon, a Tennessean who had done his year and, in fact, had missed his plane home that very day. He had been among the first short-timers to volunteer to accompany Lima Company into the field. Sergeant Brown was about five feet eight inches tall and physically and mentally tough. I believe he might have been a draftee, one of the first Marine draftees to get overseas. If he was a draftee and had made sergeant, he probably had a few years of college under his belt. I guarantee, if he was a draftee and a sergeant and had survived a whole year in Vietnam, Brown was one tough, one smart cookie. Only the tough guys got to be sergeants and only the smart ones did it in less than a year.

According to some of the troops, Sergeant Brown had crawled out through the brush at the very start of the action and had killed an NVA soldier he found crawling toward our lines. As the fight progressed, I could often hear Sergeant Brown shouting and cursing: "Get some people over here!" or "Get some ammunition over there!" or "Get over here!" I saw him at one point, up and about, leading several Marines forward.

Suddenly, there was a terrific burst of gunfire and everyone Brown was leading hit the dirt. But not Brown. As soon as he realized he couldn't get forward, we moved in among his men, making sure they were all okay. That was a tremendous display of leadership and guts.

There was a little trail leading right into our position. After a while, the NVA found the path and started folding in so they could follow it right to us. I caught a glimpse of several North Vietnamese soldiers as they eased up the trail into a thicket of head-high scrub growth that began about five meters beyond a stretch of clear ground in front of the prepared line of foxholes. At the head of the trail, on our side of the clear area, was a foxhole with two Marines in it. My foxhole—the company CP—was five meters behind that foxhole. Unbeknownst to me, however, both Marines in the foxhole had been killed. There was nothing between me and the perimeter line and nothing between the perimeter line, the clearing, the scrub, and the trail the NVA were about to use to get right into the company position.

The first inkling I had of trouble to my immediate front was when I next spotted Sergeant Brown. Son of a gun, it was like he was standing on the 200-yard line at the rifle range. He was just standing there, cool as you please, in the offhand position, with his M-16 tucked into his shoulder, shooting at NVA soldiers who were making their way up the trail. At that moment, the leading NVA were no more than 30 feet away from him. He was shooting them, one right after the other. By the time I looked up, he must have laid out about six or eight of them, all in a nice little pile. Then, just as calmly, he stopped firing, pulled his rifle from his shoulder, stared at the dead North Vietnamese for a moment, and turned around to resume yelling orders and encouragement to other Marines. When he turned away from the front, he saw something he didn't like and stalked beyond my view. A moment later, I looked again when I heard him bellowing a command. He was dragging another Marine—probably a man who was bigger than he was—by the suspender straps. "Get over there," he yelled as he *threw* the Marine toward the foxhole in front of my CP hole. The kid he threw had an M-79. As soon as the kid landed, Brown started chanting, "Shoot! Shoot! Shoot!" The kid was still dazed, so Brown stalked over, grabbed the M-79, and snapped off the 40mm grenade in the chamber. It hit an NVA soldier in the chest and blew him all over the landscape.

I couldn't believe what I was seeing. I couldn't believe it was all happening within fifteen feet of me!

Sergeant Brown disappeared and I didn't see him again for a while. I heard him yelling from time to time, which made me feel good, because things on our hill were very grim indeed. As I fought to keep control of the company, to keep Lima cohesive and viable, I needed all the encouragement I could get. And Sergeant David Brown provided most of what I needed in that regard. As long as I heard Brown yelling from time to time, I knew we were still in the running.

Somewhere along in there, I heard Sergeant Brown say, "My goddamn rifle's jammed," so I said, "Here, take mine." I wasn't shooting; I was talking on the radio. I had my pistol, which was good enough. I knew we would all be better off if Brown had the rifle.

Next thing I knew, Sergeant Brown yelled "Goddammit!" I naturally looked up. He was lying in a foxhole about 10 feet away, but suddenly he was on his feet, uncorking a hand grenade. He reared back and pitched the grenade down the trail leading into our position. There was an explosion, but Brown screamed, "Son of a bitch! I can't get it out!" And before my disbelieving eyes—the fire was as heavy as it had ever been—he stood up and took off his flak jacket and helmet and threw them down because he couldn't throw the grenade far enough with them on.

I was too stunned—too scared for Sergeant Brown—to do anything else except watch.

Brown took two grenades out of his grenade pouch, pulled both pins, and let both spoons fly. He had two live grenades and he had to be rid of them in 5 seconds. He leaped out of the foxhole, ran forward to the trail head, and threw them both at the same time while hurling himself to the ground. By the time he and the grenades hit the ground, both grenades exploded. He had done it that way so the North Vietnamese couldn't throw them back at us. If I had seen John Wayne do in a movie what David Brown did before my eyes, I would have asked for my admission money back.

Sergeant Brown's ongoing performance was not only inspirational, it was the sort of heroism that is known as "above and beyond." He kept doing it—kept uncorking grenades and running them forward. I dropped whatever I had been doing and started yelling, "Brown, get down goddammit! Brown, get down." But he ignored me. Every time he ran up to the trail head, Gunny Bailey also screamed, "Goddammit Brown, don't do that! Don't do that!"

The gunny was another one.

2nd Lieutenant JOHN PRINCE
Lima Company, 3/26—2nd Platoon Commander

I originally took over the 2nd Platoon from Staff Sergeant Marvin Bailey. He was a classic, a short guy and wiry, with a good sense of humor. He didn't hard-ass the troops, but he got the job done. He had spent 2 years in the Army and I think he had a total of 18 years in the service when I met him. He always carried a flask of whiskey in his back pocket. After a fight, I'd look in his eyes and see that the veins were showing, so quite possibly he was nipping here and there.

He told the classic story about himself. He was what he called a "dumbshit Army guy." He was probably a private in Korea. He once was given the order to go "burn the shitter." In Korea, as in Vietnam, the indoor shitter was a little screened cage in which you sat and shit into half of a 55-gallon drum. The drums had to be removed every day so the shit in them could be burned. Well, when Bailey was given the order, they naturally expected that he would pull the half-drums out into the open, put kerosene in them, and burn the shit. But he didn't do that. He went inside the shitter and poured *gasoline* into each one of the drums. Then he threw in a match. As he said, "I was pulling shit out of my eyebrows for a month." Gunny Bailey would tell stories about himself like that. The troops liked him as well as followed him.

Captain DICK CAMP
Lima Company, 3/26—Commanding Officer

Though the gunny was armed with only a pistol, he accompanied Sergeant Brown forward every time. Even then it was humorous to see Gunny Bailey with his left hand clasped across his helmet while he fired his .45-caliber automatic pistol right into the faces of NVA soldiers coming through the scrub at the head of the trail. And all the time, *he* was yelling, "Goddammit, Brown, don't do that!"—*bang-bang*—"Get back, Brown!"—*bang-bang-bang*—"Jesus Christ, Brown, cut that out!"—*bang-bang*. I knew the gunny and I knew he was scared shitless, but he ran forward every time Brown ran forward and fired his .45 while Brown hurled his grenades.

Time remained at a standstill—and whirling ahead—as these and a thousand other scenes were seared into my memory. If I had to guess, I would say that Sergeant Brown and Gunny Bailey kept it up for 20 minutes. At that point, Brown ran by my foxhole for the umpteenth time and I looked up, as always, and yelled, "Goddammit, Brown, get down." Then, as I turned to Corporal Johnson to ask for the radio handset, I heard this terrible *thunk*. It was the unmistakable sound of a bullet hitting a man in the head. I knew right away what had happened. I looked up real quick; I snapped my head around. I knew who had been hit.

Sergeant Brown was on the ground, maybe 20 feet from me. He wasn't moving. I thought or maybe said, "Oh shit!" and I crawled out of my hole, straight over to him. I put my hand on his head and ran my fingers through his hair. He had taken a bullet behind the right ear. He was dead.

David Brown was a man, like me. And, like me, he had probably reasoned that this was his day to die. He had nothing to lose, so he staked his claim to the ground on which he stood and challenged the enemy to come take his life if they dared. Well, I don't really know why he did what he did. But I know in the deepest place in my heart that I would not have lived through that bloody afternoon and evening if David Brown had not sealed his pact with God or the Fates, had not laid claim to his manhood, had not done what he felt he had to do or might as well do. I wrote him up for a Medal of Honor, which was little enough compensation for his life. Men who were far from that nameless little hill and who did not see what I saw awarded David Brown's spirit a Navy Cross.

Shortly after Sergeant Brown was killed, several more North Vietnamese crawled into the scrub growth and began throwing Chicoms from 10 to 15 feet outside our position. Suddenly, Marines directly to my front were yelling, "Grenade, grenade!" Everyone got their heads down when they heard that. Then, as soon as the Chicoms detonated, everyone who had them responded with our own M-26 grenades, which were extremely potent. I heard the *crump* of the M-26 detonations followed by the horrible screams of NVA in the brush.

Unbeknownst to me, Sergeant Marshall Jesperson, a 3rd Platoon squad leader, told his troops that the next time the North Vietnamese got close enough to throw Chicoms, he was going to lead them into the thicket to clean the NVA out. I could imagine what those young Marines were thinking about that, but Jesperson was their leader and he knew they were going to obey.

When the North Vietnamese came back up the trail, reoccupied the thicket, and started throwing Chicoms again, Sergeant Jesperson got his squad up and led them into the brush. I heard the fighting. It was horrible. Ghastly. There are no rules in a fight in which you could wind up dead. No rules. Jesperson and his men did it any way they could—bullets, knives, bayonets, rifle butts, whatever. They cleaned out the thicket that time, and again, when the North Vietnamese foolishly challenged Sergeant Jesperson's authority. The squeals of agony were almost too much to bear.

Marshall Jesperson. He realized what had to be done, and he did it. No one told him to lead the way into the thicket, no one told him to kill other human beings up close. He did what he did because it had to be done. More important, those 18- and 19-year-old Marines followed him. They could have stayed in their fighting holes. No one held a roll call. They followed Sergeant Jesperson into the thicket. That was the key. He led and they followed. How could they not?

I was out checking the lines when Sergeant Jesperson led his second counterattack into the thicket. I stopped off to speak with my 3rd Platoon commander, Gunnery Sergeant Juan Almanza. Gunny was one of the finest Marines I ever served with. A small, whip thin, dazzlingly neat man from Texas, he was one of the best Marine noncoms I ever commanded. I had put him in command of my 3rd Platoon shortly after taking over Lima Company, and I left him there so the other platoon commanders could see how it was supposed to be done. There was nothing Gunny Almanza couldn't do better than right. He was Old Corps all the way, the perfect role model for everyone in Lima Company, an utterly unflappable leader of men.

2nd Lieutenant JOHN PRINCE
Lima Company, 3/26—2nd Platoon Commander

When I first got to Vietnam, Gunny Almanza was the company gunny. We were operating at Khe Sanh and two chaplains, one Protestant and the other Catholic, came over to conduct services. Captain Camp told Gunny Almanza to call the men out and tell them to go to church. While the skipper and the chaplains waited, the gunny walked outside the CP tent and yelled, "Okay, every swinging dick, fall in." Captain Camp about died laughing.

Captain DICK CAMP
Lima Company, 3/26—Commanding Officer

When I got to Gunny Almanza's position, the firing had pretty much died down for a bit. Jesperson had just cleared out the thicket and Almanza was up with his radioman, Corporal Thomas Krispin, looking around, checking his platoon's position. As the gunny looked around and thumbed rounds into empty M-16 magazines, Sergeant Jesperson trotted up from the thicket with his tongue hanging out from the exertion. When the gunny saw me approaching, he flashed a huge smile and said, "We're getting some, Skipper. We're getting some." I said, "Right on!"

I was going to say more, but right then HM3 Larry Bratton, the company's senior corpsman, crawled up to me and blurted out, "Skipper, Skipper, come with me. We got a Marine who's dying and he shouldn't. He's been lightly wounded." I had heard of lightly injured men getting it into their heads that they were going to die, and dying. Apparently, what the kid Doc Bratton was treating needed was a little motivation. I was it; I was the company motivation machine.

I followed Bratton about 20 feet to the side of a Marine who had indeed been wounded. I looked the Marine over and thought that it probably hurt, but it didn't look like much of a wound. So I said, "Marine, you're not going to die. Snap out of it. You're going to be okay. You'll be fine. Take it easy." As I spoke, I caught sight of a little red ball tracking across the perimeter. Then there was a blinding orange flash and I found myself flat on my back. Some very heavy concussion had lifted me up and thrown me into the ground with terrific force. Before I could move a muscle, I heard Sergeant Jesperson bawl, "I'm blind, I'm blind!"

As soon as Doc Bratton and I collected ourselves, we crawled over toward the sound of Sergeant Jesperson's voice, toward Gunny Almanza's foxhole. What I saw was revolting. The RPG had hit Gunny Almanza right in the helmet or on a boulder right behind his head. Either way, everything from the neck up was gone—except for his face. Corporal Krispin had taken a major dose of shrapnel in his chest because his flak jacket wasn't zipped. He was on the ground, coughing up blood and gore, making terrible choking and gagging sounds. Jesperson had his hands over his face and was whimpering, "I'm blind, I'm blind!"

The gunny was dead, no two ways about it. Krispin was in terrible shape. However, a closer look at Sergeant Jesperson revealed that he was not actually blind. He had been blinded by the debris from the gunny's head. In fact, he had been right in front of the gunny, talking to him, when the RPG hit. The gunny's head had taken the brunt of the blast and had saved Jesperson from being sprayed with shrapnel. Everything Jesperson had been sprayed with could be washed off.

Doc Bratton, who treated the company like it was his own private medical practice, waded right into the middle of it. Before the scene had settled on me, he was working on Krispin and talking to him, trying to calm him down: "Krispin, you're not gonna die. Hear? You're not gonna die!" The other doc and I had our hands full trying to get Jesperson calmed down.

For all Doc Bratton's hard work, there was only one way to save Krispin. He and a lot of other Lima Company Marines needed an immediate emergency helo medevac or they were going to die. But there was no way. There was too much fire across the top of the hill to get helos in. I didn't even want to ask a helo crew to risk it. The only good thing that happened to Krispin was that he passed out. It was better for him, not having to be awake with all that pain.

I crawled back to my CP hole and tried to resume my normal duties, but I was really shaken. I had really liked Gunny Almanza. I thought the world of him. As I sat in the bottom of my foxhole—by then, it was nearly deep enough to stand in—I exerted all my willpower on pulling myself together. I was no longer afraid, as I had been through most of the fight. Sooner than some—but definitely later than David Brown, Marshall Jesperson, and Juan Almanza—I had passed beyond fear. I was not apathetic nor even resigned to death, but I was no longer afraid.

Chapter 17

2nd Lieutenant PAUL DRNEC
Bravo Company, 3rd Tank Battalion—2nd Platoon Commander

I was in the B-22 tank, stranded out with Mike Company by a track separation. I lost radio contact with B-25 and F-23. I couldn't raise anyone in 3/26 either. I don't know why my comm conked out; I had line-of-sight contact with them, so I should have had comm.

I scanned the distant ridgeline with my binoculars and definitely saw movement up ahead. I saw men wearing green uniforms that looked like Marine uniforms, but I guessed from the distinctive motion of their bodies that they were NVA soldiers. I also knew instinctively that the lead Marine elements would not have had time to get up that far. I looked up at the tanks on the hill and saw a bunch of people on the turret of one of them. I couldn't imagine what they were doing and I thought, "Why are they playing around on the turret; can't they *see* all those NVA?"

I had no comm, so I decided to fire on the enemy movement in the hope the other tanks would see my rounds fall and be able to find the enemy themselves. They should have been able to see what I could see if they looked in the right direction, but it looked like they weren't reacting and I was positive they weren't shooting. I was extremely frustrated; I couldn't figure out what the hell they were doing. As far as I could tell, they had perfect, beautiful targets right in front of them, but they didn't seem to see them.

What I had not seen was the RPG hits on B-25. It turned out that the men I saw on the turret were infantrymen who were pulling the three tankers out of the turret.

All the banging around in the field for over a week must have thrown both the gunner's and tank commander's sights out of line because our first HE shot landed so far off we never saw it detonate. We tried to adjust as well as we could, but the second HE round missed by a mile. We would have tried adjusting to the burst—using the fall of one round to adjust the fall of the next—but it turned out that we had no HE rounds left. We had had just the two. All we had left was a lot of canister and a few willy-peter rounds. I was holding an internal debate about what to do next when I distinctly saw one of the other tanks get hit in the turret. It was a very smoky hit, so I assumed it was the flame tank. Right then, before I could react, I saw a whole bunch of NVA soldiers approaching the tanks and grunts on the hill. The NVA were in the open and coming from across the paddyfield. As I noticed the NVA, I saw the flame tank's turret blow up.

There was nothing I could do to help the other tanks. I couldn't bring fire on the enemy who were attacking them across the paddies. All I could do was sit and watch.

*

Captain ANDY DeBONA
Mike Company, 3/26—Commanding Officer

I had placed Mike-2 on the point, Mike-1 on the right flank, and Mike-3 on the left flank. The CP group was to be in the center, halfway down the Mike-2 column and about midway between the point squads of Mike-1 and Mike-3.

The reason I gave Mike-2 the honor of being point was that its commander, Lieutenant Bob Gall, had finally arrived. On the night of September 7, in the short amount of reaction time, he had done a super job of moving his platoon over to occupy India's position. On the morning of September 8, he had aggressively swept through the treeline in front of the 81s. This was the first time that Gall was to be in a position of trust and responsibility. I was not going to hover over him.

2nd Lieutenant CHAN CRANGLE
Mike Company, 3/26—1st Platoon Commander

Mike Company was formed in a company wedge—an inverted V—with

Bob Gall's 2nd Platoon at the point of the *V,* leading the company. Lieutenant Harry Dolan, now the commander of the 3rd Platoon, was on the left (south) side of the *V* and my 1st Platoon was on the right (northwest) side.

I could plainly hear the India Company firefight, but, at that point, there wasn't much to do but wait for orders.

My platoon went to ground facing west, with me perched on a grave mound. We were at the base of a little ridge, almost into the open paddyfields. My platoon was deployed well down the west slope in echelon formation, facing the open fields.

Staff Sergeant CHARLES OWENS
Kilo Company, 3/26—Company Gunny

The 81s were just packing up and we were getting ready to follow them out. The exec, 1st Lieutenant Robert Dobies, all of a sudden looked around and said, "It doesn't feel right. It just doesn't feel right. Something isn't right. Gunny, get all those people in their holes right away!" Me and 1st Sergeant Goddard went flying up the hill and told the men to get back in their holes. Right then, the NVA hit India Company.

2nd Lieutenant CHAN CRANGLE
Mike Company, 3/26—1st Platoon Commander

My first hint that the war was about to come to Mike Company was the sound of rockets lifting off.

Staff Sergeant CHARLES OWENS
Kilo Company, 3/26—Company Gunny

The rockets hit Hill 48; me and the battalion commander and the sergeant major all jumped in the same hole. The battalion commander wound up at the bottom of the hole, underneath the rest of us. He got the whole side of his face skinned.

2nd Lieutenant CHAN CRANGLE
Mike Company, 3/26—1st Platoon Commander

I was sitting on a grave mound when the incoming started. I recall going "eenie-meenie-minie-mo" to decide on which side of the mound to dive. I went right as a rocket or mortar round hit on the left. My radio operator and I bounced off the ground a couple of times. It really rang our bells! I looked up to where my 1st Squad had halted and saw enormous clouds of flame, black smoke, and dust—obviously more than one rocket impact. My first thought was, "My God, 1st Squad is gone!" Fortunately, that wasn't so. Everyone was okay. The only significant casualty in that opening volley was one Marine in the 3rd Squad— about 60 meters north and west of me—who took shrapnel in his back.

I pulled the platoon into a semicircle facing west and tried to figure out what to do next. I tried to raise Andy DeBona on the radio, but I couldn't get any response.

Lance Corporal RON BURKE
Mike Company, 3/26, 2nd Platoon

Rockets started hitting all around. I think our squad leader got his wires crossed. On September 7, we'd been told to move from our original position to a new position. The squad leader did it again on September 10, but I think it was without orders. He moved us forward to try to flank the enemy, to cover the paddies. We just took off, the whole squad, blindly following him.

I had a radio on my back. I'd had it since the night of September 7 because I hadn't been able to find anyone to take it from me. The radio made it very difficult for me to do my John Wayne maneuvers— leapfrogging back and forth and up and down with an occasional roll— but that's how we were trained, so I did it the best I could. We were in high grass. The farther forward we got, the taller the grass got. We were in rough ground, moving toward the rice paddies.

The NVA were leapfrogging across the rice paddies, using the dikes for cover. We were going toward them and they were moving toward us. I saw what looked to me like hundreds of NVA coming at us in waves. One wave would fall down and another wave would move in front of it, and so on. That's when I began thinking we were doing something stupid. I had the radio and I hadn't heard anyone order us that far forward. I was getting concerned about the squad leader's direction. It didn't look so good to me.

Major CARL MUNDY
3/26—Operations Officer

After the rockets hit Hill 48, I ran to the edge of the brush that surrounded the battalion CP and looked out. I was struck by the almost theatrical fact that coming across from the high ground to the west of us—coming across the depression toward us—was an almost perfect formation of NVA. It looked somewhat like what Andrew Jackson might have encountered in New Orleans as the British came toward him. Here was an almost perfectly aligned NVA battalion, moving across the low ground toward us, firing their weapons as they came, being supported by mortars and rockets. The Marines in our perimeter were beginning to return the fire.

Staff Sergeant CHARLES OWENS
Kilo Company, 3/26—Company Gunny

The NVA came across the paddyfield at us just like rows of corn. We watched them come. Mike Company was in a bad place, out on our left front, out on a finger. They were right out in the open, with no holes.

*

Captain ANDY DeBONA
Mike Company, 3/26—Commanding Officer

The next thing I knew, Mike-2's point squad reported contact. I heard a lot of firing going out from directly to my right front.

2nd Lieutenant PAUL DRNEC
Bravo Company, 3rd Tank Battalion—2nd Platoon Commander

I saw masses of NVA soldiers attacking straight at me from across the paddies to my right front. When I first noticed them, they were already a third of the way across the field, about 150 meters away.

It would have been beautiful if we'd had any HE. I said, "Let's put a little willy-peter out on 'em." We fired two quick rounds at the center of the formation, the biggest group I could see. Bad choice. The willy-peter just clouded up the field, provided the NVA with a smoke screen. All we had was the .30-caliber coaxial machine gun mounted alongside the main gun tube and the .50-caliber in my commander's cupola. We couldn't see where the .30-cal was hitting—there were so many NVA out there—and the .50-cal jammed after only a few rounds. All the .50-cals in all of our tanks were useless. I got so frustrated I cranked the gun up all the way, pulled the pin, and let it drop onto the deck of the tank. That left a 3-inch hole. I popped our M-14 rifle in there and started shooting it at the NVA.

2nd Lieutenant CHAN CRANGLE
Mike Company, 3/26—1st Platoon Commander

My 3rd Squad leader said, "Holy shit! Look at that!" He was standing up, so I did the same. We could see quite clearly two or three distinct waves of NVA—20 or so in each wave, in distinct linear formation. They were sweeping across the open fields to our west, heading for my right flank. I didn't use binoculars to verify the uniforms of the enemy, but my squad leader, platoon sergeant, and radio operator said the same thing: "Those guys are wearing Marine helmets and flak jackets!" It couldn't have been India or Lima Company; these people were too far west and north of the battalion axis of advance. They were definitely NVA.

There were about a dozen of them in Marine gear, all in the lead wave. We opened fire and so did Marines to my right. The NVA formations broke into fire-and-maneuver elements, and I lost direct sight of them.

Captain ANDY DeBONA
Mike Company, 3/26—Commanding Officer

I couldn't see the NVA attack from my CP position. But Mike-2 and Mike-1 apparently had clear fields of fire into the NVA main body's left flank as the NVA attacked India and Lima. After hitting India and Lima head-on, the bad guys made a left-oblique turn so they were pointed straight down the rice paddy at Hill 48. They were heading right for us, but a little off to our right. India and Lima then had clear fields of fire into the right flank of the NVA main body, and we were shooting into their front.

Heavy mortar and small-arms fire started falling into the Mike position. It seemed to me that the tank on the high ground with Mike-2 was an aiming stake. At the same time, Lima-Six and India-Six were completely tying up the battalion tactical net. I couldn't get a word in edgewise.

Our artillery was still shut off because the Bird Dog was in the area, but, finally, fast movers started rolling in from my left to my right with nape and snake—napalm and 250-pound general-purpose bombs. About the same time, I observed at least four .51-caliber machine guns directly across the rice paddy from me, firing at the fast movers.

Major CARL MUNDY
3/26—Operations Officer

What we had at that time was what I would characterize as a pretty good, well-planned, and pretty well coordinated attack by the NVA engaging all of our elements, which were strung out. They were keeping India and Lima companies engaged over on the high ground to our southwest and keeping Mike Company pinned down between the battalion and an attempt to move onto that ground behind Lima Company.

Captain ANDY DeBONA
Mike Company, 3/26—Commanding Officer

Mike's CP group was hit by mortars. I vividly remember for the first time in my life knowing absolute stark fear. A round fell about 4 feet from me. I felt a burning sensation, and I probably screamed. I don't know; I think I did. I asked Corporal Thomas Schneider, my radio operator, to check my foot to see if it was still on there. Schneider had a small shrapnel wound in his arm. While he was checking, I recovered the fins from the mortar round, as a souvenir. I had a small shrapnel wound in my Achilles tendon.

Mike-1's radio operator came up on the company tac net and reported that Mike-1 was in heavy contact. I didn't really understand what the Mike-1 radioman was saying at first because he was epitomizing what I felt. He could barely speak. It came out garbled. It came out high pitched. The whole thing. I grabbed the radio. Where it came from, I don't know, but I told him to speak calmly. That was something I wasn't feeling.

Mike-1-Actual, Lieutenant Crangle, got on the phone and told me that he was in heavy combat.

Chan Crangle was our steady-eddie, an extremely intelligent individual. He had been a Navy submariner who had gone to college under an enlisted commissioning program. The Navy had paid for his degree in nuclear propulsion, but he had selected the Marine Corps to be a grunt! He never sounded shook. Anytime I talked to him, I got clear, concise information. He always had control of his people. He always had his fire plan in order. He was always there.

Crangle's call led me to believe that my whole right flank from Mike-2 to Mike-1 was engaged. It was still difficult to report this to Battalion because Lima-Six and India-Six were still tying up the radio. During a semi-pause, while one of them was waiting for the other to answer, I called, "Break, break, break, break, break! This is Mike-Six." I reported back to Battalion that we were in heavy contact. I also suggested that India-Six and Lima-Six get off the battalion tac net and come up on one of their company frequencies—I said I didn't care which one it was—so that they would not tie up the battalion net. This suggestion went unheeded.

1st Lieutenant HARRY DOLAN
Mike Company, 3/26—3rd Platoon Commander

We were still digging in when the first rounds started landing. Needless to say, the incoming increased excavation speed. After the first volley, we had several men wounded. I checked the men, and a corpsman moved from hole to hole patching wounded Marines. I called Andy and told him I had had no contact with anyone on my left flank. He told me to refuse the flank, which I had already done with two fighting holes. The 3rd Platoon no longer had many effectives.

Captain ANDY DeBONA
Mike Company, 3/26—Commanding Officer

As I was trying to reimpose discipline on the battalion tac net, Mike-3 was hit by mortars and some artillery fire. I received the word that Mike-3-Actual—"Zero Fingers" Dolan—and his platoon sergeant were both WIA. Shortly thereafter, I received a report that Mike-1—Chan Crangle—was also hit. However, when I checked, I found that it was not true.

*

2nd Lieutenant CHAN CRANGLE
Mike Company, 3/26—1st Platoon Commander

I had no contact with either Gall's platoon or any friendlies to my rear, nor with the company. I was alone.

Captain ANDY DeBONA
Mike Company, 3/26—Commanding Officer

Mike-1 had somehow gotten out of position. It should have been set in with its point about midway down and to the right of the Mike-2 position. However, it was a little farther to the rear and maybe farther to the right than it should have been. There was a gap. But the good part was that, from the start, Mike-1 had had clear fields of fire across the paddyfields at the NVA main body. The paddyfield was dead flat and open. The bad news was that, instead of having Mike-1 firmly tied in on its right flank, Mike-2's lead element was alone out there.

The way it looked from the Mike Company position, the NVA bounced off India and Lima, attempted to flank them, and ran smack dab into Mike-2. When they attempted to flank Mike-2, they ran smack dab into Mike-1. I firmly believe that if Mike-1 had not been where it was, there wouldn't have been a company CP.

About 10 minutes into Mike-2's contact, I received word from the Mike-2 platoon sergeant, Staff Sergeant Edward Gaytan, that Lieutenant Bob Gall was KIA. Gaytan said he was going forward to find out what had happened. About 3 minutes later, I received word that Staff Sergeant Gaytan was also KIA. As I pieced it together later, some NVA got into the Mike-2 position. The fighting was down to 5 to 6 meters. Everyone was blasting away at each other. Gall was killed as he was going forward. He was killed standing up. So was Gaytan. It was a madhouse.

Once again, trying to break in the battalion tac net, I requested permission to pull back because the situation was not looking too good. This request was denied because of the tank. They said I had to protect the tank.

The company CP group was hit again by mortars and small-arms fire. My battalion communicator was hit. In fact, everyone was hit except Lieutenant Crenshaw, my arty FO. Gunnery Sergeant Gleason Norris, my company gunny, had many holes in him.

*

2nd Lieutenant CHAN CRANGLE
Mike Company, 3/26—1st Platoon Commander

With clearly visible NVA circling my right flank and no contact with the company or any other friendlies, I pulled the platoon in even tighter. We were taking fairly stiff small-arms fire, but it didn't seem like they were making a direct assault on my position. I'm not sure that in all the confusion the NVA really realized that we were there. This went on for a few moments, until I decided that we were too exposed and too isolated. We had to rejoin the company. I figured that Andy was still at the top of the ridge to my rear, so we made a very hasty withdrawal on up the ridge. So far, we had sustained only minimal casualties—nothing serious.

Near the top of the ridge, the small-arms fire became extremely intense. I could see the brush being shot away. We came on what must have been a part of the battalion perimeter the night before and immediately occupied the foxholes we found. Unfortunately, we were one hole short! I was standing next to a filled-in trash pit and I figured it was the softest dirt between there and San Francisco. Boy, did I make the dirt fly! I scooped out enough dirt to get either my head and torso or my torso and legs in—but not both. Incoming and small-arms fire made my decision for me.

I was flat on my back with my legs out of the hole, watching the brush being shot away. I actually believed I was going to lose my legs, so, copying a story I had heard, I put my belt around one knee and a bootlace on the other. I hoped that, if the legs went, I would be able to keep from bleeding to death.

My platoon corpsman jumped into a hole face first, bent up on his hands and knees. A Chicom grenade landed on his back and everyone was yelling at him to clear the hole! Doc just stayed on his hands and knees, wriggling his fanny to shrug the damned thing off. The grenade was a dud. A few moments later, Doc was demanding to throw a grenade. We had nearly zero visibility—maybe 20 feet—through the brush and a lot of incoming small arms. After a few arguments, I said okay. Doc pulled the pin and gave it a mighty heave—for all of about 10 feet! This grenade was not a dud! By popular vote of the platoon, Doc did not throw any more grenades.

Despite the incoming, I was not convinced that we were being directly assaulted. We were returning a lot of fire, but we couldn't see any enemy due to the brush, which was quite thick, 8 to 10 feet high, and very similar to California manzanita. It was impenetrable, except on your belly. My impression was that the heaviest fire was to my right. We still had no contact with the company or anyone else. My platoon sergeant and I repeatedly checked our flanks, but we never found any friendlies. Finally, I got Andy on the radio. We couldn't figure out where I was or he was, so I stood up and waved my arms. Andy was to my right rear.

1st Lieutenant HARRY DOLAN
Mike Company, 3/26—3rd Platoon Commander

Bob Gall's platoon apparently was in the thick of it. Although my right flank reported firing on NVA in the open, I had not yet seen any NVA from my position at the center of the platoon. We detected and fired on a small group of NVA to our front. I doubt that the men could really see targets clearly in the high grass, but they fired at the movement. This was reported to Andy. He said hold what we had because he was heavily engaged.

I made one attempt to locate Crangle's 1st Platoon, to see if my platoon was tied in with anybody on our left flank. I cut across the base of our company wedge. Having moved about 100 meters, I suddenly realized that I was doing something incredibly stupid—but necessary—out there alone, so I moved back to the 3rd Platoon position. I advised Andy again that we had no friendly contact on the company left flank. We continued to detect and fire on NVA moving in the brush.

Chapter 18

Staff Sergeant CHARLES OWENS
Kilo Company, 3/26—Company Gunny

The NVA hit Mike Company and rolled off them toward us. They were after the battalion CP, so they sideslipped Mike and came straight on up at us, at Kilo and the CP.

Major CARL MUNDY
3/26—Operations Officer

I wanted to roll our two Ontos up on the line. I sent Bill Wildprett over to get them moved up into position where they could bring fire to bear on this wave of NVA that was coming towards the battalion CP location. Bill rolled them up.

Staff Sergeant CHARLES OWENS
Kilo Company, 3/26—Company Gunny

While the large group of NVA was coming at us across the paddyfield, a smaller group hit us from close in, from right off our front. Right then, we had an Ontos pull up on the top of the hill, from over the reverse slope. It stopped about 30 yards right behind our foxholes. The sergeant in the Ontos started firing his .50-cal at them, mowing those rows of NVA down like they were corn, like he was chopping corn. The ones he was shooting at were down in that big rice paddy, but my people were already taking care of NVA that were right on us. Right on us! They were nearly up to the military crest of the hill.

The Ontos fired his 106s once, down into the valley, at the big group. When he did that, the NVA who were close in hit him with an RPG. It hit right beside the driver, just about, and ricocheted off the front of the Ontos and hit the sergeant. Killed him. The driver jumped out of that thing and left. I don't blame him. They did a lot of damage—they were brave men—before the NVA got the sergeant with that RPG. There was another Ontos off to my left. He fired his 106s, too. When the one behind us got hit, he pulled back over the crest of the hill.

Lance Corporal RANDALL BROWNING
Alpha Company, 3rd Antitank Battalion
Navy Cross citation (excerpt):

Although painfully wounded by fragments from an artillery round, Lance Corporal Browning quickly had his injury treated and immediately returned to his Ontos where he learned that his was the only tracked vehicle in operation. Rapidly assessing the situation, he maneuvered his vehicle through intense hostile fire to a forward position and began delivering highly effective machine-gun and recoilless-rifle fire against the enemy. Successfully repulsing the first of several human-wave assaults, he remained undaunted by the vicious enemy fire and steadfastly continued to deliver a heavy volume of fire during ensuing fanatical attacks.

Staff Sergeant CHARLES OWENS
Kilo Company, 3/26—Company Gunny

We had one machine gun that got knocked out twice. The gun was set in right where the NVA were trying to get through to the battalion CP. They hit the gunner twice, trying to get through him. Then they hit him with an RPG—him and his weapon. I saw him knocked unconscious, but he got up again. He was bleeding. He got up and tried to fix his M-60, but he couldn't fix it. I saw him lay over the gun and die.

Major CARL MUNDY
3/26—Operations Officer

We had in the CP with us, as did all Marine Corps outfits in those days, a Vietnamese Marine Corps liaison officer, a lieutenant. He was petrified because it would have been very bad for him if he was captured with an American unit. He was quite convinced that he would have been very harshly dealt with by the NVA.

Captain TOM EARLY
3/26—Communications Officer

The noise, smells, screams, and action was, at best, indescribable. A wounded Pfc who was shooting NVA point-blank with his M-60 only 5 meters in front of the battalion command group suddenly crawled back to us and asked, "Where is Master Gunnery Sergeant McHugh?" McHugh said, "Here," and the Marine said, "Thanks. I just never saw one." Then he crawled back to his M-60. Some Marines were actually shaking hands to say farewell.

Staff Sergeant CHARLES OWENS
Kilo Company, 3/26—Company Gunny

We had an old bomb crater full of NVA troops. They were hitting us with rifles, grenades, and RPGs. It was a real big hole on the side of the hill, about 30 feet in diameter. I knew the Lord Jesus was with me—I never was hit; they couldn't get me, so I went out and carried in our wounded and dead.

One time, three or four NVA followed me in when I was carrying a wounded Marine back to the sick bay. The battalion commander was standing up on the hill in front of me, watching the battle. He was smiling! He knew I had a second line set up behind the main line, up the hill a little, right in front of the battalion CP. The NVA must have thought they had the battalion commander—until the Marines manning the second line of holes stood up and blew them all away.

Lieutenant Louis Roath, the air liaison officer, was all over the place, calling in air strikes. After he was hit—it was a big shoulder wound from one bullet that went all the way through him—he kept trying to work, but he finally couldn't go any farther and they put him over in our company CP. He didn't know how bad off he was.

Lieutenant John Holderness, the arty FO, was calling in fire missions from Camp Carroll, the Army 175mm guns there. He was moving around the whole time, looking at targets in all directions. He was doing a really good job.

Captain Wildprett, who had been the Kilo Company commander before he went up to the battalion staff, was a real hero. He was all over the place.

I was moving behind the line, checking on the troops, when I saw three NVA heading right for one of my Marines. I turned to go down to help him when he reached down in his hole and pulled up a LAAW. He hit the center NVA on the chest and about blew the guy apart. The backblast hit me. I went down there and yelled at him, "Hey, man, next time look around before you fire one of them things." He laughed, "Gunny, I didn't have time." He sure didn't, either.

Major CARL MUNDY
3/26—Operations Officer

The battalion CP was actually an observation post at that particular point, located as it was in a thicket on top of Hill 48. I could move out of the thicket and see what was going whenever I needed to.

I could hear crashing in the thicket as the NVA got close enough to toss some hand grenades in our direction or to exchange some small-arms fire with the perimeter right around us. At one quiet point, when I heard a crashing in the underbrush around the CP, I drew my .45 and pulled the slide back to put a round in the chamber. I was getting ready to repel boarders. As the crashing got close, I said, "Halt! Who goes there?" Back came an American voice and there emerged from the bushes a very beleaguered-looking young Marine who said, "We're out of .45 ammo. Does anybody have any .45 ammo that's working? Can we get a resupply?"

We had not at that point gotten a resupply of small-arms ammunition, but I had three magazines with the standard 7 rounds apiece—21 rounds. I pulled two of the magazines out and said, "Here you go." He thanked me, took the two magazines, turned around, walked back down the hill, and got in his hole. Here was this kid who had been down there fighting all afternoon. Finally there was a lull, and he came back for a resupply. There was no question whatsoever in his mind about going back down there, even though he had only 14 rounds, certainly not a lot of stuff with which to fight.

Staff Sergeant CHARLES OWENS
Kilo Company, 3/26—Company Gunny

My people always complained about carrying ammo because I made them carry 350 rounds per man. But nobody complained after that battle. At one point, we were about the only Marines on the hill who had any ammo.

The NVA got shotgun close at times. I didn't have time to look at them. They were coming and I was firing. I carried a 1917 pump shotgun loaded with double-aught buck cartridges. It was knocking them down. When I ran out of rounds for the shotgun, I left it at the CP and started using my .45. I started out with seven or eight clips for it, but when the battle died off, I had two rounds in the weapon and a clip in my hand.

*

Captain ANDY DeBONA
Mike Company, 3/26—Commanding Officer

Mike-2's contact suddenly became light. I was led to believe that they had beaten off the bad guys. Mike-1 was still in medium to heavy contact. India and Lima had finally gotten together, but they were still tying up the battalion tac net.

I attempted to break in, finally got Battalion again, and explained the situation—that I was getting cut up out there because we had no fighting holes. Mortars were hitting me pretty hard. I said that we could pull back at least Mike-2 and Mike-3. Mike-1 could be disengaged later. I said that I wanted to come back into the battalion perimeter. At least back there we had holes. Battalion responded by saying that they were being hit by small-arms fire.

With less than an hour of daylight left, I finally got my permission to fall back to the battalion CP. I then got on the company net. I told the platoon commanders who were going to pull back to the battalion CP to occupy the same holes that they had prior to pulling out. I told them to pull back their wounded and dead first and to let me know when their last people started moving.

1st Lieutenant HARRY DOLAN
Mike Company, 3/26—3rd Platoon Commander

Andy called me and said, "Zero Fingers, you are covering our withdrawal." I informed him that we didn't have many effectives left, but I knew the rest of the company was at least as bad off. We spread out a bit and waited.

2nd Lieutenant CHAN CRANGLE
Mike Company, 3/26—1st Platoon Commander

We made a mad dash into the battalion CP area. While my platoon did not waste any time moving back up the hill or rejoining the battalion, we pulled out in reasonable tactical formation. The important point was that we were not directly assaulted—either that or we laid down enough firepower to break up any direct attacks. We had taken incoming and small-arms fire, but not enough to break up the platoon. My casualties were very light. I didn't lose any squad leaders, although a couple of them took minor hits.

1st Lieutenant HARRY DOLAN
Mike Company, 3/26—3rd Platoon Commander

When I got word to pull back, I started moving WIAs and KIAs back down the tank trail to the battalion CP location. When all WIAs and KIAs had been moved out, my radio operator and I collected up some M-16s, ammo, and frag grenades from the abandoned position and started withdrawing. I realized that, in the process of getting our WIAs and KIAs out, I again had done something stupid—but necessary. The whole platoon cover force was now down to two men: myself and my radio operator.

Captain ANDY DeBONA
Mike Company, 3/26—Commanding Officer

A stream of dead and wounded started coming through the company CP position from the Mike-2 and Mike-3 positions. The company CP group ceased to exist when I sent my own wounded back with the wounded from the rifle platoons. I finally received word from all three platoons that they were pulling back in to the battalion position. By then, it had gotten a little bit lonely out there.

1st Lieutenant HARRY DOLAN
Mike Company, 3/26—3rd Platoon Commander

My radio operator and I began moving in a low squat along each side of the tank trail. I could see green .51-caliber tracers lacing the sky overhead. It was a long 10 to 15 minutes. We heard movement all around us and fired at what we were sure by location must have been the enemy. All of a sudden, coming down the trail to look for me, standing upright as if on a spring walk, I saw Andy DeBona. He had come out to find us. I told him to get down because of the .51-caliber fire. He retorted, "Oh bullshit, Zero Fingers, come on. We don't have all day."

Captain ANDY DeBONA
Mike Company, 3/26—Commanding Officer

It finally got to the point that the only people out there were myself and Corporal Schneider, my radio operator, so I decided it would be a good idea to leave the area.

I very rarely cursed and yelled, but on the way back in, I kept screaming, "Goddammit, quit shooting at me!" I was under the impression that my own people were shooting my way. However, the NVA could not understand English and they did not comply with my order.

As Mike was moving back into the battalion position, the battalion position received some more incoming artillery. I hit the deck and rolled into what looked like a very nice position—a very slight crater. There were two Marines in there who looked at me funny. I sure didn't expect them and they sure didn't expect me. I asked them if they were in the front lines and they said, "Yes." And then it was a "Yessir" when they recognized who I was. It sure felt nice to be back.

*

2nd Lieutenant PAUL DRNEC
Bravo Company, 3rd Tank Battalion—2nd Platoon Commander

Suddenly, my driver came up on the intercom: "Hey, Lieutenant, I don't think there's any friendly infantry around us anymore."

"What?"

"Yes, sir. I don't see anyone moving and it's quiet."

At about this time, I saw the NVA to our right moving out of the paddyfield and on into the line of bushes fronting Hill 48. They had flanked us.

That did it. We were pretty well out of ammunition, our track was bad and we couldn't move, the friendly infantry had abandoned us—so what the hell do we do? I tried reaching the infantry on the radio, but the net was in chaos. "Get ready to bail out again," I yelled into the intercom.

I didn't have any perspective on the battalion's situation. I could see the NVA coming across the open paddy area. I knew the companies up ahead were engaged. I wasn't sure how much stuff the NVA still had in back of the lead elements. I didn't know what kind of shape we were in.

To clear the immediate area, Sergeant Vining and the gunner sprayed the high-brush area in front of us with four canister rounds. I dropped the main-gun breech onto the deck, and then I threw three or four hand grenades to clear the high grass close in. Then we bailed out and headed back to the nearest position I knew Marines still had to be holding.

We had to run across no-man's land. There was good cover, heavy undergrowth. I brought up the rear. I had the grease gun and the others had the M-14 and several other odd weapons we had picked up along the way. I was the only one wearing a flak jacket, which I always wore as protection against being jolted against the lip of the turret hatchway when the tank was moving.

It was touch and go there for a while. We didn't know who was between us and the Marine position or if the NVA would pop a mortar round on us. I was learning that being in action outside a tank is a lot different from being in action inside a tank. The NVA artillery and rockets had lifted, but that was because the NVA infantry was so close.

I knew the Marine infantry would have pulled back to the foxholes they had dug and occupied the previous afternoon; they were the only prepared positions around there. So, after we had run most of the distance and I felt we were getting close, we all began yelling, "Don't shoot! Marines! We're Marines! Don't shoot!" Finally, we ran right through the friendly forward element.

I moved back toward the rear of the Marine position to try to link up with an officer, to find out what was going on. I finally found Captain DeBona. I was kind of pissed off at him because I felt Mike Company had bugged out on us without telling us anything. I let him know I was steamed, but I quickly realized that he had had a lot of grunts to think about without having to worry about a couple of tanks.

After reporting the disabled status of my tank to Captain DeBona, I jumped into a foxhole and found a young Marine who was just shaking all over. I asked, "What's wrong?" He said, "My rifle broke and I picked up another rifle. That son of a bitch broke and I picked up another one and *that* son of a bitch broke. They're *all* broke. I can't find anything to shoot!" I'd have been shaking too if it had happened to me.

I had had my head cracked open two nights earlier by a defective hatch lock. I probably had a mild concussion. I was feeling woozy, in no shape to be much good in a fight, so I offered the Marine my grease gun. He didn't believe me at first, but he was thrilled to get it. It was a very distinctive .45-caliber weapon. It had no range and I had no spare ammunition, but it would be great if the fighting got really close-in. I gave it to him and lay back in the foxhole. My head hurt. I was out of it.

*

Lance Corporal RON BURKE
Mike Company, 3/26, 2nd Platoon

My squad was way ahead of the company, a couple of football fields, at least. There was a whole bunch of NVA and not very many of us, so I started questioning my squad leader's order to go forward into the paddies. I told him, "It's going to be a fucking mess. What do we have here now? Seven, eight guys? Look at all the people they got out there." I asked him if he knew we were doing the right thing. I said, "Even if our people are behind us, are we doing the right thing?" Then rockets started hitting between us and the rest of the company. I told him that everyone behind us was probably pinned down and there was no way they were going to be able to give us any assistance. That got everyone else to stop and think about what we were doing. The squad leader saw the writing on the wall and ordered us to scurry up behind a line of hedges and wait until I could get a hold of somebody higher up on my radio.

It was difficult to get anyone on the radio. I'd somehow jammed the handset button and I couldn't get it unjammed. I wasn't a radioman. I didn't know how to fix it. We finally got the button working and got a hold of somebody. I think it was Captain DeBona. He gave us directions to pull back. Boy, was I glad to hear that!

As we started pulling back, I saw little fellows running around in our flak jackets and helmets. They were in the high grass, like us. They didn't look like Americans to me. I thought, "Oh, boy!" We had only one Asian in our whole platoon and there was a whole bunch of Asians out there! As we John Wayned our way back—we were pro-grammed to John Wayne anywhere we went when we were under fire—there were people all around us. They were in front of us and behind us. I didn't shoot at anyone with an American flak jacket on—just to be sure. I didn't really know who they were.

One rifleman from another fire team got hit in the throat. We all stopped and laid down a base of fire while our corpsman, HM3 James Holloway, performed a tracheotomy on him. The guy died. Two guys grabbed the body underneath the armpits and dragged him. We took turns dragging him. It really slowed us down. He wasn't a big guy, but he was heavy. We couldn't leave anything he had on him—no ammo or anything—for the enemy.

We dragged the dead Marine to the dead tank. There was nobody there. Everyone was gone. We were all by ourselves. We were exhausted. We needed to take a rest. It was then that someone figured out the little guys in the Marine flak jackets and helmets were NVA for sure. We started shooting at the ones we could see who were close to us. They were off to the left of the way the tank was facing—toward the low hills over to the south. We heard them yelling in their language, so we *knew* they were enemy soldiers. That really scared me.

Two guys were lost. They just disappeared, went their own way or something. I don't know where they went. I'm not even sure they went out with us in the first place. They just weren't there. When we stopped beside the tank, there were just five Marines, Doc Holloway, and the dead guy.

We pulled back behind the crest of the little hill the tank was on. We decided to leave the dead Marine beside the tank. He was too heavy to carry the rest of the way; he'd already slowed us down too much. The tank was a good landmark for where we left him. We couldn't lose him.

Two guys crawled back up to the crest of the rise and laid down a base of fire for the rest of us. Then we got into some cover and stopped. When we opened fire, the two guys came on back through us. Then we moved again, and then they moved again. We could hear the enemy, and periodically we could see them. They were firing at us. They shot the antenna off my radio, about halfway down.

We John Wayned our way all the way back to the battalion position and found Mike Company. I saw Marines I knew from the other squads of Mike-2, and Captain DeBona was there. Nobody else in the squad had been hit. We just had scrapes from all that John Wayneing.

Chapter 19

As always, more time had passed than anyone who was there really believes. According to Lieutenant Bill Cowan's research in late September 1967, Lieutenant Paul Drnec's tank, B-22, fired 90mm white-phosphorous rounds on the approaching NVA waves at 1700. Thereafter, Mike and Kilo companies were heavily engaged for at least one hour before Mike Company began its withdrawal. It appears that Mike Company started back to the Hill 48 perimeter at about 1815, and it is possible that the last element of the company—Lance Corporal Burke's squad—did not arrive until about 1900.

*

2nd Lieutenant CHAN CRANGLE
Mike Company, 3/26—1st Platoon Commander

As my platoon came into the battalion perimeter, Master Gunnery Sergeant McHugh jumped out of his foxhole and gave me a huge bear hug. Then he pointed to a spot about 50 meters to the north and said, ''Go get 'em,'' or words to that effect. Sure enough, there were about 10 NVA, which my 1st Squad took on in hand-to-hand fashion.

The platoon had been on a knife kick. Each Marine returning from R&R brought back an even larger, more ferocious-looking combat knife. The evenings were full of the sounds of sharpening and bragging about using them in hand-to-hand. My 1st Squad leader, Sergeant Gary Waldo, was a character over whom Andy and I despaired. We doubted that he could keep his sergeant's stripes. He was one hell of a combat Marine but a triple handful in the rear. Waldo had an especially deadly looking kris, wavy blade and all. When we roared into the CP and Top McHugh said, "Go get 'em," Waldo and his crew waded in. I saw Waldo bash one NVA with his M-16, which promptly broke in two. A little later, I found Waldo sitting on the edge of his hole, swearing a blue streak. He was absolutely fit to be tied because, in his one chance to use the kris, he had completely forgotten about it!

Captain ANDY DeBONA
Mike Company, 3/26—Commanding Officer

As soon as I got back into the battalion perimeter, my first step was to drop my pack. I saw Carl Mundy walking very calmly and nonchalantly around the area. He was wearing shined boots and, I swear to God, it looked like he had starched utilities on. Nearby was the shell of an Ontos. It looked like it had been RPGed.

The battalion CP itself was somewhat of a shambles. It appeared as if Master Gunnery Sergeant McHugh and Captain Tom Early were on the battalion radio, that they were in fact the battalion radio operators. I talked to Captain Bill Wildprett, now the assistant S-3 under Mundy, and found out just what in the hell was going on. I was told by Top McHugh that there were some troops pinned down in a bomb crater to the right flank of the battalion CP.

2nd Lieutenant CHAN CRANGLE
Mike Company, 3/26—1st Platoon Commander

There weren't a lot of NVA around the battalion position. But then, until we arrived, there weren't too many friendlies in the battalion CP, either.

Captain ANDY DeBONA
Mike Company, 3/26—Commanding Officer

I went around, checking my positions, and found quite a few gaps. Since everybody was in his own hole, the gaps pointed to the fact that we had suffered quite a few casualties. In addition, there were two companies still not in. The night before, India had been on my right flank and Lima had been on my left. So, when we got back, on both of my flanks were company-size positions not filled by anyone.

1st Lieutenant HARRY DOLAN
Mike Company, 3/26—3rd Platoon Commander

We moved back into the perimeter and found it in a state of high confusion. Andy told me to go to work sorting out the company into platoons and moving parts of Kilo Company to their assigned part of the perimeter. Then he was gone. It was upsetting. I didn't know where my hero was, and I was trying to get fighting holes filled with Marines.

Captain ANDY DeBONA
Mike Company, 3/26—Commanding Officer

The first thing I attempted to do was get tied in with Kilo. That at the time seemed to be the priority. I tried to find Kilo-Six, but I could only find his exec, Lieutenant Dobies, and 1st Sergeant Goddard. I told them that we were attempting to tie in and that it would be nice if they would move their flanks out a little bit so I didn't have to extend myself too far.

The whole scene was sort of reminiscent of a colony of prairie dogs. I'd look around and not see a soul above the ground. When the artillery stopped, I'd look around and see heads bobbing up. Then, as soon as the next booms were heard, everyone ducked back down. The booms were not friendly booms at this time. They were coming generally from due west of us, as opposed to our southwest, the direction of Camp Carroll. It was easy to tell whose was whose.

It seemed like a losing struggle to try to get tied in with Kilo, so I left. As I got near my own position, some more artillery came rolling in. I dived into my hole and a rather large body fell in on top of me. It was Lieutenant Crenshaw, my artillery FO, who I called Baby Huey because of his size.

The battalion position was receiving artillery, no mortar, and a little bit of small-arms fire. There was some heavy-caliber stuff being shot off, but it didn't appear to be impacting in the battalion area. The buzzes, the bees, the wasps—the distinctive sounds of incoming small-arms fire—didn't seem to be close to where I was.

I checked the lines again and continued to try and get the gaggle unscrewed. Generally, the position to my left flank wasn't occupied, but I felt that my right flank, out toward Kilo, was the important one to get covered up. I had to get people over there.

2nd Lieutenant CHAN CRANGLE
Mike Company, 3/26—1st Platoon Commander

Andy got the company reasonably straightened out, with my 1st Platoon on the western edge of the ridge. It was a fairly tight perimeter. We continued to take small arms and incoming. I was tied into Kilo Company on my right, with a Kilo Company M-60 team. The M-60 opened up, and by the time I got to them, it was firing furiously. But there were no visible enemy. I told the gunners that if they couldn't see anything they should stick to grenades. Visibility was tremendously limited by the brush; I could see maybe 10 meters or less.

Captain ANDY DeBONA
Mike Company, 3/26—Commanding Officer

I found a mess of wounded. I told them that if there was anyone who could still bear arms, it would be a good idea to start looking out toward the left flank, even though there weren't bad guys there yet. I told them they just might be in a firefight.

Zero Fingers Dolan eventually reported that he was tied in with Kilo on his left. However, he had lost contact with Mike-2, in my company's center. I got out and played traffic cop, trying to fill the gap. I was not successful.

I got near the battalion CP again, making my rounds. Lieutenant Crangle mentioned to me that there were troops still pinned down in the bomb crater. This was the second time I had heard this report.

It seemed to me that the lines just kept falling apart. When everybody would report in that they were all in contact, I would say, ''Make sure you check your right. Make sure you check your left.'' Inevitably, they weren't in contact anymore. I had asked Kilo to extend their lines, but I don't believe that this ever happened.

Eventually, I did get tied in with Kilo to both the left and the right. I was spread thin even after using many of the wounded as line fillers around on the back side of the hill. I also had the squad of engineers that was attached to the battalion. They were armed with M-14 rifles.

I had only one uninjured corpsman left in the company, HM1 William Meade. I told him to get in the sickbay bomb crater with the wounded and try to make them as comfortable as possible, to ransack abandoned packs to get sleeping blankets and poncho liners. I checked on the status of the medevac birds and found out that they weren't going to be coming in yet. I told the wounded and Doc Meade about the delay.

*

Lance Corporal RON BURKE
Mike Company, 3/26, 2nd Platoon

As our squad got into the perimeter, an Ontos was firing, going back behind the hill, coming back up, and firing again.

2nd Lieutenant CHAN CRANGLE
Mike Company, 3/26—1st Platoon Commander

The Ontos was magnificent. All the tanks were gone, and he was the only firepower left. His 106mm recoilless rifles with fléchette rounds or HE were awesome! I have absolutely no doubt that his firepower prevented some serious hand-to-hand work on the perimeter.

Lance Corporal RANDALL BROWNING
Alpha Company, 3rd Antitank Battalion
Navy Cross citation (excerpt):

When his recoilless rifle ammunition was expended and his machine gun became inoperable, Lance Corporal Browning unhesitatingly manned a sub-machine gun and continued to deliver devastating fire on the enemy.

*

Lance Corporal RON BURKE
Mike Company, 3/26, 2nd Platoon

Captain DeBona told us to go back to the rear and get supplies to bring forward. Everybody was running out of supplies. We went around to the back of the hill on a little trail through the bushes and trees. There were lots of supplies there. I dropped my radio, grabbed a case of grenades, and put it up on my shoulder.

Captain ANDY DeBONA
Mike Company, 3/26—Commanding Officer

As I got near the battalion CP once again, I saw Lieutenant Lou Roath, the ALO. A gunshot wound had taken off quite a slice of meat through his shoulder. His arm was in a sling, but he was working. He said he had been dinged while he was out with the Marines pinned down in the bomb crater. He indicated that the men in there were in pretty bad shape by the time he left.

I figured it was time for me to go out and help the men in the bomb crater.

2nd Lieutenant CHAN CRANGLE
Mike Company, 3/26—1st Platoon Commander

Andy came up to me and asked if I knew where any bomb craters were, that some Marines were pinned down and needed help. The Marines were pinned hard, 30 to 50 meters in front of the battalion lines. I told Andy where the crater was and started to assemble a squad to go with him. Andy was adamant—as only Andy can be—that I was not to accompany him. I knew that we were taking .51-caliber machine-gun fire from that general direction, so I told him to keep his head down.

Captain ANDY DeBONA
Mike Company, 3/26—Commanding Officer

It's difficult to explain my rationale. Why I went out is, I guess, because *somebody* had to go. So there I was, the company commander, in the attack with one radio operator, going out to the bomb crater.

The bomb crater was approximately 50 meters out in the open, toward the right front of Hill 48, in the direction of the NVA regimental assault. It was on a flat, but the ground dipped away from it to the right. Once I knew which crater everyone was talking about, it was very easy to find. It was a tad bit noisy in that area. The bad guys were in another bomb crater, approximately 25 meters away. There was a grenade-throwing contest going on, but neither side could quite reach the other with its grenades.

2nd Lieutenant CHAN CRANGLE
Mike Company, 3/26—1st Platoon Commander

The last I saw of Andy, he was moving down a trail or a break in the brush off to my right. My platoon provided cover.

Lance Corporal RON BURKE
Mike Company, 3/26, 2nd Platoon

When my squad came around to the front side of the hill carrying ammo, they told us there was a bomb crater in an out-front position and that we had some boys that were pinned down in there. Captain DeBona was striking out toward the bomb crater. There were two or three Marines along with him. Things were getting real confusing. We were taking some mortar fire. I heard DeBona hollering that we had to go back out there, that there were wounded Marines in the bomb crater.

I didn't know what to do. I saw Captain DeBona 15 to 20 yards in front of me, on the trail. We'd been taught never to call captains "Captain" or lieutenants "Lieutenant," but I had to get the captain's attention, so I yelled, "Skipper!" He dropped to his knee and turned. I asked what I should do with the case of grenades I was carrying. He asked, "Can't you handle it?" I said I could, and he said, "Well, bring 'em with us." Then we headed for the bomb crater, through bushes and trees.

At the edge of the brush, DeBona dropped down to one knee and said, "There's no cover from here to the crater. Do what you were taught."

Major CARL MUNDY
3/26—Operations Officer

I'll never forget big, hawk-nosed, profane Andy DeBona standing up there when it was time to go. He was on line with his troops when he turned and yelled, "This is Mike-Six, moving out."

Lance Corporal RON BURKE
Mike Company, 3/26, 2nd Platoon

We John Wayned our way into the open with DeBona leading.

Captain ANDY DeBONA
Mike Company, 3/26—Commanding Officer

My radioman, Corporal Schneider, and I ran out there together. I made a grand rolling dive right over the top of one of the wounded troops in the bottom of the hole. Schneider was right behind me.

Lance Corporal RON BURKE
Mike Company, 3/26, 2nd Platoon

It was very difficult for me to John Wayne with the case of grenades on my shoulder. I was very clumsy. Just as I got to the lip of the crater, I paused to take the case of grenades off my shoulder. DeBona reached out and deliberately tripped me. That made me fall into the crater. I suppose he was spooked about me getting hit just before we got there. The fall hurt, but I wasn't injured.

Captain ANDY DeBONA
Mike Company, 3/26—Commanding Officer

My first question was sort of a dumb one, but I didn't know what else to say. I just asked, "Who's in charge?" Nobody volunteered, so I relegated myself to the position of squad leader.

There were about 15 Marines in the hole. Approximately half of them were wounded. There were about a dozen M-16s and at least one M-60 laying in the bottom of the crater. Several had bullet holes through them. None of them was operable.

The small-arms fire that was being delivered by the people in our crater was not effective. A couple of the Marines would hold their rifles above their heads, above the lip of the bomb crater, and just make noise in the general direction of the bad-guy crater. I figured this wasn't a good thing to do, so I gingerly lifted my head up over the top of the crater in the direction of the bad guys and told the Marines with M-16s to do the same and crank off a few rounds. I told them that this was the way to do it.

Initially, when I peeked my head up, there were about five or six bad-guy weapons winking back at me.

Lance Corporal RON BURKE
Mike Company, 3/26, 2nd Platoon

The NVA were dug in just out from the crater. There were little craters out there, and they seemed to be using some of our old positions. Their big crater was just a little way beyond grenade range. There was a contest going on to see who could throw a grenade into the enemy crater. You'd start at bottom of the crater, pull the pin on a grenade, and then run up to the top of the crater to get as much force as you could before you threw. Sergeant Fred Sollie actually ran out of our crater before he threw. He was hit.

My buddy, Lance Corporal Frank Taggart, also got out of the crater, 10 to 15 meters, and he was shot once or twice in the butt or the back of the leg. I low-crawled out to him. Taggart was doing a lot of moaning. I don't think he knew what was going on. He had on an ammo bandoleer, and I was able to use it to drag him back. I was most of the way back in when someone else crawled out and helped me. When I got near the lip of the crater, someone inside there pulled me in. I lost track of Taggart after that. I never saw him again.

By the time I got back, someone had dug into the side of the crater so we could put steady fire on the enemy positions. I got up there and started firing. I saw a man with a helmet put his head above the lip of the enemy crater. The fire wasn't coming from that guy, though. I thought they had a system where he was an FO and other guys fired at us. The head kept coming up and going back down—in the same place! I drew a bead and fired. I could see his face when I fired. It was the first time in Vietnam that I could actually see what I was shooting at, and the first time I knew I hit my target. I know I got him. I saw the round go in. The helmet flipped and he never showed up again.

Captain ANDY DeBONA
Mike Company, 3/26—Commanding Officer

Eventually, we gained fire superiority over them. In spite of that, I kept thinking that if all of the bad-guy grenades came into the hole with us, we'd be in pretty bad shape.

While we were firing at the bad guys, I devised a plan. What we'd do is, first of all, find out how many walking wounded we had. Of the seven or eight wounded in the crater, five or six of them were walking wounded; they could get around by themselves. Of the remaining two, one was hit in the leg and the other was also hit pretty bad. I said, "Okay, what we're gonna do is lay down covering fire. The first people that are going to leave are going to be the walking wounded." After that, half of the rest of the force was going to leave with one of the wounded men who had to be carried. Then the other half of the force would leave with the other wounded Marine. The company commander would stay back and provide covering fire.

On the rifle range in the Marine Corps, before you deliver rapid fire, someone in authority always calls, "Are you ready on the right? Are you ready on the left? All ready on the firing line. Watch your targets. Targets!" It's a standard, stock piece *every* Marine has heard. For some reason, that popped into my head. I figured that it would be the best way to control the fire. Looking back on it, it might have been hotdoggish, but, by God, it worked.

1st Lieutenant HARRY DOLAN
Mike Company, 3/26—3rd Platoon Commander

Above the sound of the battle, I heard a loud voice shout, "All ready on the right!"

Captain ANDY DeBONA
Mike Company, 3/26—Commanding Officer

I gave the commands, "All ready on the right?" Three or four troops on the right nodded their heads. "All ready on the left?" They nodded their heads on the left. "All ready on the firing line. Watch your targets. Targets!" And we all started laying down covering fire.

Our fire pretty well suppressed any fire coming out of the other bomb crater and our initial rush of walking wounded got back safely. We did the same thing again, this time with two magazines instead of just one. The first group of nonwounded left with one of the nonwalking wounded and got back safely. Then I did it again, the last group got back, and I was the only one left. I was still busily cranking off rounds when my weapon jammed.

It is difficult to express how I felt at that time. I looked behind me and saw that all the Marines were out of sight. I had already cranked off about two magazines, so I figured they should have been pretty well back to the perimeter. With my M-16 "stick" in hand—it wasn't a rifle, it was no better than a stick—I got out of the bomb crater and started back.

The way back, it seemed to me at the time, took at least two hours longer than it had taken me to get out there to the bomb crater. I eventually hit the lines again, but I didn't run into any friendlies until I got right into the battalion CP.

2nd Lieutenant CHAN CRANGLE
Mike Company, 3/26—1st Platoon Commander

The whole episode took 15 to 20 minutes. It was a magnificent display of courage from the most magnificent company commander in the battalion.

Captain Andy DeBona was recommended for a Medal of Honor for his heroic rescue effort in the bomb crater. He was awarded a Navy Cross.

Chapter 20

By about 1900, as the evening light was waning noticeably, the battle had settled down to mere mutual mayhem. The weakened NVA battalions had lost their momentum and initiative, and they no longer were pressing their attacks seriously. However, 3/26 was not out of trouble.

1st Lieutenant BOB STIMSON
India Company, 3/26—Executive Officer

On my way to find Captain Caulfield at just about dusk, I stopped by the 60mm mortar position and tried to help them direct fire on the NVA in the paddyfield. When I asked what they had, they told me they were all out of HE. All they had left was willy-peter. "Christ," I said, "fire it."

The first rounds did a lot of damage—I could see the willy-pete hitting NVA out there—but I really did more harm than good. The willy-pete smoked up a big section of the battlefield for several minutes, and we couldn't see any targets. When I had done as much damage as I could, I continued on and joined Captain Caulfield and Ron Zappardino at the company CP.

1st Lieutenant RON ZAPPARDINO
3/26—Forward Air Controller

The problem I had using all the air support I had on station was that the NVA .51-caliber antiaircraft machine guns on the ridge ahead and to the left of our hill could fire *down* on our fast movers while they were making their passes. I felt obliged to keep warning the pilots about the antiaircraft guns, telling them that it was up to them to commit or not commit, adding that we really needed them.

There was no way our air could fly through the antiaircraft fire without getting hit, but the AO and I did our best to keep them out of the worst of it. We had to run flights in on specific targets, designating the targets, approaches, and ordnance. While it was still light, we were able to bring most of the air in from behind us, over the top of our hill toward the rice paddies—from our right rear toward our left front. As much as possible, that minimized exposure to most of the antiaircraft guns, which were concentrated to our left. Most of the pilots dropped high—they had to, the fire was so intense—but they were effective.

Captain DICK CAMP
Lima Company, 3/26—Commanding Officer

The fast movers dropped napalm and general-purpose bombs within 75 meters of our position. They came in, one flight of four right after another. Every time one of them streaked in, five North Vietnamese .51-caliber antiaircraft machine guns opened up.

2nd Lieutenant JOHN PRINCE
Lima Company, 3/26—2nd Platoon Commander

It was just fantastic to sit and watch them do their thing. One plane that flew in looked like it just about touched the bushes before it pulled up. I could hear many AK-47s firing at it. I saw one round, probably from a heavy machine gun—it was a green tracer—catch up with the plane at probably 800 feet in the air. The tracer round hit one of its wings and spun off.

2nd Lieutenant CHAN CRANGLE
Mike Company, 3/26—1st Platoon Commander

Two Marine F-4s rolled in to work the opposite ridgeline, to the southwest. Our ALO, Lieutenant Lou Roath, warned them not to make runs parallel to our lines because we had seen some really vicious .51-caliber antiaircraft fire on earlier strikes. The pilots, I suppose, decided otherwise. The first F-4 came over from south to north with snake—250-pound bombs. There was no incident. The second F-4 flew into a solid curtain of .51-cal. At least three positions poured green tracers into that aircraft.

Captain DICK CAMP
Lima Company, 3/26—Commanding Officer

I knew there were five .51-cals out there, because I could see their distinctive green tracers rising toward the Phantoms.

They hit one of the Phantoms.

2nd Lieutenant CHAN CRANGLE
Mike Company, 3/26—1st Platoon Commander

The plane seemed to stop in midair, with pieces flying off in all directions. Smoke and flame immediately erupted from the aircraft and he began to lose altitude.

Captain DICK CAMP
Lima Company, 3/26—Commanding Officer

I saw black smoke pour out behind it. I followed its progress with my eyes as it turned toward the coast.

2nd Lieutenant CHAN CRANGLE
Mike Company, 3/26—1st Platoon Commander

Two thoughts flashed into my mind: "The F-4 pilot is a dumb SOB," and "Even money says I'll have to go after him!" Fortunately, the pilot was able to stay in the air long enough to clear the area. It had been a rather spectacular sight!

Captain DICK CAMP
Lima Company, 3/26—Commanding Officer

Some of the troops saw a dark speck leave the airplane and announced, "He's out."

*

Lance Corporal RON BURKE
Mike Company, 3/26, 2nd Platoon

The NVA were firing artillery and mortars at us, but it was inaccurate and sporadic. It never was a barrage; just a little here and a little there.

2nd Lieutenant PAUL DRNEC
Bravo Company, 3rd Tank Battalion—2nd Platoon Commander

I was between two foxholes when a few artillery rounds landed nearby. I took cover behind what I thought was a full pallet of C-rations. It turned out the pallet was loaded with cases of hand grenades. When I realized that, I took off. I couldn't think of a worse place to hide in an artillery barrage.

2nd Lieutenant CHAN CRANGLE
Mike Company, 3/26—1st Platoon Commander

Just before dark, I was holding a short session with my squad leaders. A volley of incoming—mortars, I think—interrupted us. Everyone dived into the hole immediately available—mine. There's always room for one more!

Staff Sergeant CHARLES OWENS
Kilo Company, 3/26—Company Gunny

The 81s were on the back side of the perimeter, behind the crest of the hill. Those mortar people didn't hide. They were out there, firing, every time we called for a mission. That's what got a bunch of them killed. They got just about wiped out by rockets and mortar fire. All the dead and wounded 81mm mortarmen we found had shrapnel wounds in them.

One of the dead mortarmen was the acting platoon commander, Chief Warrant Officer Dick Holycross. Gunner Holycross, who had distinguished himself in battle on the night of September 7, was one of the best-beloved Marines in 3/26. He was about 40 years old, a Chosin Reservoir veteran, a policeman in Springfield, Ohio, and a Marine Corps Reserve officer who had volunteered to be called to active duty to serve in Vietnam. Gunner Holycross had been due to leave for R&R on September 7, but he had delayed his departure when the platoon commander and half the platoon had been dispatched to bolster another battalion. At the moment Dick Holycross was killed instantly by a direct mortar or rocket hit on the 81mm gun pits, his wife was waiting for him in Hawaii.

*

2nd Lieutenant CHAN CRANGLE
Mike Company, 3/26—1st Platoon Commander

Lou Roath was quite a character. He took a serious hit in the shoulder but refused medevac. I saw him on at least a couple of occasions, bloody as hell and with bandages, radio in hand, calling strikes and helos. He stayed with it throughout the evening.

1st Lieutenant HARRY DOLAN
Mike Company, 3/26—3rd Platoon Commander

I made a few quick runs past the battalion CP, on my way between different jobs on the line. It looked to me like Lou Roath was running the battalion. An aviator with a big bloody bandage on his shoulder looked to be running the whole thing.

Major CARL MUNDY
3/26—Operations Officer

Though Lou Roath was about half delirious, he stayed right there, calling in air support. That net was being monitored by the acting 3rd Marine Division commander back in Dong Ha, Brigadier General Lowell English. General English personally directed that Lieutenant Roath be written up for a Silver Star. Roath was, and he got it.

*

Captain ANDY DeBONA
Mike Company, 3/26—Commanding Officer

As soon as I returned from the bomb crater at about dusk, I once again started to reorganize my line and get Mike-1 spread over toward Kilo Company's position. It was a continual battle to try to keep our people tied in. As I was running around, I lost track of my pack. The significance of losing my pack was that it had my snuff in it. I was on an adrenaline high or whatever it was—I don't know. It was sort of stupid, but at the time it seemed the right thing to do: I started screaming, "Okay, what happened to my snuff? Okay, let's stop the war. Where's my pack? I can't find my pack.'' That got a little bit of a chuckle out of a few people. Once I realized what I had said, I sort of got a little bit of a chuckle out of me, also.

I started rearranging our lines, particularly in the vicinity of the battalion CP. All of a sudden, Master Gunnery Sergeant McHugh, the battalion operations chief, came walking up to me with a big shit-eating grin on his face. He had my pack, which was easily recognizable because it was the biggest thing out there. He handed it to me with a big smile and said, "Here, sir, here's your pack." I could have kissed him on the spot. I had my snuff; I was ready to go back in again. I was ready to start going.

I checked the line and found that the engineer squad that had been attached to Mike Company was on the rear slope just slightly to the right of the bomb crater we were using as an aid station for the wounded. They weren't really tied in to any other Marines. The engineers were all in the bottom of the hole, not looking out. I got the engineer squad leader and said, "Hey, what is this?" He said, "Well, my platoon commander told us that we should not be on the lines, and the rifle units can't put us on the lines." I informed him that there was no one else around to do the job. Instead of using his M-14s, for which he only had about two or three magazines each, I suggested he start arming his people with M-16s from the rather large supply of weapons that we had from wounded Marines who could not fire anymore.

I tried to organize each one of my people, tried to go around and talk to each of them, to find out what his fields of fire were, what his morale was like, how he was feeling. Not surprisingly the ones who had lasted that far were really spoiling for a fight. Morale was extremely good. It was a high—a personal high—for me, to talk to them, to see the dedication, to see their enthusiasm. God knows, I was scared shitless.

I talked to the wounded again, just after sunset. The battalion was still under intermediate artillery fire—maybe three or four rounds at a time. Small-arms fire had been knocked out, though.

Though I kept going back to Battalion to ask Mundy, Wildprett, Early, or McHugh what was happening, I sort of lost track of what was going on with India and Lima companies. In fact, I had lost track completely since trying to get my own lines tied up.

*

Staff Sergeant CHARLES OWENS
Kilo Company, 3/26—Company Gunny

Choppers started bringing in supplies and taking out the wounded, flying between us and Dong Ha. There weren't any helicopter gunships, but the H-34 choppers came in acting like they were gunships. Then the crewmen would kick out supplies onto our perimeter. After they kicked out the ammo, they'd whip around and go over to the landing zone to pick up our wounded.

Major CARL MUNDY
3/26—Operations Officer

I was struck by the exchange of fire between the NVA heavy .51-caliber machine guns, which used green tracers, and our own weapons, which used red or orange tracers. It was almost like a Christmas tree in the sky much of the time. This was particularly evident when the medevac helicopters would come in, or the resupply helicopters.

The helicopters would land behind the battalion position, which was down on the reverse slope of the ridge, and would either drop their supplies—most of the time, in fact, they'd just kick them out the door and keep going—or would land and pick up the wounded for medevac. As one helicopter broke above the top of the ridge, I stood there and watched this stream—just like a hose projecting water, green-colored water—chasing the helicopter around the sky. I got a great deal of respect for helicopter pilots that night by watching those guys turn those H-34 helicopters just like hummingbirds against the dark in various directions, turn very quickly and abruptly. I know at times that they had tracers entering a door of the helicopter and going out the other side.

Staff Sergeant CHARLES OWENS
Kilo Company, 3/26—Company Gunny

We tried to get Lieutenant Roath to take a medevac out, but he said there were too many people in worse shape than him and he wasn't going until all of them were gone. He couldn't do anything; his radio had been hit. When he finally got to Dong Ha, they were so worried about him ever regaining use of his arm—there was nerve damage—that they sent him straight back to the States for a special operation.

Lance Corporal RON BURKE
Mike Company, 3/26, 2nd Platoon

I was sent back to the LZ to help get the wounded aboard the medevacs. There were a few small-arms rounds coming in. Everyone was real nervous when we were putting casualties aboard the helicopters. We were exposed. I yelled around to see if anyone knew where my wounded buddy, Lance Corporal Frank Taggart, was. I couldn't find him anywhere. Two guys told me he was already gone, that he was okay and had been flown out already. I helped load three helos and then left to rejoin my squad.

Staff Sergeant CHARLES OWENS
Kilo Company, 3/26—Company Gunny

We had a cook, Corporal Roger Black, manning a position on the line. When I got to him, I saw he had a hole in the top of his head. I could see his brain showing. I told him to get over to the landing zone and get out of there. A corpsman came by and put a pressure bandage over the hole in Black's head and tied it under his chin. When the blood got to it, it looked like a little pink bonnet. He looked like Little Red Riding Hood. Black started walking up the hill, toward the landing zone, but then he grabbed the bandage and threw it on the ground. "I ain't going noplace, Gunny, not till the battle's over." He didn't; he stayed right there. In fact, later on, he shot an NVA who was trying to retrieve a dead NVA. Then Black went out there to pull the second dead NVA up to his fighting hole. I asked, "Black, what'd you do that for?" And he said, "I want to get more of them to come up here after him, so I can shoot them, too."

The company clerk came up to me and asked if he could help out on the line. By then, my people were hollering for more ammo, so I told him to go back to the landing zone, get ammo, and pass it out. I told the clerk to be careful, to crawl everywhere he went. On my next run down to the line from the CP, I found him *walking* along behind the fighting holes, passing out bandoleers of ammo like he was on the rifle range. I said, "Hey man, now don't do that!" And he said, "Aw, Gunny, I can't just crawl around here and give these people ammo! You hear all them people calling me?" I put him in for a medal.

*

Staff Sergeant CHARLES OWENS
Kilo Company, 3/26—Company Gunny

The NVA were still mingled with us when it got dark. They were still pushing. The fight had tapered down, but they were still pushing, trying to get through. They still had a lot of people out there.

Captain ANDY DeBONA
Mike Company, 3/26—Commanding Officer

Eventually, a little after dusk, we finally got tied in with Kilo. By that, I mean that Kilo Company was occupying the same positions it had initially, though it might have extended a little bit to the company's left. They were tied in to Mike-1, which was now in front of the battalion CP and really spread thin. Mike-1 was extended around to the left and tied in to what was left of Mike-2. Mike-2 was tied in to the engineers. The engineers were tied in to the company commander and wounded, who were occupying front-line positions and who were tied in with Mike-3, which was tied in with the other—right—flank of Kilo Company. The battalion perimeter around the battalion CP was maybe 30 meters front to back and maybe 100 to 150 meters in length, across the front.

As I reported to Battalion that we had finally tied in, Puff came on station. He turned night into day. It defies description when Puff fires. It looks like a solid stream of tracers coming down. He was working over the distant ridgeline on which I had observed the .51-calibers. We were also getting mortars from there.

Major CARL MUNDY
3/26—Operations Officer

Many of the evening hours were spent in controlling the fires, calling in and controlling Puff. One of the most impressive things that I have ever seen before or since was when Puff poured out a tube of orange tracers. The airplane would come around with a very dull roar and just defoliate the terrain in front of us. We knew that we were getting NVA with that. We knew that we were just tearing the earth up over where they were.

Lance Corporal RON BURKE
Mike Company, 3/26, 2nd Platoon

Puff was working out along the NVA ridgeline. It was a pleasant sight to see that boy! I noticed a couple of secondary explosions from where he was firing out there. Every fourth or fifth round was a tracer, but it looked like a solid tube of red was connecting the plane to the ground. I couldn't imagine anything in the vicinity living through that. He got close enough for us to see what he was hitting in the light of his tracer. His flares illuminated things almost to daylight bright. We fired at a

few things we could see in the light, but there wasn't much and it was
way out in front of us.

Major CARL MUNDY
3/26—Operations Officer

I personally spent a great deal of the evening trying to run in air support,
get flares over the other fellow's position—not ours. That was not the
easiest thing in the world to do. There's nothing more unnerving than
when you run a flare mission or fire some artillery illumination support
and the doggone things break open on your own position and illuminate
you instead of the other guy.

*

Staff Sergeant CHARLES OWENS
Kilo Company, 3/26—Company Gunny

The choppers kept coming in until every one of our wounded was gone.
Each chopper had a face painted on the front. They kept coming back
with supplies and picking up the wounded, running back and forth between
us and Dong Ha the whole time.

We had a TACP operator who worked through the whole battle, calling
in the choppers. After it was over, he went up to one of the corpsmen
and said, "Hey, Doc, scratch my back. It's itching me to death." The
corpsman saw little blood spots on the back of the TACP operator's
flak jacket, so he pulled up the jacket to look. The Marine's whole
back was covered with little shrapnel holes. It turned out he had been
wounded by one of the very first rockets that came in, but he didn't
even know it. When I found out, I told him to call in one more medevac.
He said, "Gunny, there ain't no more wounded," but I told him, "You
just call in one more medevac!" Then I took the corpsman aside and
told him to go down to the landing zone with the TACP operator and
load him aboard the medevac as soon as it came in. The Marine was
in bad shape, but he didn't know it.

*

Captain ANDY DeBONA
Mike Company, 3/26—Commanding Officer

My company CP was set up about 25 meters away from the battalion
CP, close to the wounded. We were practically on the front line. When

I finally got back to my CP position, Corporal Schneider, my radio operator, had the hole dug. In an infantry unit, you know you've arrived when your hole is dug when you come on back after doing something.

I took out my air mattress. I always carried an air mattress with me. I didn't mind the extra 3 to 4 pounds a bit. I would rather have had a good night's sleep. I had an air pillow, too, which I had managed to borrow off a medevac bird six to seven months earlier. These things were my pride and joy because I always knew I would get a good night's rest. I commenced blowing up my air mattress, but the thing wouldn't blow up. I looked at it and discovered that it had a few holes in it. I started looking around and found out that not only had the no-good lowlives holed my air mattress, they had holed my air pillow, too. I checked my pack and found a number of shrapnel holes in it, but no bullet holes. I took off my helmet to scratch my head and heard something rattling around the inside of that. There were a couple pieces of shrapnel rolling around inside my camouflage cover. I checked my flak jacket and found one or two small dings in that thing. At the time, all that really pissed me off was that my air mattress was flat and my pillow would not blow up.

I laid down beside the CP hole and ordered Corporal Schneider to wake me up if anything happened. I immediately crashed and woke up the next morning. I asked Schneider, "How did it go?" He mentioned that Kilo had had a contact during the night and killed two or three of them. I hadn't heard a thing.

Lance Corporal RON BURKE
Mike Company, 3/26, 2nd Platoon

What was left of my squad was ordered to the company CP area, to guard it. We were ordered to find a hole and share it with someone for the night. I saw one of the Ontos I had seen working out before. It was dead; it had a big RPG hole in it.

There were three of us in my hole, so we took turns standing guard and sleeping. One of the guys I was in with and I never got along well until that night. We got along fine then, though.

2nd Lieutenant CHAN CRANGLE
Mike Company, 3/26—1st Platoon Commander

Around midnight, one of my squad leaders came up to me and asked if I wanted a cigarette. He also offered some pineapple juice. I said, "Natch," and he handed me a half-gallon carton. "Where in the hell did you get *this?*" The battalion had been resupplied by helo late in the morning. Along with the resupply had come special packages with cigarettes and other goodies, such as half-gallon cartons of fruit juice. The excess had been loaded on the tanks. Somewhere in the middle of the night, my bandits sneaked out to the stalled tank in front of our lines and retrieved the loot!

Chapter 21

While the battalion command post and Kilo and Mike companies were turning the tide around Hill 48, India and Lima companies remained pinned to their hill by at least a full NVA infantry battalion.

1st Lieutenant BOB STIMSON
India Company, 3/26—Executive Officer

Our situation and disposition had stabilized by dusk on September 10. We had good tactical integrity.

After dark, around most of the India Company sector, the NVA pretty much backed off and engaged us with small arms rather than direct assault. I wasn't aware of very much indirect fire either, just a few 60mm mortar rounds every once in a while. The pressure certainly was not as intense as it had been before sunset.

Lance Corporal CHUCK BENNETT
India Company, 3/26, 1st Platoon

I don't know what happened. They were there, and then they weren't there. I guess they figured they couldn't come through us. I don't know where they went. They kept probing at us, but the big attack just ended. Just like that.

1st Lieutenant BOB STIMSON
India Company, 3/26—Executive Officer

I knew that the battalion CP, Mike, and Kilo were being engaged, but I didn't realize they were being attacked as heavily as they were. Also, I was not conscious of the continual assaults on Lima Company.

2nd Lieutenant JOHN PRINCE
Lima Company, 3/26—2nd Platoon Commander

We got orders to pull back a little and set in. I told my men to pull the line back and bring the dead and wounded with them. Then, as everyone was pulling back, I saw the Marine in charge of our company's 3.5-inch rocket team walk right past a wounded Marine. I looked right at the rocketman's eyes and I could see the fear in them. He wasn't petrified, but he was very frightened. I lined up my rifle right at his midsection—he was maybe 10 yards away—and I said, "Bring back the dead and wounded." He looked at me and his eyes got wider, but he went back and brought in the man he had walked past. In general, he was a very good Marine, an exceptionally skilled rocketman, but the confusion of the battle and fear had overwhelmed his senses and better instincts.

Corporal Patrick McBride was the company 60mm mortar-squad leader. He was a Marine everyone said was squared away. He never caused any problems and he was a good leader. He wasn't a vocal leader; he was a quiet leader who got the job done. During the early part of the fight, Corporal McBride's M-16 jammed and he had to clear the jam. While he was working, he was shot dead. When we got orders to pull back and tie in our perimeters, we somehow left McBride's body outside the lines. I didn't know about it or I would have done something right then.

After we set in our perimeter, we had contact with India Company. Lieutenant Bill Cowan's platoon of India was immediately on my left flank. My right flank went around and tied in with Sergeant Mullins's 1st Platoon, which was on the south side of the hill. Mullins's platoon had very little, if any, contact that night, and no casualties that I know of.

The bomb craters that were caused by the bombs that fell between India Company and Lima Company fit right into my platoon perimeter. They ran down along one edge of my perimeter and saved the Marines over there a lot of work digging holes.

Corporal FRANK GARCIA
Lima Company, 3/26—2nd Platoon Squad Leader

It was dark and the shooting had almost died off before I finally got my squad together. Out of eleven, there were just four of us left. Everyone else had been wounded. We had one E-tool between the four of us, so we shared it and, little by little, dug two two-man foxholes on the brow of the hill, overlooking the burned-out gun tank. As we dug in, Lieutenant Prince came by to check in and tell us where the platoon CP had been set in. The 2nd Platoon guide kept coming by all night, passing out ammo, checking to see how we were doing, making sure the perimeter was tight. He did a great job; he really knew his shit.

1st Lieutenant BOB STIMSON
India Company, 3/26—Executive Officer

Captain Caulfield was fully in control of the company. My role was a lot less dramatic than it had been on September 7. I was very concerned that we were going to be attacked, so I spent a good deal of my time working with Ron Zappardino, trying to get an ammunition resupply. I moved around our lines, making sure everybody was tied in, making sure the machine guns were emplaced to the best advantage, talking to the corpsman about the casualties, trying to encourage the casualties, and reporting the situation in to Caulfield. I moved around alone after my radioman was pressed into service as a rifleman because we had sustained so many casualties.

*

Lance Corporal CHUCK BENNETT
India Company, 3/26, 1st Platoon

I could hear NVA in the bushes in front of our position, but I never saw any live ones after the big attack ended. We all kept firing suppressive fire at them, hoping they would fire back so we could find out exactly where they were.

Captain DICK CAMP
Lima Company, 3/26—Commanding Officer

Things were slacking off, but we were still taking some sniper fire. I was about ready to begin breathing easier when Lance Corporal Terry Smith, my TACP operator, crawled up to my CP hole and said, "Skipper! Skipper, I just got the word that there's North Vietnamese in the landing zone." The zone—a little flat place undoubtedly used for that purpose by the previous tenants—was about 20 feet behind my foxhole, in the middle of the company position. Well, that caught me in the solar plexus. I thought, "Oh, shit! What do you do now, coach?" I couldn't very well merely pass the word to my Marines that there were "maybe" NVA inside the position because it was inevitable that Marines would kill other Marines who were crawling around in the dark trying to pass out ammunition or make sure the lines were okay. If we stopped doing the chores we needed to do, we would weaken our position. What to do?

As I was pondering the alternatives—and perhaps taking too much time figuring the angles—Lance Corporal Smith started crawling off toward the landing zone. "Smitty," I whispered as loudly as I dared, "Smitty, where you going, where you going?" He looked back at me and said, "Skipper, don't worry about it. I'll get 'em with my knife."

I had seen only bad things happen to brave men that day. I couldn't let him do it, especially when I saw he was indeed armed with only his K-bar knife. It took all the balls in the world to even consider such a thing, but I couldn't let him do it. "Goddammit, Smitty, get back in your hole. Get back in that hole now." He did—a little petulantly, but he did. I decided to wait a few minutes more before making a decision, to see if the NVA would act.

1st Lieutenant RON ZAPPARDINO
3/26—Forward Air Controller

The India Company CP was on the brow of the hill, overlooking the rice paddies. We had all the wounded in a big bomb crater and, to the right of that, was a platoon CP, and another one farther around to the right. I decided to go around to the platoon CPs to talk to the people there and see what their needs were. I couldn't see all the way around the hill, and I couldn't depend on the comm net, which was in undisciplined chaos. I wanted to see what they could see so I could call the air in as accurately as possible. I made the circuit around to the right and back several times, but eventually I went wrong; I zigged when I should have zagged. Eventually, I knew I had gone too far. I didn't know where I was, but I knew I wasn't where I was supposed to be. Before I took another step and landed in something I couldn't back out of, I hunkered down and started looking around for any kind of landmark. I was disoriented. There were no flares being dropped or fired by our mortars, no gunfire in or out of our position, nothing by which I could judge distance or my position. I finally decided to backtrack. All I knew was that I had to go up. I knew for sure I didn't want to go *down* the hill any farther. I realized that there was a good chance there were

NVA between me and India Company. I was as scared as I could be. I locked and loaded my M-16 and crawled back up on my hands and knees.

I eventually reached what I took to be little fighting holes, shallow dugouts somebody might have dug at the start of the battle to get down, away from the fire. I got up then and started walking up the hill. Someone saw or heard me and challenged me. I called back, "It's Zappardino, the FAC. You guys know me." Fortunately and unfortunately, I always wore a soft cover I had gotten from some recon guys when I was flying with VMO-2. It was my trademark. I never wore a steel pot. The bad part was that the NVA often wore soft covers, but the good part was that everyone in the battalion knew me by my soft cover. I pointed this out to the Marines on the hill and that eventually convinced them I was me. They passed me through their line.

Captain DICK CAMP
Lima Company, 3/26—Commanding Officer

Right after I got the word that North Vietnamese might be in the landing zone, I was standing in my foxhole with Corporal Johnson, my radioman. All of a sudden, I saw a shadow. I said, "Jesus Christ, John, watch it," pulled up my automatic pistol, and assumed the two-handed crouch. The shadow kept getting larger, so I aimed in on it. It turned into a person. I was squeezing the trigger as the shadow got close enough for me to identify. I was about ready to let the round go when I realized it was a Marine. I said, "Goddammit, who the hell's that?"

"It's me, it's me!"

"Who's 'me'?"

"Lieutenant Zappardino."

I was very close to shooting him. It was a miracle I held off as long as I did. I asked Zap if he had been over the landing zone and he told me he had just come from there. As far as he knew, no NVA had camped out there.

*

1st Lieutenant BOB STIMSON
India Company, 3/26—Executive Officer

The company radioman was a Japanese-American who, of course, looked Asian. In light of the fact that we had been engaged initially by North Vietnamese wearing American equipment and since there was word that there were NVA crawling around inside our perimeter, this guy was scared to death, and rightfully so. He attached himself to Captain Caulfield's back like a limpet. He was really crowding the captain, who finally said to him, "Look, I recognize your situation. You just stay put right here in the CP hole and I'll find you when I need you."

2nd Lieutenant BILL COWAN
India Company, 3/26—3rd Platoon Commander

We had a corpsman who had joined us on September 8. He had been in Vietnam for a while. He and I started joking about how, if we got into any more battles, we wanted to mark the zone right away. He said, "Lieutenant, what we'll do is cover ourselves with smoke grenades. As soon as one of us gets shot, a smoke grenade'll go off and that'll mark the zone so they can get us outta there." We kidded about that for two days. He was killed that night.

Lance Corporal MIKE HEFFLIN
Lima Company, 3/26, 2nd Platoon

My buddy, Corporal Robert Horton, and I were both wounded. After most of the shooting died down, we tried to take turns sleeping, but we kept getting mortar rounds in the perimeter, and Horton and I kept hearing word that the enemy was penetrating the perimeter. I heard there were NVA in the landing zone. I believed that they had penetrated, because earlier, when I'd gone down into the gully to join the M-60 teams, I'd seen a couple of them run through our line. The M-60s had picked them off that time, but I figured others probably had gotten past the machine guns. If there were no NVA *in* the perimeter, they were damn close to it.

The Marines on the line were so scattered out. They kept bringing guys from the back side of the hill to the front. During daylight, I'd seen only one machine gun and a couple guys around the back side, so there couldn't have been many left there if they kept moving them to the front side. Horton and I were scared to shit, bare to the world. All we wanted to do was take a few NVA with us if they came right at us.

Horton and I tried to get as comfortable as we could. We had one flak jacket that we threw over ourselves. Lance Corporal William O'Neill, our guardian angel, kept coming back to check on us. He was the only one. I never saw a corpsman the whole night.

The wounded guys in the crater were moaning and groaning all night long. One of the machine gunners was lying outside, on the edge of the crater. He was in excruciating pain from a stomach wound. Someone finally came by and gave him a shot.

*

1st Lieutenant BOB STIMSON
India Company, 3/26—Executive Officer

We had an ammunition problem. We had expended all of our 60mm mortar rounds and certainly most of everything else.

2nd Lieutenant JOHN PRINCE
Lima Company, 3/26—2nd Platoon Commander

As a rule, as a platoon policy, everybody carried a thousand rounds for their M-16s. At least 200 rounds had to be in magazines and the rest had to be in magazine chargers or in boxes in their packs. However, an ongoing problem we had was that as soon as we got in a firefight a lot of the troops would throw their packs away because the packs slowed them down and hindered their firing. A good portion of our ammunition was in the packs, so, when we finally set in our perimeter, there were some Marines who had maybe only two magazines left. A lot of that got used up as time went by.

Captain DICK CAMP
Lima Company, 3/26—Commanding Officer

It had been a terrific fight, and I knew it could erupt in its full glory again at any moment. We were running out of ammunition—we were critically low—so I got Lance Corporal Terry Smith up on the tac-air net to request an emergency ammunition resupply. We also had a position filled with wounded men and many of them were in danger of succumbing at any moment. But I also knew that the NVA had set in five .51-caliber heavy machine guns around us and thus could seriously endanger any helos that might respond to our call. But I couldn't worry about them. We needed the ammunition or we would all die. We made it as plain as we could that getting ammo was a matter of life or death.

1st Lieutenant RON ZAPPARDINO
3/26—Forward Air Controller

I tried calling a medevac for the wounded, but the NVA .51-cals were still out there and I couldn't get any of the helos to come in. The wounded Marines in the bomb crater were getting panicked. I decided to crawl over and reassure them as best I could, but they locked and loaded on me, wouldn't take my word that I was a Marine. We went through the whole corny baseball rigmarole you see in the war movies. I couldn't believe it was happening to me, but that's what Americans are all about. They asked me about 10 questions before they let me in. I think it was more for their own peace of mind than it was out of conviction that I was an NVA soldier. I was scared shitless. I was more scared of our own hurt and wounded guys than I had been when I passed through our lines into no-man's-land earlier.

We finally got one helo pilot who would risk a resupply. I told him, "We need you, but it's bad and I'm not going to tell you you have to do it." He came in anyway.

Captain DICK CAMP
Lima Company, 3/26—Commanding Officer

Goddamn if a Marine H-34 pilot didn't come back with, "Get somebody in the LZ and mark it for me."

That was Terry Smith's job. Despite my fears that the zone might be crowded with NVA, I ordered him to crawl down there and climb into a foxhole or a shell hole so he could flash his strobe light to mark the zone. Terry sure enough crawled back out of sight and encountered no opposition. He turned on the strobe—which flashed straight up and could not be seen from the ground—and pretty soon we heard the helo. A second later, all five of the NVA .51-cals began hurling green tracer toward the sound. Pretty soon, I couldn't hear the helo.

I was in the bottom of my hole, only 20 feet from the landing zone. I was scared to death for the helo crew. Then I started thinking about what would happen if he was shot down over our position. We would have burning fuel, exploding ammo, and a great big fire to mark us for every rifle and machine gun out there.

As I waited and worried, I heard the H-34's engine again above the roar of the NVA small-arms fire. He was right over the zone. As I looked up, I could make out the dim outline of a human form laying prone in the hatchway in the helo's side. I could see a head, chest, and arms. It looked like the man was down, wounded or even dead.

1st Lieutenant BOB STIMSON
India Company, 3/26—Executive Officer

The H-34 helicopter attracted fire like a magnet. I saw someone in the chopper lying down, kicking stuff out.

Captain DICK CAMP
Lima Company, 3/26—Commanding Officer

It seemed that green tracer rounds were penetrating the body of the H-34 from all angles.

Lance Corporal CHUCK BENNETT
India Company, 3/26, 1st Platoon

I was surprised the helo stayed over us as long as it did. It was an easy target—I saw it get hit—but we needed the ammunition resupply.

2nd Lieutenant JOHN PRINCE
Lima Company, 3/26—2nd Platoon Commander

NVA machine guns on three sides of us fired at the helicopter. I didn't think he'd make it, but he did get out. Immediately he dropped down below a hill into the rice paddy behind us and got away.

1st Lieutenant BOB STIMSON
India Company, 3/26—Executive Officer

We had taken so many casualties, we didn't have the liberty of detaching a lot of people to retrieve and hump the ammunition the helicopter dropped, so I crawled out into the zone with Zap and a few other headquarters men to get it. The zone was under heavy fire as soon as the helicopter arrived, and it remained so.

Captain DICK CAMP
Lima Company, 3/26—Commanding Officer

A minute or two later, Terry Smith returned to the CP area and told me the crew chief apparently had stacked the ammo cases right in the hatchway and had kicked them out on the run as soon as the helo edged in over the strobe. The ammo had nearly brained Terry, but it hadn't and he and a handful of volunteers had grabbed it. It was being distributed as Terry was reporting to me.

1st Lieutenant BOB STIMSON
India Company, 3/26—Executive Officer

We got some useful small-arms ammunition, but most of the resupply was linked .50-caliber ammunition and a demolitions kit. Of course, we had no .50s and the demolitions kit was of no use. We were very upset.

1st Lieutenant RON ZAPPARDINO
3/26—Forward Air Controller

At terrible risk to his life, he dropped ammo we couldn't use. We were down to about 10 rounds of 5.56mm ammo for our M-16s and they sent that shit to us!

1st Lieutenant BOB STIMSON
India Company, 3/26—Executive Officer

As always, fire discipline had to be strongly imposed and I particularly was very strict about it. As on September 7, my main reason for moving around to the troops as much as I did was to remind them to maintain strong fire discipline. The resupply had been disappointing and no one knew if another helo would reach us.

1st Lieutenant RON ZAPPARDINO
3/26—Forward Air Controller

Another helo pilot, flying a medevac bird, kept asking me if he could come in, but I kept telling him how bad it was. The last thing any of us wanted was a dead, burning helo in the landing zone, marking our perimeter for every NVA gunner in range on both sides of the DMZ. That was a tough decision. I visited the crater filled with wounded Marines. I saw the kid with the leg half severed, the kids with the head wounds, the Marines who would die for lack of hospital treatment. But I knew that if we lost a bird in the zone we'd never get *any* of them out by air. I had to wait until the firing died down and it was at least halfway safe to land a bird and load the wounded. We agonized over that one all night, but there really wasn't any choice. The medevac pilot wanted to land, but I couldn't risk it. I couldn't risk it.

Captain DICK CAMP
Lima Company, 3/26—Commanding Officer

Only one helo got over our position that night. We never got one of our WIAs lifted out. The worst case remained Corporal Thomas Krispin, the 3rd Platoon radioman. Doc Bratton refused to give up on him; he even set up a shelter half and worked over Krispin's wounds in the light of a hooded penlight. But only the best trauma care in a real hospital could save Krispin, and he died during the night. So did several other WIAs who might have survived if we could have gotten them out in time.

1st Lieutenant BOB STIMSON
India Company, 3/26—Executive Officer

Our biggest job through the night was remaining vigilant and saving the lives of our casualties. The wounded were incredibly disciplined. Many of them were in grave condition, but they'd just grit their teeth and bear it.

Corporal FRANK GARCIA
Lima Company, 3/26—2nd Platoon Squad Leader

Late at night, I was crawling around in the dark, trying to find Lieutenant Prince to tell him something, but I came across these *things* wrapped in ponchos. I couldn't make out what they were and I hit one, which rolled over. It was a dead, burned body. I asked a Marine who was sitting right there, "Who is this?" and he said, "It's one of the tank guys."

2nd Lieutenant JOHN PRINCE
Lima Company, 3/26—2nd Platoon Commander

The tanker who had been killed when the gun tank had been RPGed was laid out next to what became my CP. He was on his back and his right arm, from the elbow, was sticking up and his hand was sort of bent 90 degrees from his arm, sort of in a death claw. It so happened he was situated in such a way that, when I was in my hole that night, every time I'd look out into the shadows cast by the illumination, I'd see this death claw.

2nd Lieutenant BILL COWAN
India Company, 3/26—3rd Platoon Commander

The crew from the gun tank was in my perimeter. The commander was injured badly and laid out on the ground. There were three or four other wounded tankers there, sitting in the little spot we wanted to use as a landing zone. I went back there a few times. The staff sergeant lay there quietly all night on a poncho. He knew it was a bad situation and that nothing could be done. I didn't know the guy, but it was frustrating to know all night that I had a man there who was not complaining, who was hurting bad, who was conscious the whole time, who was willing to be quiet and lie there patiently while we tried to sort out the problem. He never said a thing and then he quietly died. It was sad.

*

Captain DICK CAMP
Lima Company, 3/26—Commanding Officer

The air strikes and resupply were far from the only support we received from around sunset on. When pressure eased on the battalion main body, they were able to devote some time and energy to saving Lima and India. The biggest effort came from friendly artillery bases. We were close to Dong Ha, Camp Carroll, and C-2, so we had a hell of a lot of artillery available to us. I'll bet it was a regiment's worth of artillery by the time they got done laying it all on. We were by far the biggest show out there that night. We rated it. Someone told me later that the artillery fired 10,000 rounds to support us. The battalion FO boxed us in and fired constant box barrages to keep the NVA out. We had a curtain of steel around us.

1st Lieutenant BOB STIMSON
India Company, 3/26—Executive Officer

We were not *in extremis* after sunset. It was nothing like it had been the night of September 7 and not like it had been late in the afternoon and early in the evening. Puff the Magic Dragon, for example, was an insurance policy, not a necessity. I don't know if Puff took much of a toll on the North Vietnamese or if it just scared the hell out of them, but everything seemed to stabilize around the time he started firing. I no longer had the uneasy feeling I had had earlier.

Captain DICK CAMP
Lima Company, 3/26—Commanding Officer

Puff flew back and forth firing 6,000 rounds a minute with his 7.62mm minigun. The show he put on was awesome. He could literally hose an area down with what appeared to be a solid stream of red tracer—a flexible tube of death. It was even more awesome when I realized that the tracer represented only one round in four. Also, the sound Puff made was scary. The whole night was suffused with an eerie, continuous *AWWWWWW*. I was told that a minute of firing could plow up every square inch of a regulation football field. I heard we used up two Puffs— 125,000 rounds apiece.

1st Lieutenant RON ZAPPARDINO
3/26—Forward Air Controller

We had a 30-minute period in which Puff was firing his minigun without flares. He had the coordinates and just orbited and sprayed rounds into the NVA areas. There is nothing like Puff, nothing in the world, especially close in. Once he has his position fixed, there is nothing like it—not artillery, not fast movers, *nothing!*

Captain DICK CAMP
Lima Company, 3/26—Commanding Officer

The big problem we faced was marking targets. We couldn't just bring an aircraft in and say, "Okay, shoot up the terrain." We had no 60mm ammunition—no willy-pete—so we decided to do the marking with our M-79 grenade launchers. Any old flash would do, so the grenadiers fired their 40mm grenades at targets the platoon commanders designated. The pilots overhead were alert—we maintained very good radio contact— and they completed run after run without hitting any of us.

Lance Corporal CHUCK BENNETT
India Company, 3/26, 1st Platoon

Puff firing his minigun at night was a hell of a sight. All I could see was his tracer rounds. It looked like a straight, solid orange line from the sky to the ground. It was just one line. It was hard to believe there were four or five rounds between each tracer round. He was tearing up everything. If it was out there, Puff was hitting it. He was a *beautiful* sight. Puff had to be the baddest thing over there.

*

1st Lieutenant RON ZAPPARDINO
3/26—Forward Air Controller

Someone came up on my air net and said he was making a photo pass. I couldn't believe it! A photo pass! I said, "Give me some ordnance instead!" Then the whole sky lit up.

2nd Lieutenant CHAN CRANGLE
Mike Company, 3/26—1st Platoon Commander

We heard nothing coming. All of a sudden, "flashbulbs" started going off. My first reaction was a total blank; I had absolutely no idea what had hit us. Nuclear weapons? Harry Dolan and I aged a century until our hearts started beating again!

2nd Lieutenant PAUL DRNEC
Bravo Company, 3rd Tank Battalion—2nd Platoon Commander

When the photo-reconnaissance plane made its pass dropping all those flares, I thought, "Shit! Now what?" I didn't know what the hell it was—or whose.

Captain DICK CAMP
Lima Company, 3/26—Commanding Officer

The photo-reconnaissance airplane gave me one of the truly big frights of my life. I didn't hear him come on station, and no one told me he was there. All of a sudden, the darkness was overwhelmed by a *whoof* and a flash so brilliant I thought we had been nuked. It turned out that the photo plane had launched a brilliant carbon-magnesium flare—followed by four or five more. We found out later that the pictures he took showed hundreds of North Vietnamese bodies scattered around our position. Hundreds of them.

*

Captain DICK CAMP
Lima Company, 3/26—Commanding Officer

The normal illumination Puff put out for us also had its scary side. The flares went off with a *whoof-whoof-whoof* noise followed by a *thunk* when the expended flare canister hit the ground. The empty ceramic canisters could kill anyone they hit. No one was hit, but several canisters landed inside the company position.

2nd Lieutenant JOHN PRINCE
Lima Company, 3/26—2nd Platoon Commander

It seemed like Puff ran out of ammunition and flares about the same time, so the artillery at C-2 or Camp Carroll took over firing illumination for us. The illumination rounds made a strange sound. The round goes up, then it explodes, then the flare pops and starts burning, and the shell casing tumbles down and goes *whoo-whoo-whoo*. The illumination flare canisters and illumination shell casings became the major danger in our part of the perimeter that night. We knew that if they fell on anyone, that person probably would be killed. So, for a couple of hours, that's what I worried about.

*

2nd Lieutenant JOHN PRINCE
Lima Company, 3/26—2nd Platoon Commander

We hadn't eaten all day. And I was as tired as I had ever been at any time in my life—the fatigue of battle.

Captain DICK CAMP
Lima Company, 3/26—Commanding Officer

Unfortunately, the gunfire was too hot to risk a ration run. So, we had nothing to eat. It sounds petty, I know, but none of us had eaten since breakfast, and many of us, including me, had not eaten since dinner the evening before. The gun tank that had been hit and incinerated at the start of the action had been carrying our rations, but it had rolled back down the hill into the paddyfield. Naturally, as we later discovered, the North Vietnamese facing us had scavenged the rations. We found empty C-rations cans in NVA fighting holes right around our position. I hope it was all ham and limas.

*

Corporal FRANK GARCIA
Lima Company, 3/26—2nd Platoon Squad Leader

We got rocketed and mortared during the night, but they were just feeling us out. They'd mortar us—a couple rounds now and then—but there was no direct assault. We knew they were there; there was a lot of movement. I figured that if we had killed anyone, they were taking them away.

2nd Lieutenant JOHN PRINCE
Lima Company, 3/26—2nd Platoon Commander

Corporal Jimmy Beckwith, an M-79 grenadier, was a short, stocky guy and his best friend, Lance Corporal William Ochoa, was a big, tall, lanky guy. During the night, Beckwith got real edgy and fired his M-79 at any little noise or suspected noise he heard. He managed to wound Ochoa. Finally, when he was hit by Beckwith the second time, Ochoa said, ''Screw it,'' and went back to stay with the wounded people.

*

Lance Corporal CHUCK BENNETT
India Company, 3/26, 1st Platoon

The gun tank, which was right out in front of my position, was on fire. Rounds inside it were going off now and then all through the night. At first we thought it was enemy fire, but we could see some of the rounds going off inside the tank. They were .50-cal rounds, I think.

2nd Lieutenant BILL COWAN
India Company, 3/26—3rd Platoon Commander

The destroyed gun tank was up by my platoon when it got hit, but by the time it started rolling back it was in front of Lima. During the night, my troops reported there were NVA on it, stripping it.

Corporal FRANK GARCIA
Lima Company, 3/26—2nd Platoon Squad Leader

I could hear them fucking with the tank that had rolled down the hill in front of our line. It sounded like they were unscrewing it, taking it away piece by piece. There was a lot of noise.

2nd Lieutenant BILL COWAN
India Company, 3/26—3rd Platoon Commander

Because it was in front of Lima's lines, we couldn't do anything, so I went up to Captain Caulfield and said, ''Hey, sir, my guys see NVA on the tank out there. Can we get Lima Company to go out there and clean 'em out or blast the tank away, or do something?'' Word was sent to Lima Company, but the answer was, "No, we're not going to fire on that tank because it's U.S. government property." I went back to Captain Caulfield and said, "If they won't do it, sir, we'll do it." He told me to go ahead.

I told Lima Company I was going to send two men over in front of their lines. One of them was one of my squad leaders, and he took another man. Lima Company said, "Roger, no problem. We'll let everybody know."

2nd Lieutenant JOHN PRINCE
Lima Company, 3/26—2nd Platoon Commander

Apparently Captain Caulfield was really worried about the .50-caliber rounds that were cooking off from the tank into our lines every half hour or so. The rounds weren't hitting anybody, but they made movement within our lines seem quite perilous.

1st Lieutenant BOB STIMSON
India Company, 3/26—Executive Officer

Captain Caulfield and I wanted to destroy the gun tank because we believed there was some ammunition aboard it that the NVA might have been able to use. Also to deny the enemy access to anything else on it.

2nd Lieutenant JOHN PRINCE
Lima Company, 3/26—2nd Platoon Commander

Captain Caulfield finally sent a rocketman down to knock the burning tank out with a LAAW. The rocketman arrived at my CP with a sergeant from India Company, and the sergeant told me that the India Company commander wanted the rocketman to blow up the tank. I left the sergeant at my CP and led the rocketman down to a place on my line from which he could hit the tank.

When we got to the line, the rocketman said he wanted to go out in front of the line to find a better place to shoot from. I said I would wait for him.

2nd Lieutenant BILL COWAN
India Company, 3/26—3rd Platoon Commander

The Marine went out in front of the lines with a LAAW.

2nd Lieutenant JOHN PRINCE
Lima Company, 3/26—2nd Platoon Commander

Well, he didn't shoot the LAAW. And when he came back in through my platoon's line, he came back in a different place.

Corporal FRANK GARCIA
Lima Company, 3/26—2nd Platoon Squad Leader

He said something as he was coming back into our lines.

2nd Lieutenant JOHN PRINCE
Lima Company, 3/26—2nd Platoon Commander

He walked right into one of my machine-gun teams. The assistant gunner, who was sitting beside the gun, shot him with his .45.

2nd Lieutenant BILL COWAN
India Company, 3/26—3rd Platoon Commander

Some fucking guy from Lima Company shot him right in the chest with a .45. Fortunately, he had a flak jacket on and the bullet ricocheted right off him.

2nd Lieutenant JOHN PRINCE
Lima Company, 3/26—2nd Platoon Commander

The rocketman got only a broken collarbone. He was extremely lucky. If the M-60 gunner had fired the M-60 or if any of the ammo humpers had fired their M-16s, he would've been dead.

2nd Lieutenant BILL COWAN
India Company, 3/26—3rd Platoon Commander

There was still fighting going on, but the kid stood up and started screaming at Lima Company, walked right over to my hole, and said, "Sir, those motherfuckers just shot me!" The story ended up in *Stars and Stripes,* but, as it was written there, he was shot by an NVA.

*

Captain DICK CAMP
Lima Company, 3/26—Commanding Officer

Between 0300 and 0400, September 11, things really quieted down. When I realized how quiet it had become, I began thinking, "Hey, maybe I'm going to live through this.'' I did not know if it was the calm before the storm, or what, but I couldn't help thinking—hoping— it was as good as over.

Corporal FRANK GARCIA
Lima Company, 3/26—2nd Platoon Squad Leader

After the heavy action died down—all that night—I was shaky scared. I sat in my foxhole thinking, "Oh fuck, when's it gonna end? Are they gonna attack? Is this the big rush?'' I couldn't leave it alone.

PART IV

Parting Shots

Chapter 22

Major CARL MUNDY
3/26—Operations Officer

By about 0300, all was quiet. The NVA had disengaged. The troops at the front reported hearing the sound of what they described as bodies being dragged back. The NVA routinely carried meat hooks and they would oftentimes send their troops back out and literally meat hook the dead—hopefully not the wounded—and drag them back to a common burial site. They were often found in mass graves. The next morning, when we surveyed the area, we saw many signs, many blood trails, where the NVA had come up and recovered their dead under the darkness, when there was no fire going on.

About an hour or so before daylight, I spent probably too much time on the radio, talking to the company commanders, trying to prepare for what we would do at first light. The first thing I wanted was an accurate situation report. Even though you think you know what's going on at night, it's oftentimes very difficult to know exactly where you stand. I wanted an accurate situation report; I wanted an enemy body count to determine what we had, and estimates of the numbers they had engaged—all sorts of reportable statistics. We talked about that and we talked about how we would ease out to get it.

Captain DICK CAMP
Lima Company, 3/26—Commanding Officer

I passed the word that at first light we were going to fire a 10-second mad moment just in case there was anybody out there who needed to be cleared out. I alerted Battalion and we got all set to go. As the very first glimmer of dawn appeared, I ordered, "Okay, shoot it out." We all fired for about 10 seconds—that was a lot of bullets—and then we started moving around.

Corporal FRANK GARCIA
Lima Company, 3/26—2nd Platoon Squad Leader

Somebody spotted three gooks on the other side of the rice paddies. I had an M-60, so I started shooting at them, but they told me I missed.

1st Lieutenant BOB STIMSON
India Company, 3/26—Executive Officer

Everybody was pretty weary, to say the least. We had been through a lot. However, we were well-disciplined infantry; we all knew our having gone through a lot didn't mean the war was going to stop so we could relax. In fact, I always felt particularly vulnerable around the time the shock and fatigue set in at the conclusion of an action. As always, I made sure all the normal housekeeping was accomplished—weapons cleaned, ammunition reallocated, security positioned.

Captain DICK CAMP
Lima Company, 3/26—Commanding Officer

After the mad moment, as I roved through the company area, I immediately began finding dead Marines. I found two Marines who had been killed in the foxhole dead ahead of my foxhole, at the head of the trail through the thicket. It looked as if two or three grenades had gone off between them. I also ran across Sergeant Brown's body, Gunny Almanza's, and Corporal Krispin's. There were a lot of others.

2nd Lieutenant JOHN PRINCE
Lima Company, 3/26—2nd Platoon Commander

We found the body of Corporal Patrick McBride, the mortar-squad leader who had been shot dead while clearing a jam from his M-16. His body had been left behind when we moved back to tie in with India Company. His skin was that waxy gray color.

Captain DICK CAMP
Lima Company, 3/26—Commanding Officer

The smell of blood tinged with singed tissue and hair was almost overpowering. I told Gunny Bailey, "I want to send these dead Marines out of here cleaned up, at least wrapped up.'' He got them all under poncho liners—as well as he could, since they were all frozen in grotesque attitudes.

Lance Corporal MIKE HEFFLIN
Lima Company, 3/26, 2nd Platoon

The hill was a horror scene when the sun came up. We could see all the guys laying around dead. Horton and I went back down the slope to the crater and got in with all the other wounded. People started running around checking on everybody, taking a nose count to see who was dead and alive, wounded and okay. A couple H-34 choppers came in and dropped off supplies. They came in *real* fast, dropped their supplies as fast as they could, and got the hell out. Then they started sending medevacs. By then, a lot of the wounded guys were yelling, "When the hell are they gonna get us outta here?" I was one of the guys yelling. I was afraid the NVA was going to come back for seconds, and I didn't want to be there when that happened.

No one came by with any water and I never saw a corpsman the whole time, but they were too busy with the guys who had been hit really bad. My guardian angel, Lance Corporal William O'Neill, came by to check on me, and Lieutenant Prince stopped by once to see how I was doing. So did my squad leader, Corporal Frank Garcia. My spirits were low. I wanted to get the hell out of there.

The medevacs finally came, and some guys got me on a stretcher and threw a sheet over me. I kept my .45 with me. By the time they got me off the ground and into the helicopter, I had been hit for about 16 hours.

Captain DICK CAMP
Lima Company, 3/26—Commanding Officer

After we got all the wounded lifted out, we staged the dead on the landing zone and waited until there was a free helo to carry them out. After a while, my TACP operator, Lance Corporal Terry Smith, got word that he had a helo coming in for the dead. As Terry guided the helo in, the terrific downdraft from the main rotor blew the ponchos off. It was a mess. It really got to me—along with my hunger, sleeplessness, and the downer following the nightlong adrenaline rush. I felt the sting of tears in my eyes. Though I lowered my head to try to hide the tears, I noticed that many of the Marines in the zone were crying too.

Corporal FRANK GARCIA
Lima Company, 3/26—2nd Platoon Squad Leader

I happened to see them loading Corporal Tony Sawicki's body aboard one of the helicopters, and I thought about how happy he'd been about winning that 15 grand, how it was going to turn his life around. It always seemed like the guys who had the most to live for were the guys who got killed, and down-and-out guys like me always seemed to come through.

*

Major CARL MUNDY
3/26—Operations Officer

September 11 was a beautiful day—very hot, but a nice day.

Captain ANDY DeBONA
Mike Company, 3/26—Commanding Officer

I got to work reorganizing Mike Company. I called up my platoon leaders and got head counts and made sure everybody was there. Medevac birds finally started coming in. For the two actions, September 7 and September 10, Mike had a total of 12 KIAs and 115 WIAs. Of the 115 WIAs, a little over 30 of them were actually medevacked.

We moved out to the bomb crater. There were still a few things left in the bottom. I saw a blown apart M-60; it had a bullet hole through it. Next, I gingerly proceeded over to the bad-guy bomb crater. I found three lines of enemy dead; each line was formed of bodies stitched together by a meat hook. The meat hooks were on ropes that extended through the shoulders of the NVA dead. There were no weapons. Apparently, their priorities were to take away their weapons first and their dead later. I counted 39 dead NVA around or on the meathook line. I looked inside the bomb crater. There were a total of seven fighting positions inside, neatly dug in.

1st Lieutenant BOB STIMSON
India Company, 3/26—Executive Officer

We could see many dead NVA and a lot of their equipment on the battlefield. We sent some troops down to look them over and bring documents and other intelligence matter back. They didn't go far for fear of running into trouble. I don't think we turned up anything really significant in our sector.

Lance Corporal CHUCK BENNETT
India Company, 3/26, 1st Platoon

After we sent our killed and wounded out, we went down and policed the area below the hill, recovering NVA weapons and lots of other gear. There were a lot of bodies down there—as many as I ever saw at one time in Vietnam. I found a man I know I had shot the previous afternoon. He was on his back with an RPG launcher on his chest. He was a big man in an NVA uniform, but he was larger and fairer than most Vietnamese I had seen. I'm sure he was Chinese. He was wearing brand-new gear. It looked like it had just been issued. In fact, all the dead NVA out there looked like they had brand-new uniforms and gear. It wasn't even dirty. They were better equipped than we were; they had newer stuff. The men were clean shaven and had fresh short haircuts. Those who had boots had new boots. Most of them had new-looking steel helmets.

2nd Lieutenant BILL COWAN
India Company, 3/26—3rd Platoon Commander

We policed the battlefield up a little bit, but we didn't get much of a chance to look things over. All the NVA bodies I saw had on very clean clothes and good shoes. They all had short haircuts and were well shaven. They were not ragtag at all. They were very sharp. There were no black pajamas or beat-up old rifles. They were very sharp. It was a big surprise. They looked much better than we Marines looked. Our uniforms were old and beat-up. A lot of us needed to shave.

Staff Sergeant CHARLES OWENS
Kilo Company, 3/26—Company Gunny

We had to go out and sweep the area, to pick up information or maps or other things the Intelligence Section could use. We also had to pick up weapons; we didn't want to leave them for the enemy. We had to be real careful turning over the enemy bodies, in case they were booby trapped.

The night before, after the battle died down, I had gone around to find if anybody was missing. The Guamanian platoon sergeant told me all his people were accounted for. But it wasn't true. The next day, when we had our sweep around the perimeter, I found Lance Corporal Raymond LaPointe, a machine-gun squad leader, a really good man we called Frenchy. He was dead. He looked like he'd been trying to crawl into our lines. He was stabbed and shot.

I ran up the hill and grabbed the staff sergeant and started to hit him with my pistol. Lieutenant Dobies stopped me and said, "I told him not to tell you." So I put the muzzle of the pistol underneath the lieutenant's chin and told him, "You do anything like that again and I'll blow you away." If I'd have known where Frenchy was, I would have gone after him. The lieutenant knew that and had told the staff sergeant to tell me everyone was accounted for; he didn't want me making another trip out there.

2nd Lieutenant CHAN CRANGLE
Mike Company, 3/26—1st Platoon Commander

I took a patrol out to the southwest of Hill 48 to sweep a portion of the battlefield. Some 2nd Platoon folks found Bob Gall and his command group. I got to the scene shortly thereafter. Gall, his platoon sergeant—Staff Sergeant Edward Gaytan—and another man were in a small clearing against the brush, alongside the disabled tank. They looked like they had just curled up against each other when the shit hit the fan. They were pretty badly chewed up. My impression was that the focus of the fire was the tank—it was shot to hell—and that Gall was killed by extremely intense incoming mortars and rockets. But it was difficult to tell whether they were killed by incoming or small-arms fire.

Lance Corporal RON BURKE
Mike Company, 3/26, 2nd Platoon

I helped recover the body of the Marine from my squad we had had to leave out by the tank. He had not been molested at all by the NVA. We set up a landing zone at the crest of the little hill, near the tank, and helped load him and other dead Marines we found in the area.

2nd Lieutenant CHAN CRANGLE
Mike Company, 3/26—1st Platoon Commander

Very near the spot where Bob Gall had been killed, we found a North Vietnamese FO. Found, hell—this gent came running out of the brush firing a pistol at us. He promptly bit the dust. We took maps, a compass, and a pistol from him. Andy DeBona got the compass and the pistol went somewhere else. I took the maps to the S-2, but I retrieved them later.

Major CARL MUNDY
3/26—Operations Officer

There was evidence in whatever form—bodies and parts of bodies—to indicate about 144 enemy dead. That's what we reported.

During the afternoon and evening hours of September 10, 1968, the 3rd Battalion, 26th Marines, lost 34 Marines and corpsmen killed; 192 Marines and corpsmen were wounded.

*

2nd Lieutenant PAUL DRNEC
Bravo Company, 3rd Tank Battalion—2nd Platoon Commander

My crew and I went out to B-22 at daybreak. We decided that its separated track could be repaired, which we did. The tank was driven back to the 3/26 battalion perimeter under its own power. It occurred to me then that we probably could have driven it a thousand miles if we had thought of it the previous afternoon.

Major CARL MUNDY
3/26—Operations Officer

We arranged for some LVTs to come out, escorted by tanks. We wanted to use the LVTs to carry back our loose gear and captured NVA equipment, of which I might say we were quite surprised we took so very little.

2nd Lieutenant PAUL DRNEC
Bravo Company, 3rd Tank Battalion—2nd Platoon Commander

At approximately 1000, September 11, a tank-recovery group from Alpha Company, 3rd Tank Battalion, reached the battalion perimeter from Gio Linh. They had some LVTs with them.

Captain TOM EARLY
3/26—Communications Officer

As the LVTs approached to take our casualties away, we all shuddered.

We knew who else was watching. As we got the LVTs loaded, over the battalion tac net we heard, ''Good-bye, Three-Twenty-six.'' Once again, it rained shells on us. Even in death and carnage, the NVA persisted in showing resolve and professional class.

Captain ANDY DeBONA
Mike Company, 3/26—Commanding Officer

This reinforced my belief that moving vehicles were artillery aiming stakes. A two-gun platoon of the bad-guy guns were shooting at us. Each volley, we got one HE round and one smoke round in. My initial thought was that they were starting to register in on us, which did not make me too happy.

Major CARL MUNDY
3/26—Operations Officer

The artillery battery at C-2 provided counterbattery fire.

2nd Lieutenant CHAN CRANGLE
Mike Company, 3/26—1st Platoon Commander

Apparently, the NVA prisoner taken on September 7 had been unable to locate Hill 88—the site of the 812th NVA Regiment's CP—on our maps. But, when we got the NVA maps off the dead FO, Hill 88 stood out like a sore thumb. The real problem was that the grid alignment on the NVA maps was not the same as on our maps. Our S-2 and an artillery FO had to do some fast math to make a conversion, but the NVA map was used to excellent effect when the shelling started.

2nd Lieutenant JOHN PRINCE
Lima Company, 3/26—2nd Platoon Commander

A few LVTs came out to our position. They brought food.

Captain DICK CAMP
Lima Company, 3/26—Commanding Officer

Immediately after we completed the evacuation of our dead and wounded, we started to get ready to move out. Battalion had not told me what was next on our agenda, but I knew there were only two choices: Either we were going to continue on or we were going to get the hell out of there. Finally, word arrived that we were going to pull back to C-2. I cannot describe the feeling of elation I had when that message came in.

We still faced the problem of what to do about the two disabled tanks at the base of our hill. Battalion called me and asked for a status report on them. I told them what the tanks looked like, how charred they appeared. Battalion hemmed and hawed a little and finally told me they were going to send up a tank retriever.

2nd Lieutenant PAUL DRNEC
Bravo Company, 3rd Tank Battalion—2nd Platoon Commander

While the LVTs proceeded directly to the India-Lima position, the recovery-team leader and I went out to survey F-23 and B-25. The gun tank appeared to be capable of moving under its own power. We decided to call the tank retriever ahead to tow F-23 to the rear.

2nd Lieutenant CHAN CRANGLE
Mike Company, 3/26—1st Platoon Commander

After I returned from the morning patrol in front of Hill 48, Andy DeBona shifted us around to prepare for a withdrawal to C-2. I was going to be the lead platoon, so I deployed on the southeast side of the ridge. We were very anxious to get moving. About the time we were set to go, a tank retriever came roaring up the road. A hatch popped open and a major inside the retriever yelled at me, ''Where are the tanks?'' I pointed to the west and told him that the effort wasn't worth it—that we had been taking incoming and expected more and that he was going to get more tanks blown away trying to retrieve the hulks. So much for advice from a second lieutenant. He roared away.

2nd Lieutenant PAUL DRNEC
Bravo Company, 3rd Tank Battalion—2nd Platoon Commander

As soon as the tank retriever moved out of the battalion position, however, incoming rockets or artillery started hitting around it. With no thought at all, I dived straight underneath B-25—my famous maneuver.

Captain DICK CAMP
Lima Company, 3/26—Commanding Officer

The tank retriever waddled toward us, drawing the artillery with it. At that time, I wanted nothing more to do with artillery, so I grabbed the battalion radio and yelled, ''Get that fucking thing out of here. If it comes any closer, *I'm* going to knock it out! You know, I don't give a shit about these goddamn tanks. They're destroyed!''

2nd Lieutenant CHAN CRANGLE
Mike Company, 3/26—1st Platoon Commander

In nothing flat, the tank retriever came roaring back up the trail and flew by me at top speed! At the same time, Andy DeBona yelled at me to get moving. Encouragement I did not need! Thoroughly loaded down with NVA equipment—I was carrying about six AK-47s and other equipment—we took off at a speed that would have done credit to Stonewall Jackson's "foot cavalry"!

2nd Lieutenant PAUL DRNEC
Bravo Company, 3rd Tank Battalion—2nd Platoon Commander

When the shelling lifted, the recovery-team commander and I decided that B-25, which was a firepower kill—its turret was blown and burned out—should immediately be driven to the rear, under its own power. We put in a driver and a man to guide it from the turret and sent it back. F-23 was just a burned out hulk. On second thought, in view of the danger from enemy shelling, we decided to abandon it rather than expose the tank retriever and the men to more enemy artillery.

*

Corporal FRANK GARCIA
Lima Company, 3/26—2nd Platoon Squad Leader

All the rifles from our dead and wounded guys, and all the ones that didn't work, were piled up in a square. The pile was 4 to 5 feet high. Just rifles. I kept the M-60 I had been given the previous afternoon. It worked.

2nd Lieutenant JOHN PRINCE
Lima Company, 3/26—2nd Platoon Commander

As the wounded were being taken away, all their gear was thrown in one place, in a big pile. I happened to need a mosquito net for my helmet. Since I had used my own head net to wrap up my oil can in my pocket, so it didn't make any noise, anytime I put my net on, I smelled oil. Smell was one of the senses that was very good to have in Vietnam, so I was on the lookout for another mosquito net.

Normally, the troops kept their head nets rolled up inside their helmets, between the liner frame and the helmet. I went over to the pile of discarded gear from the wounded and dead Marines who had been evacuated and started looking through the helmets until I found one with a head net in it. I pulled the head net out and saw that it had something that looked like snot all over it. Then I took a better look at the helmet. There were bullet holes in it. I knew then that there were brains all over that head net. I started retching.

*

Major CARL MUNDY
3/26—Operations Officer

We did not do an extensive sweep in front of our positions, because the word came that we were to be pulled out and relieved by the 2nd Battalion, 4th Marines (2/4). We were to be relieved because we had taken extensive casualties in the two engagements—or, indeed, in the single running engagement between September 7 and 11.

When all the wounded and dead were gone from Hill 48, we began to move out of the position, back toward C-2. The battalion commander led the initial elements out. Then we got the line companies in trace.

Captain ANDY DeBONA
Mike Company, 3/26—Commanding Officer

We received word that we were going to move out. Mike Company was given the point.

I called in my platoon leaders, such as they were. Of the three lieutenants who had commanded my rifle platoons on September 7—Chan Crangle, Bob Gall, and John Manzi—only Crangle was still with the company. Manzi and Gall were dead. Gall's platoon sergeant was dead and Manzi's platoon sergeant had been medevacked. A sergeant was in command of Mike-2, and my new acting company gunny was a sergeant I pulled out of my M-60 machine-gun section.

We started out with Mike-1 on the point. I put what was left of Mike-2 on my left flank. I wanted to go out in a company wedge. I figured if any contact was going to be made, it would probably come from our right front, which was the most critical position. I put Mike-3 over on the right.

2nd Lieutenant CHAN CRANGLE
Mike Company, 3/26—1st Platoon Commander

Prior to Con Thien, we had been pretty much a jungle outfit, without much dispersion on the march. Until that morning, the most repeated command from myself and my platoon sergeant was "Spread out! Spread out!'' Con Thien had really convinced each individual Marine that, if two Marines bunched up, the NVA artillery was on immediate reaction! I didn't have to order folks to spread out on this trip. We had an easy 50 meters between individuals.

1st Lieutenant RON ZAPPARDINO
3/26—Forward Air Controller

As soon as it began to turn light, I had marched out to rejoin the battalion CP on Hill 48. I was moving fast when I ran right into Andy DeBona, who told me that Lieutenant Bob Gall had been killed during the battle. Bob and I and John Manzi had been planning to go to Sydney together for R&R. John had been killed on the night of September 7, and now Bob was dead.

As I fell in beside Andy, we picked up a hurt Marine who was down and started him on his way. Then Andy started picking up loose gear, adding it to his load, so I followed suit. It ended up that the officers came out carrying more gear than the troops. We were also cheering the kids on—''Come on guys, let's get outta here. A little farther and we're outta here.''

Captain ANDY DeBONA
Mike Company, 3/26—Commanding Officer

We moved on out at a rather rapid pace and had gotten 300 to 400 meters out of the perimeter when I got a call from Battalion. Battalion said there were three 60mm mortars left in the battalion perimeter. I turned to my acting gunny, the sergeant who had come from the machine-gun section, and asked him where the 60s section was. It turned out no one had told him that, in Mike Company, the gunny was in charge of the 60s. We found two people left in the 60s section. The senior of the two was a lance corporal, who I promoted on the spot to become the 60s section chief. My new gunny, the new 60s section chief, and the other remaining member of the 60s section humped on back to Hill 48, got the three 60mm mortars, and came back after us. They caught up with us about three-quarters of a mile later.

1st Lieutenant RON ZAPPARDINO
3/26—Forward Air Controller

I saw kids who couldn't take another step until their buddies or sergeants shook them and maybe slapped them around a little. Marines were crying and whimpering, unable to pull themselves together. The battalion was a wreck, a ragtag organism running through the enemy fire with its tail between its legs.

Captain ANDY DeBONA
Mike Company, 3/26—Commanding Officer

We hit the road coming back out from Hill 48 and then made a right turn toward C-2. This was the same area in which Lima Company had been bombarded when it came in on September 8, so I figured the bad guys would have it pretty well zeroed in. We spread out on both sides of the road, along the treeline, and set rather large intervals between Marines—10 to 12 meters. At that time, we were still a klick and a half from the gates of C-2. I looked back at my Marines and they reminded me of the "Marines' Hymn." They were dirty. They were scraggly. Quite a few of them were walking wounded. One thing, though—they *all* had their heads up and they were looking around the area, scanning it.

We got out to the MSR—there was normal traffic flowing up and back to and from Con Thien—and hooked a right toward C-2.

Major CARL MUNDY
3/26—Operations Officer

Some sporadic mortar fire was coming in. It was a hot day. One of the mortarmen who was moving along in a column in front of me collapsed. He didn't physically collapse; he psychologically collapsed. He just fell down and said, "I can't go on any further. I gotta have some water. I'm out of water. I can't carry my pack." I was enraged at him. In anger, I took my remaining canteen out. It was about half full. I poured it all over his head to refresh him, but also to impart some degree of my anger. Well, that refreshed him enough to where he got up, but he didn't feel that he could carry his pack. So I swung his pack up on top of mine and walked in with it. Probably one of my more foolish moments, but it seemed to me the right thing to do. He followed along behind me, insisting that he could carry his pack, but I was so angry with him I toted it on in.

*

Captain DICK CAMP
Lima Company, 3/26—Commanding Officer

The battalion command group was back with two companies; we had two companies, India and Lima, where we were. I knew that Matt

Caulfield of India Company was senior to me—just waiting for his gold major's leaves—but I had more time in-country, so I decided to take charge. I stalked out of our perimeter with my command group and entered India's lines. Caulfield's CP was only 60 feet from where we had been. I couldn't believe it. We could have joined up during the night if I had known.

Matt Caulfield turned out to be a very cool customer, very confident, but I believe he was a wee bit shaken at the start of his third full day in the field. I suggested, "Look, you guys go ahead and we'll follow you." He agreed, and that was that. Without further ado, I formed the company up and moved it out. After a while, my company radioman, Corporal Johnson, pointed out that we were leading and India was following. I snapped at Johnson, told him to shut up, and he gave me a hurt look. When I saw Johnson's face, I knew the pressure was getting to me. I decided to maintain the lead. We were getting off the hill; nothing else mattered.

2nd Lieutenant JOHN PRINCE
Lima Company, 3/26—2nd Platoon Commander

We headed directly for C-2. This was probably the one time in my career in Vietnam I didn't have to tell people to spread it out. Everybody automatically spread out.

2nd Lieutenant BILL COWAN
India Company, 3/26—3rd Platoon Commander

We walked back out to the MSR. It seemed like a million miles. Bob Stimson and I stopped and drank the filthiest, scuzziest water I ever drank in my life, right out of the rice paddy. I mean, it was scuzzy! It had to be the best-tasting water I ever had. We were ragged and beat and tired.

Captain DICK CAMP
Lima Company, 3/26—Commanding Officer

A lot of the people I talked to later thought the retrograde from our position back to C-2 was the toughest, most physically demanding march they had ever done. No wonder. We had all been without sleep or food for two days, and some men's physical reactions to the adrenaline rushes were shocking. But I didn't see it that way. I was so happy to be going to C-2 that I had an energy rush that would have allowed me to do anything. I was walking on air. I was physically fit and ready to go.

*

Major CARL MUNDY
3/26—Operations Officer

When I arrived at C-2, the press was on hand interviewing Lieutenant Colonel Alderman. We were still running some air strikes in on the tank hull that we could not recover because it was too badly damaged. Pretty soon, the contact ceased.

1st Lieutenant RON ZAPPARDINO
3/26—Forward Air Controller

The press was out in force. Everybody—AP, UPI, CBS, all the major newspapers. I didn't want to play. I just wanted to get into the fire base so I could start seeing who was still alive.

2nd Lieutenant CHAN CRANGLE
Mike Company, 3/26—1st Platoon Commander

When we marched into C-2, there was a raft of TV crews from all the major networks and foreign stations as well. They wanted to interview us and all we wanted to do was find a deep bunker! We were still in the V Ring, and nobody wanted to stand around and tell war stories. By the time I got to the wire, the newsmen were waiting with a vengeance. I was standing there talking to a bunch of cameras, with NVA gear hanging all over me, dirty, clothes torn up, a real mess. My intelligent remarks were along the lines that every time we went left, the NVA went right and every time we went right, they went left. We had just kept on colliding with them for the previous three days. About the only real difference was we had air and the NVA didn't—but they had more artillery, especially rockets.

By then, I was antsy about standing on top of the ground. Andy DeBona had come through the gate and was sitting on a bunker, laughing his fanny off at me, so I said, "You guys need to interview a real hero. Go ask *him* about the bomb crater." They immediately took off like a pack of wolves, and I found a congenial bunker. I am told by my family that the interview appeared on the "CBS Evening News"— Walter Cronkite!—but I have never seen it.

Captain ANDY DeBONA
Mike Company, 3/26—Commanding Officer

I answered a few questions, but I didn't really have time for that, so I told them to go start talking to the troops because that's what it was all about.

Lance Corporal RON BURKE
Mike Company, 3/26, 2nd Platoon

The reporters were ambushing everybody, trying to get stories. I talked to a reporter who sold the interview to my hometown paper in Spokane, Washington. My folks read it.

Staff Sergeant CHARLES OWENS
Kilo Company, 3/26—Company Gunny

I saw the photographer I'd grabbed the film off of out on the MSR on September 8. He took my picture, but he steered clear of me, so I never had a chance to give him his film back. When I left Vietnam a few weeks later, it was still in my pack when I handed it in.

2nd Lieutenant BILL COWAN
India Company, 3/26—3rd Platoon Commander

There were lots of people waiting around for us. Among them was the battalion commander of 3/4, who had been on the staff at the Naval Academy when I was a midshipman. I talked to him briefly. Then I heard there was a reporter from the *Sacramento Bee,* my hometown paper. I sought him out and spoke with him for a few minutes.

1st Lieutenant BOB STIMSON
India Company, 3/26—Executive Officer

There was *a lot* of press waiting for us as we were about to enter C-2. It opened my eyes to the fact that our battle was one of the most significant events going on in Vietnam just then. One of the newsmen accosted Bill Cowan and me. He was John Lawrence, of CBS. I spoke to Lawrence because it was my policy to cooperate with the press on the rare occasions they asked me questions. Generally, I thought the reporters who took the trouble to go out with us were good men. Lawrence asked us what had happened, how large a unit we had engaged. He tried to get us to speculate on what we had run into, had us describe the weapons they had and the types of fire we were taking, and asked us about our casualties. He was a veteran combat correspondent who had a good feel for what we had endured. He asked good, informed questions.

2nd Lieutenant BILL COWAN
India Company, 3/26—3rd Platoon Commander

Lawrence's question to me was, "What was the enemy like?" I told him they were tough, well equipped, had clean uniforms, were newly shaven, and had good haircuts. I told him that we had hit them with everything we had until they did the only thing they could do: "bugged out." In contrast to my impression of them, we looked pretty humble. We were dirty; we hadn't shaved; many of us needed haircuts; and our utilities were, for the most part, ragged—except for the new guys'. We had been shelled by our own artillery two nights earlier and bombed by our own aircraft the previous afternoon. We were out of water, low on ammunition, and we had suffered incredible casualties. We were being moved to the rear to recoup and refit. It was hardly what I would consider a resounding victory over the NVA. However, despite the bad news, we were still a proud bunch of Marines who had held together well, who had been supported totally by whatever forces could be brought to bear against the enemy. We were walking out proudly.

2nd Lieutenant JOHN PRINCE
Lima Company, 3/26—2nd Platoon Commander

When Bill Cowan had been in Lima Company early in my tour, I had posed for several photographs with him to send home to my parents. My parents saw him on TV and recognized him from my photos. When they saw Bill and not me, they got very worried about me. I got a letter from them about that.

Corporal FRANK GARCIA
Lima Company, 3/26—2nd Platoon Squad Leader

A whole line of reporters and cameramen was walking up to the guys, asking them about the fight. Nobody tried to talk to me. I wondered, "What happened? Was I in something very major?" I knew we'd been in a battle, but that was the first hint I had that it must have been a *major* battle. Why else would all those reporters have been there waiting for us? I thought, "Something must have happened," but I had seen only one small corner of it.

Captain DICK CAMP
Lima Company, 3/26—Commanding Officer

A civilian with a microphone accosted me and said he was with the Reuters news service. He shoved the microphone in my face and said, "How was it?" I just told him that it had been tough out there. I let him off easy.

I later found out that somebody in our little town in upstate New York walked up to my dad about a week later and asked, "Hey, isn't your son in the Marine Corps?" When Dad said I was, the other man said, "Well, he's in the newspaper." He gave Dad a copy on which the front-page headline read, "Captain Camp Involved in Fight Against North Vietnamese Regiment—Heavy Casualties." That went over real big in the Camp household until my next letter arrived.

Lance Corporal CHUCK BENNETT
India Company, 3/26, 1st Platoon

One of the newsmen asked me a question, but I was busy looking around to see how many of my buddies had made it. That's all I was worried about. One of the lieutenants I hardly knew—Lieutenant Cowan—grabbed me and asked, "Hey, how are you doing, Bennett?" He sort of embraced me. I asked him if he knew what happened to certain guys, and he asked me about others. We talked a little bit, but I was dead tired and I hardly knew what either of us was saying. A reporter came up and asked, "Was it hell out there?" And I answered, "No, it was *pure hell*."

I sat down by a bunker and someone gave me a canteen of water. It tasted great. I wanted to sleep right there.

Chapter 23

2nd Lieutenant PAUL DRNEC
Bravo Company, 3rd Tank Battalion—2nd Platoon Commander

My mind was a blank by the time I reached C-2. I was tired, dirty, unshaven, and my head still hurt from its collision with the faulty turret hatch on September 8. I probably had a concussion. I left all the tanks and some crewmen at C-2, which featured a forward repair shop, and the rest of us grabbed a truck for the drive back to Camp Carroll.

As a novice tank platoon commander I had been assigned the 1801 Military Occupation Specialty [MOS] classification. Immediately after I got my whole platoon blown away, my MOS was upgraded to 1802: qualified master tank officer.

1st Lieutenant HARRY DOLAN
Mike Company, 3/26—3rd Platoon Commander

When I got to C-2, my hand was swollen to the size of a grapefruit from an infected wound. I have no idea when or where I picked up the wound—a little piece of shrapnel in the tip of my left index finger—but I had red lines running from it part of the way up my arm. Andy DeBona ordered me onto one of the first trucks out of C-2 bound for Dong Ha. When I got up on the truck, I asked Andy for a rifle and maybe one or two hand grenades. I didn't want to be riding on those roads without a rifle. He gave me the rifle and I left.

Captain ANDY DeBONA
Mike Company, 3/26—Commanding Officer

Mike Company spread out in the C-2 bunkers. We got there just about the time 3/9 was leaving to go up to Con Thien. About an hour later, we received word on the radio that a platoon of trucks was waiting outside C-2 to pull Mike Company down to Cam Lo.

Major CARL MUNDY
3/26—Operations Officer

We began moving India and Mike companies by truck convoy back to the rear. Lima and Kilo companies were to remain at C-2, pending relief in a day or two by 2/4.

Captain ANDY DeBONA
Mike Company, 3/26—Commanding Officer

We went out and found about 10 trucks sitting there. That was normally just enough to transport a company. We filled only seven of the trucks. We put one empty one in the rear and two empty ones in the front, and then we moved on out.

Lance Corporal RON BURKE
Mike Company, 3/26, 2nd Platoon

Everyone was in a big daze. I didn't know what to think or say. We'd lost a lot of people. There were just three of us left in my squad. I don't know where everyone else went; I never found out.

Captain ANDY DeBONA
Mike Company, 3/26—Commanding Officer

Mike Company got down to Cam Lo to spend the night. They had cold soda and cold beer waiting for us. Word was passed—the typical thing—that there would be no more than two beers per man and that all beer drinking would cease at 2000. We came rolling in about 1800. By the time we got set up, it was about 1930, so I rescinded the order to quit drinking at 2000. I decided they could each have two beers and two cans of soda pop. It turned out that there was enough beer and soda for our normal complement, about 160 people. I came back with about 110 men in the company, counting attachments. We had two beers and two sodas for 160 men, and 110 people consumed all of it.

Next day, I found that many of the men still had cans of beer and soda with them. That gave us all a little chuckle.

1st Lieutenant BOB STIMSON
India Company, 3/26—Executive Officer

They drove India Company straight to Dong Ha. Once there, I felt secure for the first time since I had been flown out of Khe Sanh on September 5, only six days earlier. My concerns were very basic— getting a shower and a shave, getting a little rest. The battalion mess sergeant had steaks grilled up for everybody. It was a welcome change from the ordeal we had just experienced. I went visiting, checking in with friends to learn what they had seen and gone through. I spent a lot of time with Bill Cowan, talking, comparing notes.

*

Lance Corporal MIKE HEFFLIN
Lima Company, 3/26

After we were medevacked off the hill, they flew us to Dong Ha and treated us real fast at Delta-Med. They pulled out all the shrapnel they could and sent me on to the big hospital at Phu Bai. I was there for two weeks because my right foot got infected and none of my wounds were healing good. Next, they sent me on to Danang for two or three days, and then they loaded me on a C-130 for a flight to the Philippines. From there, they flew me to Japan. I stayed in the Yokosuka Naval Hospital until early December. I didn't get home to Los Angeles until right before Christmas, over three months late. I had been declared Missing in Action at one point.

Staff Sergeant RUSS ARMSTRONG
India Company, 3/26

From Delta-Med, they shipped me south on September 9 to Phu Bai and, from there, I was sent south again to Danang. Each layover was for about two days. Along the way, men with lesser wounds were retained and men with heavier wounds were sent on a road that eventually led to Stateside hospitals.

HN Robert Davis, the platoon corpsman who had lost his arm in the September 8 rocket barrage on the MSR, was sure to go home. We traveled out together, but I eventually outpaced him because he had to recuperate from major surgery. As I was getting ready to go, I asked one of the corpsmen to take me in to see him, a request that was granted without protest. Most of Davis's left arm was gone. What was left was being held aloft in a harness. I felt terrible, but his attitude was incredibly positive. He was from Pennsylvania, and he told me that they had him slated to go to the Philadelphia Naval Hospital. I asked him, "Are you going to be all right?"

"Oh, yeah, Staff Sergeant, I'll be okay." I believe he really meant it.

A machine gunner who had lost most of the fingers of one hand on September 7 was another who went through the medevac cycle with me. Though he was from Texas, he wound up with me in Balboa Naval Hospital, in San Diego. After about a week, when they had done all they could for him, he got the word that he was going to be shipped to another hospital, nearer to his home. He was thrilled. When we were saying our good-byes, he told me that he had about a year left on his enlistment. He asked if I could do anything to get him put on duty with the Reserve unit in his hometown. He was a good Marine, but he wasn't the smartest kid I ever ran into. I knew for sure that he was going to be surveyed from the Marine Corps, but he had not realized it yet. I almost fell apart. What could I tell him? I stared at him for a moment and finally said, "That sounds like a good idea. Let me see what I can do." I didn't have the guts to tell him the truth. On the way out, I got angry with the people whose job it was to tell Marines like him what to expect from life. Those people were around, but I guess they weren't around for us.

My family was living in San Diego. As soon as I arrived at Balboa, my wife and son came to see me. I was assigned to the hospital for about three months, but I only spent three weeks there. The doctor in command of the ward had always served with the Marines and he was partial to Marine NCOs. I talked him into rushing me through my physical therapy, which was simply learning to walk with crutches and then a cane until my leg healed.

I guess because I could walk so well—nerve damage left me without feeling from my knee to my ankle—the Marine Corps reassigned me to duty as a drill instructor at the Recruit Depot in San Diego.

*

Staff Sergeant CHARLES OWENS
Kilo Company, 3/26—Company Gunny

They left Kilo and Lima companies at C-2. They fed us a hot meal. I sent my men to get their food one at a time so we wouldn't be all clumped up if any rockets came in. C-2 was a dangerous place.

Captain DICK CAMP
Lima Company, 3/26—Commanding Officer

C-2 was on top of a knoll, with no cover whatsoever. They had deep, strong DMZ bunkers, and a trench digger had cut very deep trenches all over the place, each about 7 feet deep and very narrow. They were perfect for covering up during an artillery or mortar attack, but we couldn't have fought from them. When we formed up and learned that Lima Company was going to stand fast to guard C-2 while the rest of the battalion moved somewhere else, I ordered everyone to get into the trenches. There were NVA artillery and rockets all over the place out there—as we well knew—and I wasn't about to give their FOs a company-size target.

2nd Lieutenant JOHN PRINCE
Lima Company, 3/26—2nd Platoon Commander

The rest of the battalion left C-2 right away, but Lima Company had to stay behind. We set in the perimeter, but everybody was just exhausted so I had just one man stand watch and let everybody else crap out. I was so hungry that I started going through garbage cans to get thrown-away food to eat. I found some—and I ate it.

Captain DICK CAMP
Lima Company, 3/26—Commanding Officer

As the company hit the trenches, I really started winding down. Everything started to hit. The downside of the manic euphoria I had experienced getting to C-2 really started to hit me. I went into a bunker my radiomen had turned into a CP, and I stayed there all day and all night. I was too numb with exhaustion to think straight. As soon as I got inside the bunker, I sat down on a cot, shed all my gear, and pulled open one of several cases of C-rations I found stacked up along one bulkhead. I placed the case of C-rations at the foot of my cot and gulped down one complete ration. Then I fell back onto the cot and went to sleep. I half remember waking up periodically during the night, famished. Each time, I sat up, opened up another can of C-rations, and gulped it down. It sounds strange, but I swear that by the time morning rolled around, I had eaten the entire case of C-rations.

2nd Lieutenant JOHN PRINCE
Lima Company, 3/26—2nd Platoon Commander

We slept most of the day. That evening they brought us hot chow from Dong Ha. It was so good it sort of reaffirmed my pleasure in being alive again.

Corporal FRANK GARCIA
Lima Company, 3/26—2nd Platoon Squad Leader

That night at C-2 was the first time I ever smoked in my life. I used to save up cigarettes and trade them to smokers for extra food, and I had a bunch with me when we came in after the battle. I started smoking the day we got to C-2—a lot. I wasn't a smoker after Vietnam either, but I was then.

I thought a lot about the guys who didn't make it. I came from a broken home; I didn't really have anything to go home to. I had gotten a Dear John while I was over there. I had nothing to live for, nothing to look forward to. I didn't give a shit about living or dying. I began thinking that the good guys all were dead. The guy I had replaced as squad leader had been killed. He was a rich kid whose father owned a ranch in Texas. Sawicki had had that 15 grand he'd won gambling. It looked like his life might be turning around. He was real happy about that, but he was killed in front of my eyes. A couple other guys who were killed were married or had sweethearts. It seemed that all the good guys, all the guys with something to live for, were dying out there. I thought about it all night. I also wondered why Lima Company had to stay out there in C-2, why we weren't allowed to go back with the rest of the battalion.

*

Captain DICK CAMP
Lima Company, 3/26—Commanding Officer

Higher headquarters had promised us relief the next day, September

12. As promised, an advance party from a company of 2/4 arrived early, and I started briefing them by describing the danger from NVA artillery and rockets. "Lookit," I warned, "this place is under observation and subject to artillery fire. Whatever you do, make sure you bring your people in and don't let them bunch up, particularly on the skyline." The skyline was the big danger because the road from Cam Lo ran right up to the top of the knoll and continued on up to Con Thien.

The appointed hour of the relief approached, and I ordered Lima Company to stand by in the trenches. Everybody had their gear on and we were all set to go. My command group was down by the base headquarters bunker, in the open but spread well apart. Everyone was waiting for my signal, and I was waiting for the relief company to arrive. I strolled to the top of the knoll to see what was going on. I happened to look back toward Cam Lo, which was to the south, and I spotted the dust clouds from the trucks bringing up our relief.

The trucks drove into C-2 through the wire, ran right up to the top of the knoll, and parked, radiator to tailgate.

Staff Sergeant CHARLES OWENS
Kilo Company, 3/26—Company Gunny

The convoy commander lined his trucks up bumper to bumper, so I went out there, screaming and hollering, telling the drivers to get their trucks spread out. I said, "We're gonna get hit here anytime!" They didn't believe me.

Captain DICK CAMP
Lima Company, 3/26—Commanding Officer

They were right out in the open. I couldn't believe it.

Staff Sergeant CHARLES OWENS
Kilo Company, 3/26—Company Gunny

I had my people in covered positions. I'd told them we were going out with big intervals between each man and would load outside the perimeter. The convoy commander wanted to load right in there, with the trucks bumper to bumper. I told him we wouldn't do it. I told him he'd have to get his trucks out there and park them 50 meters apart before I'd load my men on them. I threatened him and he said he was going to court-martial me.

I *knew* we were going to get hit, but he said, "Aw, we're old hands at this. We know what we're doing." I said, "All right, buddy, you know. But we're not going to load here." I gave my people the signal, and they got up and walked straight back out of C-2. When they got 50 meters back, I motioned for them to turn. That's when we heard the rockets leaving their launchers.

Captain DICK CAMP
Lima Company, 3/26—Commanding Officer

As I ran over to tell them to get the hell off the knoll, I happened to glance over to the side in time to see an artilleryman jumping up and down on his bunker. I distinctly heard him yell, "Incoming!"

I pivoted back around toward my command group. "Incoming!" I screamed.

They all recognized my voice and made like prairie dogs going into their holes. My people disappeared so fast even I couldn't believe it. On the other hand, the 2/4 company apparently had not been around the DMZ before. The Marines jumping off the trucks just stood there with expressions on their faces that seemed to say, "What the hell are you talking about?"

Corporal FRANK GARCIA
Lima Company, 3/26—2nd Platoon Squad Leader

We all ran for cover as soon as we heard the incoming being fired, but the guys in the relief company started laughing at us, telling us there was nothing happening, that we all had jungle fever, combat fatigue. Then—*boomboomboom*—the incoming started hitting and they started running. Then *we* started laughing, yelling, "Hey, we're leaving and you're staying. Hah!"

Captain DICK CAMP
Lima Company, 3/26—Commanding Officer

I grabbed the two nearest 2/4 Marines and yelled at them, "Get in that culvert." We jumped into the culvert by the road—it was a regular drainage culvert—just as the first artillery rounds impacted. The three of us lay there, hunched over, and I thought, "My God, if there's a close round, it's going to kill us with concussion." I turned to the two Marines and said, "Lookit, I'll listen, and if I don't hear anything, I'm going to run to the trench. You guys follow me because of concussion." I was sure I was confusing them, but they nodded their heads.

I stuck my head out and listened. I didn't hear anything, so I said, "Let's go," and went roaring out of the culvert toward the nearest deep trench. I was well along into a two-and-a-half gainer when, evidently, a round came in and knocked me ass over teakettle. A sliver grazed my forearm, just enough to draw blood. As soon as my body tumbled onto the ground—I was still in the open—I bounded back up, just like that. There was no hesitation. I executed a pretty nice swan dive into the 7-foot-deep fire trench, right on top of a couple of the kids from my company. I said, "Excuse me," and they chorused, "Yessir!"

2nd Lieutenant JOHN PRINCE
Lima Company, 3/26—2nd Platoon Commander

One of my men was wounded. A rocket landed 2 feet away from him and blew off the ring finger on his right hand. I don't know how it blew off just his ring finger, but that's what it did. He had a ticket home.

Staff Sergeant CHARLES OWENS
Kilo Company, 3/26—Company Gunny

My men all got up and left there. The trucks that were left came after us and picked us up.

Captain DICK CAMP
Lima Company, 3/26—Commanding Officer

When the artillery attack slackened off enough, I started yelling for Lima to get the hell out of C-2. As the shells continued to fall intermittently, my people raced down the road, a fire team at a time. The relief company had arrived; we were no longer responsible for C-2. As I ran down the road beside my radioman, I glanced down and saw that several trucks were on fire, two 105mm howitzers were burning in the gun pits, and a lot of people were laying all over the ground. It was too bad, but the relief company just hadn't understood what the hell was going on up there.

Corporal FRANK GARCIA
Lima Company, 3/26—2nd Platoon Squad Leader

Lima Company just picked up and walked out of there. We got up and left in the middle of the barrage. We'd had enough; we didn't have to be there. We walked down the road, got in the trucks, and left.

Staff Sergeant CHARLES OWENS
Kilo Company, 3/26—Company Gunny

When we counted everyone aboard the trucks, we were missing a man. The skipper said, "Find him," so I went back to the morgue, the sick bay, everywhere in C-2 I thought he might have been. I couldn't find him. Finally, someone said he thought the missing man had gotten on a truck we'd sent back to Cam Lo the day before. Nobody had told him he could, but he had. I got down to Cam Lo and found him sitting on the back of that truck. I pulled him off the truck and banged his head against it about three times. I'd been at C-2, dodging rockets, looking for him, and he'd been at Cam Lo the whole time, sitting in the back of that truck.

2nd Lieutenant JOHN PRINCE
Lima Company, 3/26—2nd Platoon Commander

As soon as we got off the trucks at Camp Evans, young Vietnamese kids came out to sell us Cokes. I got so pissed! We'd just been out fighting their war for them and those kids come out and sell us Coke— hot Coke for a dollar a bottle. I almost shot some of those sons of bitches.

*

1st Lieutenant BOB STIMSON
India Company, 3/26—Executive Officer

3/26 needed to be rebuilt. We were in no shape to go right back out to the war. Also, a very large proportion of the officers and men were due to rotate home at the conclusion of our 13-month tours. I had less than three weeks before I was to leave. So, after pulling ourselves together, we left Dong Ha to go down to Camp Evans.

Captain ANDY DeBONA
Mike Company, 3/26—Commanding Officer

They moved us to Camp Evans to reorganize the battalion. The 3rd Battalion, 26th Marines, had been about the original tenants of Camp Evans, which, in fact, was named for the first member of the battalion who was killed in Vietnam.

2nd Lieutenant JOHN PRINCE
Lima Company, 3/26—2nd Platoon Commander

About this time, 3/26 was rotating its original members home. The battalion had been overseas for exactly a year—afloat for three months and then landed en masse in Vietnam. So we lost about half of our people at one time. I had, as I recall, 3 killed and 12 evacuated wounded, plus the rotations from the original 3/26. For a while, I was down to 10 or 11 men in my platoon, until the wounded started coming back.

Captain ANDY DeBONA
Mike Company, 3/26—Commanding Officer

When the rest of the battalion pulled into Camp Evans a few days after Mike Company, I was told that, since I was due to rotate home in a few weeks, I was to turn Mike Company over to a newly arrived captain, Bill Dabney. I had a little company formation, an emotional one—at least on my part. It looked like we had a reinforced platoon out there in company formation. I received a report from my platoon leaders and the acting company gunnery sergeant. I thanked them for a great job. I told them I was going to be leaving. I sort of felt like a stranger at that time, after all we'd been through. It was sort of weird; I felt like a stranger when I turned around and walked away from the company. I was no longer a part of it, even though a part of me would always be there.

Reflections

The 3rd Battalion, 26th Marines lost 20 Marines and corpsmen killed and 70 Marines and corpsmen wounded in action at The Churchyard on September 7, 1967. One Marine was killed and 28 Marines and corpsmen were wounded in the rocket and artillery attack on the MSR on September 8; another Marine was killed by friendly fire that night. During the afternoon and evening of September 10, the battalion lost 34 Marines and corpsmen killed and 192 Marines and corpsmen wounded. In all, 3/26 and the attached tank and Ontos units sustained losses of 56 killed and 290 wounded. Given a *high* estimate of 700 effective combat troops in the battalion on September 6—that is, subtracting troops assigned to the various rear echelons, troops on R&R, troops undergoing routine medical treatment, half the 81mm mortar platoon, and other routine attrition from an authorized strength of 950 men—3/26 lost well over 40 percent of its fighting strength in four days. A unit is considered "decimated" if it loses 10 percent of its strength. In other wars, 3/26 would have been considered ineffective by the afternoon of September 8. However, in Vietnam, higher headquarters considered a battalion in name a battalion in fact; they doggedly stayed with a vague plan that had obviously gone awry.

TOM EARLY: From September 7 to September 10, we changed India Company commanders from Coulter to Caulfield. Wildprett had just left Kilo Company, so Kilo Company had a brand-new commander. DeBona, in Mike Company, was continuity. Camp wasn't there for September 7, but he arrived for September 8, 9, and 10. The battalion commander had changed only a few weeks earlier and the battalion exec—Mundy—wasn't in the field on September 7. Then, on September 9, we pushed Mundy down to S-3 because a senior major had arrived. You can conclude that we were a unit thrown into intense combat during a period of tremendous personnel turmoil. I'm sure that contributed in some way to a bit of what might be called lack of total coordination. So many key billet changes certainly didn't make 3/26 the most effective outfit before and while we were being thrown into what I would call a feces sandwich.

BILL COWAN: I have no idea why we were out there. What did we have to show for it when it was over? Body count. That's the only thing we had. They had had some photo birds come over during the night, taking a number of recce shots. The mythical number of confirmed North Vietnamese KIAs—they said it was 300—came from the photos. None of us ever saw the photos, and we didn't come close to counting 300. The photo people said they'd all been dragged away during the night. I have no idea what we really inflicted on the enemy. About three months later, in *Stars and Stripes,* there was an article quoting NVA propaganda reports that said what the NVA claimed they lost. Their number was much lower than our number, and I found their numbers consistently more accurate than I found ours.

Were there better ways to do what we did? Hell yes, there were!

The map Chan Crangle took off the dead North Vietnamese FO on the morning of September 11 couldn't have been the first of its kind ever captured. If someone had shown us a captured map while we were out there, I'd have known where Hill 88 was when I interrogated the young NVA prisoner on September 8. Then we'd have had more than a battalion wandering around out there with a platoon—my platoon— leading it into an ambush. If we had known then where the NVA regimental CP was, maybe someone higher up would have hit it with some B-52s or maybe moved some bigger units around to try to force them into the open. But my platoon blundered in a direct line toward their CP, and I never knew about it. No one in the battalion knew about it.

CHAN CRANGLE: I cannot say that we were lulled to sleep or misled, but it is clear that 3rd Marine Division and 9th Marines knew a hell of a lot more than anyone told us. Some of what they knew I found out later in my tour, when I was on the 3rd Marine Division Forward staff at Dong Ha, in February 1968. I did some research on my own. I don't know how much the 3/26 command group knew, but it was clear to me that Division and 9th Marines had a pretty clear picture of what was about to happen. I didn't.

Harry Dolan and I agree that we were briefed that our battalion was to move into the area southwest of Con Thien, generally stay out of trouble for a few days, and then move into the Con Thien Combat Base as the palace guard. I do not recall any briefings indicating substantial NVA activity or any warning of what we were about to step into. Indeed, the first day, September 6, the departing platoon commander from Bravo Company, 1/9, told me there had been no activity in the area for some time. Certainly, there was no briefing about a buildup before we went out.

India Company was attacked near the spot from which my patrol had been withdrawn early on the morning of September 10. Several years after the battle, another officer in the battalion griped that I should have continued the patrol and uncovered the "ambush" that India Company ran into. I guess it depends on who's in the barrel. I followed my instructions, and I can't say that I'm sorry for not triggering the fight instead of India Company.

In some circles of the Marine Corps, 3/26 still has the reputation of having been clobbered on the DMZ, almost wiped out, and unable to cut it in the big league, the DMZ. We took some hits, to be sure, but we gave back more than our share, and I think we could have gone right back, just like any of the other battalions that saw some pretty stiff action up there.

CARL MUNDY: What you had in this whole episode was a contact on the same ground 1/9 had gone into, then we went into, and that 2/4 subsequently went into. This, to anybody's calculation, would sound like extremely poor tactics. We put three battalions successively into an operating area that was about 16,000 square meters, which may sound like a big number but was really only 4 klicks by 4 klicks. That's not a lot of maneuver area, and the NVA very apparently had every piece of ground in that operating area targeted with rockets, mortars, and artillery. The result was that, even when we moved to another hill, they could target us. They could pick any target they wanted to, lay in on it, and inflict significant casualties.

I am certain that the strategy behind our being there was the defense of the MSR leading up to Con Thien. After-action deductions concluded that the NVA were attempting to cut the road that supplied Con Thien. If you accept this thesis, which the historic recording of the action does, then it might be logical to infer that 3/26 upset NVA intentions by blunting their thrust. If the NVA had cut that MSR, they would have surrounded Con Thien. They would have cut Con Thien off from resupply up the road by way of C-2. So, ours was a fairly important mission involving three battalions successively placed in the same restricted operating area.

I doubt that I could support the contention that either side ambushed anybody. If that was the case, it would seem to me that it was we who got ambushed, although, again, ambush does not seem to fit the scenario that evolved on September 10. My belief is that the NVA attacked the battalion on September 7 and then took advantage of the move of 3/26 in daylight on September 10 to attack us as we were strung out. That conclusion is not glamorous, but it was clearly we who received the incoming prep fires followed by an on-line infantry assault.

In sum, as a "newbie" on the scene that day, I don't for a moment want to suggest the lack of a tactical scheme or the absence of intelligence—I was not there long enough to get a full grasp of the situation before we became heavily engaged. My impression was that we were attacked by a carefully coordinated NVA effort and that we were successful in blunting that attack and giving no ground. The bottom line: There was individual valor and heroism, and I believe that all of us can be proud of our performance, but the notion that there was well-thought-out strategy or tactical brilliance in the design of the action is not something I can support.

JOHN PRINCE: This particular battle didn't have any effect on putting an end to the war. But, it was typical in the sense that three of our companies and the battalion CP had gotten mauled fairly badly on September 7. It is ironic that the Marine Corps could field only one battalion when they knew where the NVA was. They had so many people tied up—at fire bases like Gio Linh, Camp Carroll, Camp Evans, The Rockpile, Con Thien, C-2, Cam Lo, Dong Ha, and Khe Sanh, plus everything down south—that they didn't have enough people out in the field. One of the principles of war is mass, but the Marine Corps couldn't mass any more than one battalion for this particular fight.

BOB STIMSON: There was nothing in my previous 11 months in Vietnam that compared with the actions on September 7 and 10. Other, earlier actions, while violent and costly, were nowhere near the intensity of these battles.

The NVA troops we engaged were professionals. Certainly, they made some mistakes, but they were very professional soldiers. I always maintained that an NVA company could literally outrun a Marine company, with all its vaunted equipment and assets. An NVA unit could inflict damage and be in the next county before a Marine unit could react. I believe that American combat units in general were heavily burdened with a logistics tail and reporting and communication requirements that seriously degraded our ability to carry out assigned missions. We were overly dependent on air and supporting arms. The NVA, by and large, were far more able to fight without that extensive logistics tail and supporting-arms array. They could certainly fight better in small units that were generally in coordination with one another.

We're talking about a regimental action here, but this wasn't Waterloo, where everybody was lined up on both sides. The North Vietnamese regiment that hit us had the same command structure as we had—down through battalions, companies, platoons, and squads. Certainly, they didn't have the communications gear that we had, and yet they had an ironclad doctrine by which everyone knew exactly what to do in relation to what everyone else was doing. This was a large unit that was able to deploy and coordinate very effectively—despite what it lacked in communications equipment and other support, such as aerial observers. They could make an entire regiment disappear. A Marine platoon could never evaporate into the ground the way that regiment did.

When I was a Marine fighting in Indochina, I knew nothing significant about the peoples in whose country I was waging war. Realizing that somehow sparked in me a desire to fill a void left over from my typical American education, which was oriented toward European and U.S. history, culture, and languages. After I left the Marine Corps, I went to graduate school and studied Asia and Asians. After graduate school, I wound up in Vietnam with a civilian job. I also did some work for the government after all our military advisors were withdrawn. I saw the war on a much deeper level then and came into contact with all levels of the society—Americans, Vietnamese, Europeans, even Communists. When I think of Vietnam, my tour with 3/26 is only one part of it, although a rather significant part. Since then, I have spent almost my entire adult life working and living in Asia.

At the time of my combat tour in Vietnam, I was very well equipped to do what I had to do, which I credit to my training at Quantico and my time living in the field with fellow Marines. It was not until years later, long after I was out of the Marine Corps and back from my second Indochina experience, that, for some unknown reason, the real horror of my Vietnam experience and these two battles in particular hit home. The violence in which I had had the misfortune to participate worked its way to the surface.

To this day, I don't know why they sent us out there. Why were we bouncing around in that small area without a reaction force ready to pounce on any enemy we turned up? We were struck by an NVA regiment twice in four days, and no one was prepared to help us.

RON ZAPPARDINO: There was a lot of joy in getting back, but a lot of anger quickly erupted among the officers about how we had come to be put in that position. As soon as the pressure was off, as soon as we felt safe, we started feeling the depth of the experience. We felt betrayed. No one had been sent to our aid, no one had been sent to relieve us of our "vital" mission. If our being there was so vital, why were we pulled in without being replaced?

Updates

In 1969, Russ Armstrong was awarded his Navy Cross and commissioned a second lieutenant on the same day. After working for several years in Explosive Ordnance Disposal, he completed a master's degree program and left the Marine Corps. Today, he works for the government in Nevada.

After many years of working as a union representative, Ron Burke works the night shift for Alcoa Aluminum in Washington State.

Dick Camp retired from the Marine Corps as a colonel in 1988 and found immediate employment as an executive in Ohio.

Matt Caulfield is a major general on active duty.

Bill Cowan spent the second half of his first tour in Vietnam as an advisor with the Vietnamese Marine Corps—and a total of five years in Vietnam. Bill went into military intelligence work and, to put it mildly, had an exciting career. He retired from the Marine Corps in 1986 as a lieutenant colonel. Following a stint as military advisor to a United States senator, Bill went to work for a private counterterrorism consulting firm in the Washington, D.C., area.

Recognizing the degree in nuclear propulsion Chan Crangle earned while serving in the Navy, the Marine Corps sent him to law school. He was promoted to the rank of colonel in 1989.

Andy DeBona returned to Vietnam in 1972 as an advisor to the Vietnamese Marine Corps. During the 1972 Communist Easter Offensive, he was the last U.S. Marine out of Con Thien and, during the same flight, the last member of 3/26 to see Ambush Valley. Andy retired as a lieutenant colonel after his doctors told him he was going to die of cancer in six months. Every year since, he has held a party on the anniversary of his death. Today, he lives in a town on the Madison River, in Montana, whose road sign reads, "Population: Human—660; Trout—11,000,000."

Harry Dolan retired from the Marine Corps as a major and owns a farm in Alabama.

Paul Drnec retired from the Marine Corps as a major and obtained an advanced degree in business.

Tom Early is a colonel on active duty.

Frank Garcia went to work for the Los Angeles Sheriff's Department when he got out of the Marine Corps, just in time for the Los Angeles riots. He is now a private investigator in L.A.

Mike Hefflin left the Marine Corps and went back to work at McDonnell Douglas.

Carl Mundy is a lieutenant general on active duty.

John Prince left the Marine Corps at the end of his tour and is a real estate agent in Arizona.

Bob Stimson left the Marine Corps at the end of his tour and attended graduate school. Following a civilian tour in Vietnam, he has been employed continuously as an engineering consultant throughout Asia.

Ron Zappardino left the Marine Corps at the end of his tour and flew for Air America in Vietnam at about the time Saigon fell. He got into restaurant management and now owns a world-class restaurant in La Jolla, California.

Bibliography

PUBLISHED SOURCES

Camp, Colonel Richard D., Jr., with Eric Hammel. *Lima-6: A Marine Company Commander in Vietnam.* New York: Atheneum Publishers, 1989.

Caulfield, Major M. P. "India Six," *Marine Corps Gazette,* July 1969.

Davidson, Lieutenant General Philip B. *Vietnam at War: The History, 1946–1975.* Novato, CA: Presidio Press, 1988.

Shulimson, Jack. *U.S. Marines in Vietnam: An Expanding War, 1966.* Washington, D.C.: United States Marine Corps, 1982.

Telfer, Major Gary, Lieutenant Colonel Lane Rogers, and V. Keith Fleming, Jr. *U.S. Marines in Vietnam: Fighting the North Vietnamese, 1967.* Washington, D.C.: United States Marine Corps, 1984.

All quotations attributed to Captain Dick Camp and Captain Matt Caulfield are excerpted with permission from the preceding sources.

OFFICIAL SOURCES

Only three official documents pertaining to the battle described in this book could be uncovered by the author. The most important was the 3/26 Command Chronology for the month of September 1967. This uncharacteristically detailed and vivid official account was researched and written in early October 1967 by Lieutenant Bill Cowan, who was then a member of the battalion operations staff. Unfortunately, despite Cowan's best efforts, the official account is not entirely accurate. This is owing to the fact that about half the survivors completed their tours and were sent home in the three weeks before Cowan began his research.

The other two official documents are the largely illegible 3/26 unit roster and unit diary. About half the names on each list could not be deciphered, and it appears that neither list is complete in any case. Still, these were extremely valuable resources to the extent they could be deciphered.

UNOFFICIAL SOURCES

The bulk of the material contained in this volume was gleaned from exhaustive interviews with the men named. A first round of interviews was conducted in 1983, and the final round was conducted during the first half of 1989. Edited, largely corrected transcripts of the interviews have been donated to the Marine Corps Historical Division, located at the Washington, D.C., Navy Yard.

EDITORIAL NOTE

For purposes of clarity, style, and consistency, most of the passages appearing in this book have been edited or corrected by the author. However, the substance of the quotations has not been altered except in the case of errors of fact corrected by the author.

Acknowledgments

I owe a special thank you to my dear friend and partner in at least one crime, Dick Camp. It was Dick who first told me about this brutal battle, and he is the one who introduced me to many of the survivors.

Andy DeBona also deserves a special thanks. Valiantly and unselfishly taking time out from important fishing, Andy browbeat many former 3/26 comrades into cooperating with my research effort. He also browbeat me into completing it.

I wish to offer my heartfelt thanks to the following men for sharing their experiences and reliving their pain and trauma for the sake of this book: Russell P. Armstrong; Charles Bennett; Ronald W. Burke; Richard D. Camp, Jr.; Raymond J. Chiappelli; William V. Cowan III; Chandler C. Crangle; William H. Dabney, Jr.; Andrew D. DeBona; Harry C. Dolan; Paul F. Drnec; Thomas M. Early; Francis M. Garcia; Michael L. Hefflin; Carl E. Mundy, Jr.; David M. Nugent; Charles T. Owens; John F. Prince, Jr.; Robert E. Stimson; Walter L. Whitesides; and Ronald R. Zappardino.

Finally, I would like to thank my good friends at the Marine Corps Historical Division, notably Danny Crawford, for answering inquiries and forwarding mail.

Index